E-Evidence: Mastering the Science of Digital Forensics

Esterino Falcone

In today's hyper-connected world, where every interaction, transaction, and activity leaves a digital trace, the importance of digital forensics has never been greater. From cracking high-profile cybercrime cases to uncovering hidden corporate scandals, digital forensics lies at the intersection of technology, law, and justice. Yet, for many, this field remains an enigma, misunderstood and underestimated in its complexity and potential.

E-Evidence: Mastering the Science of Digital Forensics is designed to demystify this fascinating discipline, offering readers an in-depth guide to uncovering the secrets embedded in bytes and code. Whether you're a budding investigator, an IT professional looking to sharpen your skills, or someone fascinated by the intricacies of modern crime-solving, this book will equip you with the knowledge and tools to navigate the digital evidence landscape with confidence.

Digital forensics is more than just recovering files or cracking passwords; it's a meticulous science that demands precision, ethical responsibility, and a mastery of ever-evolving technology. With cyber threats growing in sophistication and digital footprints expanding to the farthest corners of our lives, the ability to analyze and interpret e-evidence has become an indispensable skill.

This book is structured to take you on a journey—from the foundational principles of digital forensics to the cutting-edge tools and techniques that define the field today. Along the way, you'll learn to tackle real-world challenges, such as preserving evidence integrity, deciphering encrypted data, and presenting findings in a court of law.

As we embark on this journey, it's worth remembering that digital forensics is not just about technology. It's about solving problems, seeking truth, and delivering justice. Behind every byte of evidence lies a story waiting to be told—a story of trust betrayed, crimes committed, or mysteries unraveled. And it is the digital forensic investigator who ensures that these stories are told with integrity and precision.

The future of investigations lies in the mastery of digital evidence. By the time you turn the final page of this book, you will have a firm grasp of the skills, tools, and mindset required to succeed in this critical and rapidly advancing field.

Welcome to the world of E-Evidence. It's time to master the science of digital forensics.

Esterino Falcone is a seasoned expert in digital forensics and cybersecurity, with a career spanning over two decades. As a trailblazer in the field, Esterino has dedicated his life to unraveling the complexities of digital evidence, helping law enforcement agencies, corporations, and legal professionals uncover the truth hidden in the digital realm.

Esterino's journey into the world of digital forensics began during the early days of personal computing, when the potential of technology to both enable and disrupt society was becoming clear. Fascinated by the intersection of technology and justice, he honed his expertise in data recovery, cryptography, and network analysis, eventually becoming a trusted advisor for high-profile cases involving cybercrime, corporate espionage, and fraud.

A passionate educator and mentor, Esterino has trained countless professionals worldwide, sharing his knowledge through workshops, conferences, and now this book. Known for his ability to break down complex concepts into accessible insights, he has a talent for empowering others to see the story within the data.

In E-Evidence: Mastering the Science of Digital Forensics, Esterino combines his wealth of practical experience with a forward-thinking approach to address the challenges and opportunities in today's digital forensics landscape. Whether it's investigating mobile devices, analyzing malware, or tackling the intricacies of cloud computing, his expertise is both deep and wide-ranging.

Beyond his professional achievements, Esterino is a lifelong learner and innovator, always exploring the cutting edge of technology. When he's not solving digital puzzles, he enjoys sharing his passion for technology and justice through writing, speaking engagements, and mentoring the next generation of forensic investigators.

With this book, Esterino Falcone invites you into the world he has devoted his life to mastering, equipping you with the tools and knowledge to succeed in the ever-evolving domain of digital forensics.

1. Introduction to Digital Forensics

In a world increasingly driven by technology, digital forensics has emerged as a critical discipline in the pursuit of justice and truth. This chapter lays the foundation for your journey into the field, exploring its origins, evolution, and vital role in modern investigations. From solving cybercrimes to uncovering fraud and protecting organizational integrity, digital forensics touches every corner of our connected lives. By understanding its core principles, tools, and methodologies, you'll gain insight into how digital evidence is collected, analyzed, and presented, setting the stage for deeper exploration in the chapters ahead.

1.1 The Evolution of Digital Forensics

Digital forensics is a rapidly evolving field that has emerged in response to the growing complexity of technology and its integration into every aspect of modern life. It is a specialized discipline within forensic science that focuses on the recovery, analysis, and preservation of digital evidence, which may be used in legal investigations, cybersecurity matters, or criminal justice. The evolution of digital forensics has been driven by several factors, including advancements in technology, the increase in cybercrimes, the rise of mobile and cloud computing, and the growing reliance on digital evidence in legal and corporate environments.

The Early Years: Pre-1990s and the Birth of Digital Forensics

The roots of digital forensics can be traced back to the early 1980s, though it did not gain recognition as a distinct field until later. In the early years, digital devices were relatively simple compared to modern technology. Personal computers, introduced in the 1970s and 1980s, began to play a central role in personal and business activities, but their impact on crime and investigation was still limited. The need for specialized techniques to recover and analyze data from digital devices was not yet apparent, as the majority of criminal investigations relied on physical evidence.

The first significant step in the evolution of digital forensics occurred during the 1980s and early 1990s, when law enforcement and the legal system began to encounter crimes that involved digital evidence. The most notable early cases involved unauthorized access to computer systems (hacking) and the theft of intellectual property. During this time, forensic investigators faced many challenges, as computers were not yet considered reliable sources of evidence, and there were no established methodologies or tools for examining digital systems.

By the late 1980s and early 1990s, digital forensics began to take shape with the development of the first digital forensic tools. The initial tools were often homegrown, created by investigators or hackers themselves to extract, analyze, and preserve data from digital systems. These tools were rudimentary and often depended on simple file recovery techniques. The need for a formalized process for acquiring and handling digital evidence was recognized, which laid the foundation for future developments in the field.

The 1990s: Establishing the Discipline

The 1990s saw the emergence of digital forensics as a formal discipline. During this time, as personal computers became more widely used and interconnected through the early internet, cybercrime became more prevalent. Hackers, cybercriminals, and fraudsters exploited the growing dependence on digital technology, creating new challenges for law enforcement and forensic investigators. Investigations into digital crimes, such as unauthorized access, data theft, and fraud, required specialized knowledge and techniques that traditional forensic methods could not address.

One of the most significant milestones in the evolution of digital forensics came in 1995 with the creation of the first digital forensic laboratory at the FBI. This laboratory, known as the FBI Computer Crime Squad, marked the official recognition of digital forensics as an essential part of law enforcement. The FBI's investment in digital forensic expertise reflected the increasing recognition that digital evidence was becoming integral to criminal investigations.

Additionally, the 1990s saw the development of several key forensic software tools that laid the groundwork for modern digital forensics. Tools such as FTK (Forensic Toolkit) and EnCase emerged, enabling forensic investigators to examine, recover, and analyze data from hard drives, floppy disks, and other digital media. These tools introduced the concept of creating forensic images—bit-for-bit copies of digital devices that preserve the integrity of the original evidence and allow for detailed analysis without altering the original data.

During this period, the legal system also began to acknowledge the importance of digital evidence. Laws surrounding computer crime, such as the Computer Fraud and Abuse Act (1986) in the U.S., were updated to address new forms of digital criminal activity. These legal developments led to the formalization of procedures for handling digital evidence, including rules for preserving evidence in a manner that would ensure its admissibility in court.

The 2000s: The Rise of Cybercrime and the Expansion of Digital Forensics

The early 2000s marked a significant shift in the role of digital forensics due to the explosive growth of the internet, social media, and mobile devices. As the internet became an integral part of business, personal communication, and everyday life, cybercrime also began to evolve and diversify. Identity theft, online fraud, child exploitation, and cyberattacks emerged as some of the most significant threats in the digital realm.

This expansion of digital crime increased the demand for digital forensic expertise, and forensic professionals were required to address new types of evidence. The rise of email communications, online activity logs, and social media interactions created new challenges for investigators. Moreover, the growth of encryption technologies, which aimed to protect the privacy of online communications and transactions, posed additional hurdles for forensic experts who needed to bypass these security measures in their investigations.

Another milestone in the 2000s was the development of mobile forensics. As mobile phones became ubiquitous, investigators realized the value of extracting digital evidence from mobile devices. The first mobile forensics tools appeared in the early 2000s, enabling investigators to extract information from mobile phones, including call logs, text messages, photos, and location data. Mobile forensics quickly became a vital subfield within digital forensics, with tools like Cellebrite and XRY emerging as industry standards for mobile device data extraction.

With the increasing use of cloud computing, the 2000s also saw the introduction of cloud forensics. The growth of online storage, web-based applications, and cloud computing platforms raised new challenges in terms of accessing and preserving digital evidence. Investigators had to learn how to work with data spread across multiple servers and jurisdictions, which required an understanding of cloud infrastructure and its implications for data privacy and security.

The 2010s: Advanced Tools, Big Data, and Emerging Threats

The 2010s saw an explosion of new technology, with the proliferation of smartphones, the Internet of Things (IoT), social media, and cloud computing further complicating digital investigations. Cybercrime became more sophisticated, and attackers increasingly targeted critical infrastructure, financial systems, and personal data. In response to these emerging threats, digital forensics continued to evolve, with advanced tools and techniques being developed to handle the new complexity.

The rise of big data meant that forensic investigators had to process vast amounts of information from numerous sources, including cloud-based storage, mobile devices, and network logs. This required the development of new data analytics tools and techniques to sift through massive datasets and identify relevant evidence. Additionally, the emergence of artificial intelligence (AI) and machine learning (ML) began to play a role in helping forensic investigators analyze data more efficiently and effectively.

Another trend during this time was the rise of cybersecurity forensics, with a greater emphasis on detecting, analyzing, and mitigating cyberattacks. Digital forensics became integral to incident response teams, who relied on forensic tools and expertise to investigate breaches, track down attackers, and determine the scope of the damage. High-profile incidents, such as data breaches involving large corporations, further highlighted the importance of digital forensics in maintaining the integrity and security of digital systems.

The 2020s and Beyond: The Future of Digital Forensics

Looking forward, the future of digital forensics promises continued innovation and adaptation to emerging technologies. As the world becomes increasingly interconnected through IoT devices, artificial intelligence, and decentralized systems like blockchain, forensic experts will need to develop new strategies to collect and analyze evidence from these technologies.

The rise of encrypted communication platforms, along with privacy concerns, will likely continue to challenge investigators. At the same time, new tools that leverage AI and automated systems will likely streamline the process of identifying, collecting, and analyzing digital evidence. As cybercrime becomes more sophisticated, digital forensics will need to evolve to stay one step ahead of cybercriminals.

In conclusion, digital forensics has come a long way since its inception, driven by technological advancements and an ever-growing need to address digital crimes. As technology continues to evolve, so too will the tools, techniques, and methodologies that define the field. Digital forensics will remain at the forefront of cybersecurity, criminal investigations, and legal proceedings, adapting to the challenges of the digital age.

1.2 Key Applications in Modern Investigations

Digital forensics has become a vital tool in modern investigations, providing essential insights into a wide range of criminal and civil matters. As technology continues to advance and permeate every facet of daily life, the role of digital evidence in solving cases has become increasingly critical. From cybercrime and fraud to corporate espionage and national security, digital forensics plays a crucial role in uncovering the truth. This section explores some of the key applications of digital forensics in modern investigations, highlighting how this discipline is applied to various fields and industries.

1. Cybercrime Investigations

One of the most prominent applications of digital forensics is in investigating cybercrimes, which have surged in recent years. Cybercriminals use a wide array of digital tools to perpetrate illegal activities, including hacking, identity theft, fraud, phishing, and the distribution of malware. The primary goal of digital forensics in cybercrime investigations is to identify, collect, and analyze digital evidence that can help trace the origin of cyberattacks, identify the perpetrators, and uncover the methods used.

Digital forensic tools are used to track malicious activity, recover deleted files, and analyze logs from servers, networks, and personal devices. For example, in cases of hacking or data breaches, investigators may analyze network traffic, look for traces of unauthorized access, and gather evidence from compromised systems. The growing sophistication of cyberattacks, including ransomware and Distributed Denial of Service (DDoS) attacks, requires forensic experts to have advanced knowledge and specialized tools to properly analyze these incidents.

2. Fraud and Financial Crimes

Financial crimes, including fraud, embezzlement, insider trading, and money laundering, often leave behind digital traces that can be uncovered through digital forensics. In financial investigations, forensic experts examine financial records, transaction logs, and other digital artifacts that might point to illegal activity. Digital forensics can be used to track money flows, identify fraudulent transactions, and recover hidden assets.

For example, in cases of embezzlement, investigators may look at email communications, financial spreadsheets, accounting software, and transaction records to trace the movement of funds and identify discrepancies. In money laundering cases, forensic experts can analyze bank statements, wire transfers, and cryptocurrency transactions to uncover illicit financial activities.

Moreover, with the increasing use of digital platforms in the financial sector—such as online banking, e-commerce, and digital payments—digital forensics has become essential in identifying fraudulent activity and securing financial systems. Investigators often use digital forensics to identify vulnerabilities in financial institutions and prevent future attacks.

3. Corporate Investigations and Intellectual Property Theft

In the business world, intellectual property (IP) theft, corporate espionage, and insider threats are growing concerns. Digital forensics plays an essential role in investigating these types of crimes, which often involve the unauthorized access, theft, or distribution of sensitive corporate data. Investigators use digital forensic tools to track access to confidential information, analyze data exfiltration methods, and identify suspects who may have stolen trade secrets or other proprietary materials.

Forensic experts might examine email correspondence, file-sharing platforms, and cloud storage accounts to determine how sensitive data was compromised. In cases of intellectual property theft, forensic investigators can examine network traffic, analyze access logs, and recover deleted files to uncover the perpetrators and assess the impact of the theft on the company's operations.

Digital forensics is also used in investigating employee misconduct, such as inappropriate use of company resources, data breaches, or policy violations. In such cases, investigators often look into email communications, employee computers, and network activity to identify wrongdoing. By securing and analyzing digital evidence, forensic experts help businesses protect their assets, mitigate financial losses, and ensure regulatory compliance.

4. Digital Evidence in Criminal Investigations

In traditional criminal investigations, such as homicide, assault, and robbery cases, digital forensics plays an increasingly important role in uncovering evidence that can either confirm or challenge the facts of a case. Investigators use digital evidence from mobile phones, computers, tablets, and other devices to corroborate witness statements, track the movements of suspects, and identify potential leads.

Mobile forensics is particularly valuable in criminal investigations, as mobile phones often contain a wealth of evidence, including call logs, text messages, emails, photos, and location data. Forensic investigators may recover deleted texts or trace the suspect's movements via GPS data to help build a timeline of events. In some cases, even the metadata associated with files, photos, or documents can reveal critical information, such as the date and time the evidence was created or modified.

Furthermore, social media platforms play a significant role in modern investigations. Digital forensics is used to retrieve and analyze social media data, such as posts, comments, private messages, and connections, which can be instrumental in building a suspect profile or verifying alibis. Investigators also use digital evidence to track down criminals who may be using the dark web or encrypted communication tools to engage in illegal activities.

5. Digital Forensics in Child Exploitation Cases

Digital forensics has become a cornerstone in the fight against child exploitation and online child abuse. Law enforcement agencies, as well as non-profit organizations, rely on digital forensics to investigate cases of child pornography, online grooming, and trafficking. Investigators use digital tools to identify and recover illicit materials from computers, mobile devices, and cloud storage, often uncovering evidence that leads to the identification and arrest of perpetrators.

Forensic investigators also examine social media interactions, chat logs, and email communications to track online grooming activities and identify networks involved in exploitation. They use advanced tools to trace the distribution of illegal material, map connections between suspects, and disrupt criminal networks. Moreover, the use of metadata, file hashes, and forensic imaging enables investigators to accurately preserve and present evidence, ensuring that it is admissible in court.

With the increasing use of encrypted communications and the rise of new technologies like cryptocurrencies, investigators face new challenges in combating child exploitation online. Digital forensics continues to adapt to these challenges by developing innovative tools and techniques to trace evidence in even the most complex and hidden digital environments.

6. National Security and Counterterrorism Investigations

Digital forensics plays a crucial role in national security and counterterrorism efforts, where intelligence agencies and law enforcement use digital evidence to prevent and investigate terrorist activities. Digital forensics allows investigators to track the activities of terrorist organizations, monitor communications, and uncover plans for attacks.

Investigators also analyze data from seized devices, such as laptops and smartphones, to identify key operatives, uncover hidden messages, and dismantle terrorist networks.

Forensic techniques are also used to analyze data from digital communication systems, such as encrypted emails, chat applications, and social media platforms. In counterterrorism investigations, digital forensics often aids in identifying individuals involved in recruiting, radicalizing, or financing terrorist activities. In some cases, investigators work with cybersecurity teams to uncover cyberattacks launched by hostile state actors or terrorist organizations.

The role of digital forensics in national security has become more critical as cyberterrorism and digital espionage continue to rise, necessitating the development of advanced forensic tools to protect against these threats.

7. Legal and Civil Disputes

Digital forensics is also widely used in legal and civil matters, particularly in cases of divorce, child custody, and employment disputes. Digital evidence can provide insight into issues like financial misconduct, harassment, or infidelity. For example, investigators may examine email communications, text messages, or browsing history to uncover relevant information. In custody disputes, forensics can be used to verify claims made by either party regarding their online behavior or communication patterns.

Moreover, in civil litigation, digital forensics can be used to uncover evidence related to intellectual property violations, breach of contract, or defamation. Investigators often work with legal professionals to identify relevant digital evidence, analyze it, and present it in court in a way that complies with evidentiary standards.

Digital forensics plays an indispensable role in modern investigations across a variety of sectors, from law enforcement and cybersecurity to business and legal disputes. The growing reliance on digital data, coupled with the increasing sophistication of cybercrime, has made digital forensics essential in uncovering the truth and solving complex cases. As technology continues to advance, digital forensics will remain a critical tool in the fight against crime and the pursuit of justice.

1.3 Challenges in the Digital Age

The rise of digital technology has transformed nearly every aspect of life, from how we communicate and store data to how we work, socialize, and conduct business. While these advancements have brought significant benefits, they have also created a new set of challenges for digital forensics professionals. As cybercrime becomes more sophisticated and the volume of data increases exponentially, investigators are confronted with a host of difficulties in obtaining, preserving, and analyzing digital evidence. This section explores some of the key challenges faced by digital forensics practitioners in the digital age, including the evolving nature of technology, privacy concerns, encryption, the sheer volume of data, and jurisdictional issues.

1. The Growing Complexity of Technology

One of the most significant challenges in digital forensics is the growing complexity of technology itself. Digital devices are no longer simple machines but are increasingly interconnected, multi-functional, and capable of performing a wide range of tasks. From smartphones and tablets to smartwatches, gaming consoles, and IoT devices, the digital landscape has expanded to include countless different types of devices, each with its own operating systems, applications, and data formats.

As technology evolves, so do the tools and techniques used by cybercriminals. Modern cybercrimes, such as hacking, ransomware, and data breaches, often involve complex methods that can obscure traces of malicious activity. Investigators must constantly adapt to these new technologies, learning how to extract relevant data from devices and systems that may not have existed just a few years ago. In addition to traditional computers, data is now stored across multiple platforms, including cloud services, mobile apps, and distributed networks, requiring investigators to have a broad range of skills and tools at their disposal.

The rapid pace of technological advancement means that forensic tools and methodologies must continually evolve. Software tools that are effective today may become obsolete in a few years as new technologies and operating systems are introduced. This ever-changing landscape demands that forensic professionals engage in continuous learning and stay current with the latest developments in technology and digital forensics techniques.

2. Encryption and Data Protection

Encryption has become one of the biggest challenges for digital forensic investigators. As data privacy and security concerns continue to grow, individuals and organizations have increasingly adopted encryption technologies to protect sensitive data. While encryption plays a vital role in safeguarding personal and corporate information, it also presents significant obstacles for law enforcement and forensic investigators who need to access encrypted data in the course of their investigations.

Criminals and cybercriminals often use encryption to hide their activities, such as communicating via encrypted messaging apps or storing illicit files in encrypted containers. In many cases, investigators are unable to access critical evidence without the proper decryption keys or passwords. Even with advancements in cracking encryption, decryption methods can be time-consuming, resource-intensive, and, in some cases, impossible, especially with the use of strong, modern encryption algorithms.

The debate over encryption and law enforcement access has become a hot topic in recent years, with some arguing that backdoors or weaknesses in encryption should be built into software to allow authorities to decrypt data when needed. However, such measures could undermine the security of the digital ecosystem, leaving users vulnerable to exploitation. This presents a delicate balance between ensuring privacy and enabling effective investigations.

3. The Volume of Data

The sheer volume of data generated in the digital age is another major challenge for forensic investigators. Every day, billions of emails, text messages, social media posts, transactions, and other forms of digital communication are created and stored across the globe. As individuals and organizations generate more data than ever before, investigators face the daunting task of sifting through enormous amounts of information to uncover relevant evidence.

The explosion of data is particularly problematic in cases involving large organizations or cybercrime syndicates, where terabytes or even petabytes of data may need to be analyzed. Manually reviewing and analyzing such vast quantities of information is time-consuming and may lead to missed evidence or delayed investigations. To address this, forensic experts increasingly rely on advanced data analytics tools, machine learning algorithms, and artificial intelligence (AI) to help process and analyze large datasets efficiently. These technologies enable investigators to identify patterns, detect anomalies, and flag potentially relevant data for further examination.

Despite these advancements, the sheer scale of data remains a challenge, particularly in cases where investigators may be working with outdated or incompatible data formats. The ability to quickly extract, index, and review data in a meaningful way is essential to ensuring timely and accurate conclusions in digital forensic investigations.

4. Privacy Concerns and Legal Issues

Privacy concerns are an inherent challenge in the digital forensics process, particularly as governments and organizations collect vast amounts of data about individuals. Balancing the need for security and the collection of digital evidence with respect for privacy and civil liberties is a difficult task. Investigators must navigate a complex web of privacy laws and regulations that govern how digital evidence can be collected, stored, and used.

In many jurisdictions, there are strict rules governing the search and seizure of digital evidence, and investigators must obtain proper authorization, such as a warrant, before they can access a suspect's devices or online accounts. These legal requirements help ensure that evidence is collected in a manner that respects the rights of individuals. However, the increasing use of cloud storage and remote computing has complicated this process. Data that is stored in the cloud, for example, may be hosted in another country, raising questions about jurisdiction and the application of local laws.

Furthermore, the vast amount of personal data stored on modern devices presents ethical and legal dilemmas for investigators. In some cases, sensitive information—such as medical records, private communications, or financial details—may be inadvertently exposed during an investigation. Ensuring that investigators act within the bounds of the law while also respecting individuals' privacy rights is an ongoing challenge in the digital age.

5. Jurisdictional Issues and Cross-Border Investigations

The global nature of the internet has created significant jurisdictional challenges in digital forensics investigations. Unlike traditional criminal activity, where the crime typically occurs within the boundaries of a single country or jurisdiction, digital crimes can involve perpetrators, victims, and evidence scattered across multiple locations worldwide. A single cyberattack could involve servers in one country, stolen data in another, and a suspect in yet another location.

Forensic investigators are often required to work across borders, but differences in legal systems, data protection laws, and international agreements can complicate cooperation. For instance, some countries have strict privacy laws that prohibit the sharing of digital evidence with foreign governments or organizations. In contrast, other jurisdictions may have more relaxed data protection laws, leading to potential conflicts over the handling and transfer of evidence.

To address these challenges, international cooperation and treaties, such as the Budapest Convention on Cybercrime and the General Data Protection Regulation (GDPR), have been established. These agreements aim to create a unified approach to handling digital evidence and ensure that countries can collaborate on cross-border investigations. However, the lack of a universal legal framework for digital forensics means that investigators must navigate a complex array of laws and regulations when conducting cross-border investigations.

6. The Dark Web and Anonymity

The rise of the dark web and anonymous communication tools has introduced new challenges for digital forensics professionals. The dark web, a hidden part of the internet where illegal activities such as drug trafficking, human trafficking, and cybercrime are often conducted, is designed to be difficult to trace. Criminals use anonymizing technologies such as Tor and cryptocurrencies to obscure their identities and activities, making it difficult for investigators to track perpetrators and gather evidence.

While digital forensics experts have developed techniques for tracking online activity and identifying suspicious behavior on the dark web, anonymity tools and encryption continue to pose significant obstacles. Investigators must employ specialized techniques to de-anonymize individuals, trace cryptocurrency transactions, and link illicit activities to real-world perpetrators. The evolving nature of these technologies makes it a constant challenge to stay ahead of cybercriminals who are continuously adapting to new methods of evading detection.

The digital age presents both opportunities and challenges for forensic investigators. While the increasing reliance on digital devices and data has opened up new avenues for solving crimes and uncovering evidence, it has also introduced a range of technical, legal, and ethical challenges. As technology continues to evolve, digital forensics will need to adapt, leveraging new tools and techniques to address the complexities of modern investigations. To be successful, forensic professionals must stay informed about emerging technologies, navigate privacy concerns and jurisdictional issues, and continue to develop innovative strategies to uncover the truth in a rapidly changing digital landscape.

1.4 The Role of a Digital Forensic Investigator

Digital forensics has become an integral part of modern investigations, playing a critical role in uncovering digital evidence that can make or break a case. As the world becomes increasingly digital, the role of a digital forensic investigator has evolved into one that combines technical expertise with investigative skills. These professionals are tasked with identifying, preserving, recovering, and analyzing digital evidence from various electronic devices to help solve crimes, resolve disputes, and protect organizations from security breaches. This section explores the core responsibilities, skills, and challenges faced by digital forensic investigators in today's fast-paced and ever-evolving technological landscape.

1. Identifying and Acquiring Digital Evidence

The first and foremost role of a digital forensic investigator is to identify and acquire digital evidence. This could include anything from computer hard drives, smartphones, and tablets to cloud storage, email accounts, social media profiles, and other online repositories. A thorough understanding of where digital evidence may reside, and how it can be collected without altering or damaging it, is essential.

A digital forensic investigator must be skilled at identifying various types of data sources that may contain important information. For instance, in a criminal investigation, evidence could include email correspondence, deleted files, location data, or chat logs. They also must be able to recognize the relevance of data from seemingly unrelated devices, such as network routers, surveillance cameras, or even smart home devices.

Once evidence is identified, the next challenge is to ensure that it is acquired properly. Digital forensics is governed by strict procedures to preserve the integrity of the evidence. Investigators must use proper tools and techniques to avoid tampering with or contaminating the data, ensuring that the evidence remains admissible in court. This often involves creating forensic images of storage devices, which are exact bit-by-bit copies of the original data, allowing for further analysis without risking the alteration of original evidence.

2. Preserving and Protecting the Integrity of Digital Evidence

Preserving the integrity of digital evidence is one of the most critical aspects of a digital forensic investigator's job. Digital evidence is highly volatile and can be easily altered, deleted, or corrupted if not handled properly. A key principle of digital forensics is the concept of "chain of custody," which refers to the documentation and tracking of evidence from its collection to its presentation in court. This ensures that the evidence has not been tampered with and can be verified as authentic.

Digital forensic investigators must follow strict protocols to ensure evidence is preserved without any alteration. This includes making write-protected copies of data, securing physical and digital access to the evidence, and maintaining proper documentation of each step of the process. Any lapse in the chain of custody or failure to protect evidence could render the investigation compromised or inadmissible in court.

In addition to physical security measures, digital forensic investigators must also ensure the confidentiality of sensitive data. For example, in cases involving financial records, medical data, or personal communications, investigators must take care not to expose or share information that could violate privacy laws or ethical standards. The investigator's role extends beyond simply finding and preserving evidence to ensuring that it is handled in a manner that respects legal and ethical guidelines.

3. Analyzing and Interpreting Digital Evidence

Once the evidence has been acquired and preserved, the next step in the digital forensic process is to analyze and interpret the data. This is often the most complex part of the investigation, as digital evidence can be fragmented, encrypted, or hidden within large volumes of irrelevant data.

Forensic investigators use specialized software tools to examine and process digital evidence. These tools allow them to recover deleted files, reconstruct data fragments, and analyze file metadata to uncover valuable information. For instance, an investigator may use a tool to recover files that were deleted from a suspect's computer or smartphone, or they might trace the history of internet browsing activity to establish a timeline of events.

Digital forensic analysis also involves understanding the context in which the data was created. Investigators need to examine not just the files themselves, but the underlying systems, applications, and networks that generated the data. For example, in the case of a cyberattack, a forensic investigator might analyze network traffic, server logs, and file access records to determine how the attack occurred, who was responsible, and what impact it had on the system.

The ability to identify patterns, anomalies, and inconsistencies in large data sets is essential. Investigators must be able to filter out irrelevant information while recognizing key pieces of evidence that can drive the investigation forward. This requires not just technical expertise, but also analytical thinking and problem-solving skills.

4. Reporting Findings and Testifying in Court

A digital forensic investigator's work does not end with data analysis. One of their key responsibilities is to clearly and effectively communicate their findings, both in written reports and orally in court. Digital forensics plays a vital role in legal proceedings, where investigators must present their findings in a manner that is understandable to non-technical individuals, including judges, attorneys, and juries.

In many cases, forensic investigators must prepare detailed reports documenting their findings, the methods they used to analyze the data, and the conclusions they have drawn. These reports are critical for building a case, whether in criminal or civil court. The investigator must also be prepared to explain their findings in the courtroom, often under cross-examination. This requires strong communication skills, attention to detail, and the ability to explain complex technical concepts in simple terms.

Forensic experts must be impartial and objective in their reporting. Their role is not to advocate for either side in a legal dispute, but rather to provide an accurate, unbiased analysis of the digital evidence. This makes credibility and professionalism paramount in the role of a digital forensic investigator.

5. Staying Updated with Emerging Technologies

The field of digital forensics is constantly evolving as new technologies emerge and criminals develop more sophisticated tactics to hide their activities. A key responsibility of a digital forensic investigator is to stay up-to-date with the latest trends, tools, and techniques in the field. This requires ongoing training and education to keep pace with advancements in hardware, software, and cybercrime tactics.

Investigators must continually develop their skills and knowledge of new digital environments, such as mobile devices, cloud storage, and the dark web. They must also stay informed about the legal and ethical challenges that arise with new technologies, such as issues related to privacy, data protection, and cross-border jurisdiction.

For example, as the use of encrypted messaging apps, cryptocurrency, and blockchain technology grows, forensic investigators must find new ways to recover and analyze data from these systems. In addition, as artificial intelligence and machine learning tools become more prevalent, investigators may need to integrate these technologies into their forensic toolkit to efficiently process and analyze large datasets.

6. Collaborating with Other Investigative Professionals

Digital forensics is often part of a larger investigative effort that involves law enforcement agencies, attorneys, cybersecurity experts, and other professionals. Digital forensic investigators frequently collaborate with these other specialists to share information, strategies, and resources.

In a large-scale investigation, a digital forensic investigator might work alongside a cybersecurity expert to track down a cybercriminal, with an attorney to ensure the evidence is admissible in court, or with law enforcement officers to ensure proper legal procedures are followed during evidence collection. Effective communication and teamwork are essential, as the investigator must be able to coordinate their efforts with other professionals to build a comprehensive case.

The role of a digital forensic investigator is multifaceted and requires a unique blend of technical expertise, analytical skills, and legal knowledge. These professionals are tasked with identifying, preserving, analyzing, and interpreting digital evidence in a way that can help solve crimes, protect organizations, and ensure justice. As technology continues to evolve, so too does the role of the digital forensic investigator, making their work critical to the ongoing efforts to combat cybercrime, protect privacy, and ensure the integrity of digital systems. It is a challenging, dynamic field that requires a constant commitment to learning and adapting, but also one that offers the potential to make a meaningful impact on society.

1.5 Case Studies: Milestones in Digital Forensics

Digital forensics has come a long way from its early days, with the evolution of technology constantly shaping the methods and tools used by investigators. Over the years, high-profile cases and significant breakthroughs in digital forensics have helped to shape the field into what it is today. These milestones have not only advanced the science of digital forensics but also demonstrated its power and relevance in the real world, influencing both legal and investigative practices. This section explores several landmark case studies that highlight key moments in the development and application of digital forensics.

1. The BTK Killer Case (2004)

One of the earliest high-profile cases where digital forensics played a pivotal role in solving a crime was the investigation of the BTK (Bind, Torture, Kill) serial killer in Kansas, USA. For years, the BTK killer eluded authorities, sending taunting letters to the police, detailing his gruesome crimes. Despite an extensive investigation, the killer remained unidentified for over 30 years.

In 2004, the killer resurfaced, sending a floppy disk to a local television station. Forensic experts were able to extract metadata from the disk, which contained information about the computer it was used on, including the name of the user: "Dennis." The data led investigators to a specific computer at a local church, which eventually led to the arrest of Dennis Rader, the BTK killer.

This case marked a significant turning point in the use of digital forensics in criminal investigations. It demonstrated the power of seemingly trivial digital evidence, such as metadata embedded in a file, and underscored the importance of thorough digital evidence analysis in solving complex cases. The BTK killer case helped to establish digital forensics as a vital tool in modern criminal investigations, showcasing how even the smallest digital footprint could unravel a long-unsolved mystery.

2. The Enron Scandal (2001)

The Enron scandal, one of the largest corporate fraud cases in history, involved the manipulation of financial statements and the concealment of billions of dollars in debt. When the company collapsed in 2001, investigators turned to digital forensics to piece together the vast amounts of financial and email data stored on Enron's computers. The evidence revealed that key executives had used fraudulent accounting practices to mislead shareholders, regulators, and employees.

Digital forensic experts played a crucial role in uncovering the scale of the fraud by recovering deleted emails, financial spreadsheets, and other critical data from the company's servers. Investigators used specialized tools to recover evidence that had been intentionally erased by employees, including data hidden on hard drives and backup systems. This data was crucial in bringing charges against top executives, including former CEO Jeffrey Skilling and CFO Andrew Fastow.

The Enron case highlighted the importance of digital forensics in corporate investigations and illustrated the need for robust systems to ensure the integrity of electronic records. It also brought to light the dangers of digital data manipulation in high-stakes corporate environments and underscored the growing need for companies to implement proper digital records management and cybersecurity protocols.

3. The Sony PlayStation Network Hack (2011)

In 2011, hackers targeted Sony's PlayStation Network (PSN), a major online gaming platform, compromising the personal data of over 77 million accounts. This breach included sensitive information such as names, addresses, credit card numbers, and passwords. The attack resulted in Sony temporarily shutting down the PSN, and the company was forced to deal with the fallout of a massive data breach that affected millions of users worldwide.

Digital forensics investigators played a critical role in identifying the nature of the attack, tracing the breach back to a group of hackers known as LulzSec. Forensic analysis of the compromised systems revealed the techniques used by the attackers, including the use of SQL injection vulnerabilities to infiltrate the network. Investigators also tracked down the hackers by analyzing IP addresses, examining logs of the attack, and recovering data that had been deleted or altered by the perpetrators.

The PlayStation Network hack marked a significant moment in cybersecurity history, as it exposed the vulnerability of large online platforms and underscored the need for stronger data protection measures. It also highlighted the increasing importance of digital forensics in investigating cybercrimes and understanding the methods used by cybercriminals. The case prompted changes in how companies approach cybersecurity, digital evidence handling, and incident response.

4. The Ashley Madison Hack (2015)

The 2015 hack of Ashley Madison, a website designed for facilitating extramarital affairs, was another high-profile cybercrime case that relied heavily on digital forensics. The attackers, known as "The Impact Team," exposed personal data of millions of users, including names, email addresses, and payment details. The hackers demanded the site be shut down, threatening to release the personal information of its users unless their demands were met.

Forensic investigators were tasked with analyzing the data dump and identifying the methods used by the hackers to breach the site's security. The investigation revealed that the attackers had exploited weaknesses in the website's security, including unencrypted user data and poor password management. By analyzing server logs, metadata, and other digital traces, investigators were able to trace the origins of the attack to specific IP addresses and determine the tools used to carry out the hack.

In the aftermath, the Ashley Madison hack raised serious questions about privacy, security, and data protection, particularly with regard to websites that store sensitive personal information. It underscored the need for digital forensics professionals to be well-versed in analyzing data breaches and cyberattacks in order to identify culprits and prevent future incidents. The hack also highlighted the growing role of digital forensics in dealing with cyber extortion and other types of online crime.

5. The Silk Road Investigation (2013)

The Silk Road was an online black market that facilitated the sale of illegal goods, including drugs, weapons, and stolen data, using cryptocurrency such as Bitcoin. Operated on the dark web, it was designed to be anonymous and resistant to traditional law enforcement detection. However, in 2013, the FBI successfully shut down the Silk Road and arrested its founder, Ross Ulbricht, thanks in part to the work of digital forensic investigators.

Digital forensics played a pivotal role in the investigation, as investigators analyzed the online transactions, server logs, and digital evidence left behind by Ulbricht. Through detailed examination of Ulbricht's computer, emails, and the Bitcoin transactions associated with Silk Road, investigators were able to trace the operations of the site, track the flow of money, and identify the individuals involved in the illegal activities. In particular, forensic investigators analyzed metadata from Ulbricht's laptop, uncovering evidence that linked him to the Silk Road's creation and operation.

The Silk Road case was a landmark moment in the use of digital forensics for investigating dark web activities and cybercrimes. It showed how even encrypted, anonymous systems could be infiltrated by skilled digital investigators. The case also raised important questions about the future of digital currency, online anonymity, and the role of digital forensics in combating illicit online marketplaces.

6. The 2016 Democratic National Committee (DNC) Email Leak

In 2016, a massive cyberattack targeted the Democratic National Committee (DNC) in the United States, resulting in the theft and public release of thousands of emails. These emails, which exposed potential bias in favor of Hillary Clinton's campaign during the primaries, were leaked by WikiLeaks. Digital forensic investigators, including those from cybersecurity firms and government agencies, played a crucial role in determining the origin of the attack and the perpetrators behind it.

Forensic analysis revealed that Russian state-sponsored hackers were responsible for the breach, using techniques such as spear-phishing emails to gain access to the DNC's networks. Investigators traced the malware used in the attack to known Russian hacking groups, including APT28 and APT29, and used digital forensics tools to track the movement of data and uncover the methods used to exfiltrate information from the DNC's servers.

This case was significant not only because of the high-profile nature of the breach but also because it highlighted the intersection of cyberattacks and geopolitics. Digital forensics played a central role in attributing the attack to specific actors and providing evidence for the subsequent investigations into election interference and cyber espionage. The case further reinforced the need for digital forensics expertise in investigating cyberattacks that have broader political and national security implications.

The milestones discussed in this chapter showcase the growing importance of digital forensics in solving crimes, identifying perpetrators, and ensuring accountability. From the investigation of serial killers to the analysis of massive data breaches and cyberattacks, digital forensics has proven to be an essential tool in uncovering the truth. These case studies highlight not only the power of digital forensics to extract valuable evidence but also the challenges and complexities investigators face in an increasingly digital and interconnected world. As technology continues to evolve, digital forensics will remain an indispensable part of modern investigations, ensuring that justice can be served in even the most challenging and complex cases.

2. The Fundamentals of E-Evidence

Digital evidence, or e-evidence, is at the heart of every digital forensic investigation. This chapter delves into the foundational concepts that define e-evidence, exploring what it is, where it comes from, and why it is both powerful and challenging to handle. You'll learn about the different types of electronic evidence, its sources—from devices to networks—and the critical importance of maintaining its integrity throughout an investigation. By grasping these fundamentals, you'll build a solid understanding of how e-evidence serves as the backbone of forensic science in the digital age.

2.1 What Qualifies as Digital Evidence?

In the digital age, evidence is not confined to traditional physical forms like fingerprints, DNA, or documents. With the increasing reliance on electronic devices and online platforms, digital evidence has become a critical component of modern investigations, impacting everything from criminal cases to corporate disputes. But what exactly qualifies as digital evidence, and how do investigators determine its relevance?

Digital evidence refers to information or data stored or transmitted in a digital form that can be used in legal proceedings. This evidence is typically found on electronic devices, such as computers, smartphones, servers, and even cloud storage systems, and can include anything from files and emails to digital footprints left on websites and networks. Understanding what qualifies as digital evidence is essential for anyone working in the field of digital forensics, as it governs how investigators collect, preserve, analyze, and present information in a way that is legally admissible and reliable.

1. Types of Digital Evidence

Digital evidence can be broadly classified into several categories, depending on the source, content, and relevance to the case at hand. Below are the primary types of digital evidence:

a. Files and Documents:

Files and documents stored on electronic devices are the most common forms of digital evidence. These can include text documents, spreadsheets, presentations, and PDFs, which may contain relevant information such as emails, memos, contracts, or financial records. Files can be retrieved from local storage devices (e.g., hard drives, SSDs), as well as from cloud storage services.

b. Emails and Messaging:

Emails, chat messages, and social media conversations are powerful forms of digital evidence, particularly in cases involving communication and intent. Investigators can access these records to examine conversations, timestamps, attachments, and metadata that could reveal intent, conspiracies, or provide context for specific actions. Messaging apps, email services (Gmail, Yahoo, etc.), and even direct messages on social media platforms can contain valuable evidence.

c. Internet History and Browser Data:

Web browsing data, including search history, cookies, and cache files, provides insight into an individual's activities on the internet. This data can help investigators understand where a suspect has been online, what they have been researching, and whether they have visited relevant websites. Browser history can also include timestamps and URLs that indicate when a person visited a particular site, which can be crucial for building a timeline.

d. Metadata:

Metadata is often referred to as "data about data." It includes information embedded in files that provides details such as the date and time a file was created, modified, or accessed, the author or user who created the file, and the devices used to create or modify the file. Metadata is critical in many investigations, especially when it comes to verifying the authenticity of digital evidence, as well as establishing a timeline of events or activities.

e. Digital Footprints:

Digital footprints are traces left behind by a user's online activities. These can include IP addresses, login records, GPS coordinates, location tracking, and timestamps associated with website visits or social media interactions. These footprints are especially important in tracking the movements and actions of suspects or victims, often providing essential evidence in cases like stalking, cyberbullying, or fraud.

f. Logs and System Data:

System logs (e.g., operating system logs, application logs, security logs) and event logs are records that track the actions or events on a system. These logs can provide crucial evidence in cases of system breaches, cyberattacks, or unauthorized access. For instance, a security log might contain records of login attempts, failed passwords, or the use of administrator privileges to access sensitive data.

g. Digital Images and Videos:

Images and videos stored on devices or captured through digital cameras, smartphones, or surveillance systems can serve as powerful pieces of evidence. These digital files can include photographs, screenshots, and video recordings that may capture criminal activity, evidence of a suspect's whereabouts, or physical evidence at a crime scene. The metadata associated with these files, such as geolocation data, timestamp, and device information, further enhances their reliability as evidence.

h. Audio Files:

Audio recordings, whether from phones, recorders, or online platforms, can be a significant form of digital evidence. In criminal investigations, audio files can contain conversations, confessions, threats, or discussions related to the crime. Just like other types of digital evidence, the integrity of audio files, including the origin, authenticity, and editing, must be verified through forensic analysis.

i. Cloud-Based Evidence:

Cloud storage platforms (Google Drive, iCloud, Dropbox, etc.) have become repositories for vast amounts of digital data. Digital evidence from cloud services can include documents, images, emails, and backups that are crucial to investigations. Data stored in the cloud may also contain data synchronization logs or metadata indicating when a file was uploaded, modified, or shared, making it an important source of evidence. Legal challenges related to cloud data often involve jurisdictional issues and the privacy laws of the country where the cloud service is based.

j. Digital Currency Transactions (e.g., Bitcoin, Ethereum):

In cases involving financial crimes, such as money laundering, fraud, or ransomware, digital currency transactions often provide valuable evidence. Transactions made via blockchain technology, like those involving Bitcoin or Ethereum, are recorded publicly, though they are anonymous. Digital forensics experts can track and analyze these transactions to identify suspects, trace funds, or uncover patterns of illegal activity.

2. Requirements for Digital Evidence to Be Admissible

While digital evidence can be incredibly valuable, it must meet certain criteria to be admissible in court. The legal admissibility of digital evidence is governed by established rules and protocols to ensure its integrity and reliability. These requirements are similar to those applied to physical evidence and include:

a. Relevance:

For digital evidence to be admissible, it must be relevant to the case at hand. This means that the evidence should have a direct connection to the allegations or the dispute in question. Evidence must demonstrate its importance in supporting claims or disproving the defense.

b. Authenticity:

Digital evidence must be shown to be authentic, meaning it must be proven that the evidence is what it claims to be and has not been altered or tampered with. This is where forensic tools and techniques come into play to verify the integrity of the data, including the use of hash values, metadata analysis, and the chain of custody documentation.

c. Chain of Custody:

The chain of custody is a record that documents every instance of access, transfer, or handling of digital evidence. This ensures that the evidence has not been tampered with or altered during the investigation and handling process. Maintaining an unbroken chain of custody is vital for digital evidence to be admissible in court, as it helps establish the credibility of the evidence.

d. Accuracy and Integrity:

Digital evidence must be accurately represented and maintained to ensure that it retains its integrity. Any alterations or destruction of digital evidence during collection, analysis, or storage could compromise its credibility and render it inadmissible.

e. Preservation:

Once identified, digital evidence must be preserved in its original form, ensuring that no data is overwritten, lost, or corrupted. This involves the use of write-blockers during acquisition, creating bit-by-bit copies (forensic images) of devices, and storing evidence in secure, controlled environments.

3. Challenges with Digital Evidence

Despite its importance, the use of digital evidence presents several challenges. These include issues related to the rapid advancement of technology, the complexity of data recovery, the sheer volume of digital data available, and the legal and ethical concerns surrounding privacy and data protection. Some of the major challenges include:

- **Encryption and Password Protection**: Many devices and data are encrypted, making it difficult for forensic investigators to access them without the correct passwords or keys.
- **Data Volatility**: Digital evidence can be easily altered, deleted, or corrupted, particularly on devices that are still in use. Thus, time is often of the essence when collecting digital evidence.
- **Data Storage and Retrieval**: The vast amounts of data available on cloud platforms, personal devices, and servers present a logistical challenge. Investigators must be able to locate and retrieve relevant data efficiently.
- **Jurisdictional Issues**: Digital evidence can span multiple jurisdictions, especially when dealing with cloud storage or cross-border communications, creating legal challenges and delays.

Digital evidence is any data stored, transmitted, or captured in a digital format that can be used in an investigation. It comes in various forms, including files, emails, metadata, images, and even digital currency transactions. For digital evidence to be admissible in court, it must be relevant, authentic, and handled according to strict legal protocols. With the rise of technology and the digital transformation of almost every aspect of society, digital evidence has become indispensable in modern investigations, but it also requires careful handling to ensure its integrity and reliability in legal proceedings.

2.2 Sources of Digital Evidence: Devices and Systems

Digital evidence is increasingly found across a variety of devices and systems. As technology has evolved, digital forensics has had to adapt to new sources of evidence, ranging from traditional computing devices like desktops and laptops to mobile devices, cloud systems, and the Internet of Things (IoT). Understanding where digital evidence can be found is critical for investigators, as it allows them to identify, preserve, and analyze relevant data in a way that meets legal and forensic standards.

This section explores the primary sources of digital evidence, focusing on the devices and systems that are most commonly encountered in digital forensics investigations. By understanding these sources, investigators can optimize their approach to collecting and analyzing evidence and ensure that all potential evidence is considered during an investigation.

1. Personal Computers (Desktops and Laptops)

Personal computers, including desktops and laptops, are one of the most common sources of digital evidence in forensic investigations. These devices typically store a large volume of data and can provide critical information related to a suspect's activities, communication, and digital footprints.

Key Evidence Sources on Personal Computers:

- **Files and Documents**: Personal computers are home to a wide range of documents, from word processing files to spreadsheets, presentations, and images. Investigators often recover these files from a device's hard drive or storage devices.
- **Emails and Communications**: Email clients (e.g., Outlook, Thunderbird) on desktops often store local copies of emails, including deleted messages. Additionally, evidence related to instant messaging or chat services (e.g., Skype, WhatsApp Desktop) can be recovered from computers.
- **System and Application Logs**: Logs detailing system events (such as login times, system errors, or application crashes) are often stored on a computer's hard drive. These logs can provide a timeline of activity and point to particular events that may have occurred.
- **Web Browsing History**: Browsing history, including visited websites, search terms, and cookies, is stored by web browsers and can reveal a user's online behavior. Evidence such as cached pages, bookmarks, or autofill data can help investigators build a suspect's timeline.

Personal computers typically contain vast amounts of data that can be vital to an investigation, but they also pose challenges due to the wide variety of file formats and applications used. Investigators must use specialized tools to recover deleted files, examine hidden or encrypted data, and create accurate forensic images of the device's storage.

2. Mobile Devices (Smartphones and Tablets)

Mobile devices, including smartphones and tablets, are increasingly central to investigations due to their widespread use and the significant amounts of personal data they contain. Mobile devices can serve as a rich source of evidence, providing insight into an individual's communication, location, and behaviors.

Key Evidence Sources on Mobile Devices:

- **Call Logs and Text Messages**: Phones store records of calls made and received, along with detailed information about the sender, receiver, and duration of the call. Text messages, including SMS and MMS, are often critical in investigating communication between suspects.
- **Contacts and Calendar Entries**: Data related to contacts, appointments, and reminders can offer valuable context in an investigation, revealing relationships or planned activities.
- **Photos, Videos, and Audio Recordings**: Mobile devices often store multimedia files, including photographs, videos, and voice memos. These can serve as direct evidence, such as photos of crime scenes or videos that capture criminal activity.
- **App Data and Social Media Activity**: Mobile applications, including social media apps (e.g., Facebook, Instagram, Twitter), messaging platforms (e.g., WhatsApp, Telegram), and even location-based services (e.g., Google Maps), store a wealth of evidence. These apps often retain user interactions, posts, geolocation data, and conversations that can be critical in a case.
- **Geolocation Data**: Most smartphones contain GPS functionality, allowing them to track and store precise location data. Geolocation information from mobile devices can be used to trace a suspect's movements or verify alibis.

While mobile devices are a rich source of evidence, they also present unique challenges, including encryption, locked screens, and evolving operating systems. Forensic investigators must have the expertise to bypass security measures like passcodes, perform logical or physical extractions of the data, and preserve data integrity.

3. Cloud Storage and Online Accounts

Cloud storage services, such as Google Drive, iCloud, Dropbox, and OneDrive, have become essential to the daily operations of individuals and businesses. These services enable users to store files remotely, access data across multiple devices, and back up their information. In a forensic context, cloud storage can serve as a treasure trove of evidence, with a wealth of data that may be difficult to recover from physical devices alone.

Key Evidence Sources in the Cloud:

- **Files and Documents**: Cloud services often store a copy of files such as documents, photos, videos, and spreadsheets. Investigators can search through these files for relevant evidence, including deleted versions or modified documents.
- **Emails and Communication Records**: Many cloud storage services integrate with email accounts (e.g., Gmail, Yahoo, Outlook). Emails stored in the cloud can provide critical evidence related to communication between parties, especially when emails are stored across multiple devices.
- **Backup Files**: Many individuals and organizations use cloud services to back up their devices. These backups can provide a copy of data that might have been lost or deleted from the original device, including app data, contacts, messages, and other personal information.
- **Shared Files and Collaborations**: Cloud storage platforms often allow for file sharing and collaborative work. Investigators can examine shared files, communication logs, and collaborative documents to uncover additional evidence related to the case.

Cloud services also introduce complexity in digital investigations, particularly regarding issues of jurisdiction and data privacy. Depending on where the service provider is based and the nature of the data, law enforcement may face challenges in accessing data across borders. In some cases, legal orders may be needed to access a user's cloud data, and investigators must be mindful of privacy laws.

4. Networked Systems and Servers

Networked systems, including servers, routers, and cloud-based infrastructure, are another critical source of digital evidence. These systems can contain logs, communication data, and system records that provide valuable insight into the activities of individuals or organizations involved in a particular investigation. Servers hosting websites, email services, or online applications can store records of user activities and interactions.

Key Evidence Sources in Networked Systems:

- **Server Logs**: Servers that host websites or applications typically generate detailed logs of access, including user IP addresses, timestamps, and the pages or files that were accessed. These logs can help investigators trace a suspect's online activities, pinpoint the time of a crime, or track unauthorized access.

- **Network Traffic Data**: Routers, firewalls, and other network devices track the flow of data across a network. Investigators can analyze network traffic to identify patterns of activity, including communication between devices, data transfers, or cyberattacks.
- **Database Files**: Servers that host databases, such as those for websites, financial systems, or customer information, can contain vital evidence. Forensic experts can analyze database logs and data entries to uncover relevant transactions, interactions, or evidence of manipulation.
- **File Servers and Shared Network Drives**: In organizational settings, shared file servers often store critical files, emails, and backups. These files may contain valuable evidence related to corporate fraud, intellectual property theft, or insider trading.

Server-based evidence often requires specialized skills and tools to extract and analyze, particularly given the large volume of data involved and the technical complexity of network configurations. Investigators must ensure that they follow proper protocols to preserve the integrity of the data and comply with legal and ethical standards.

5. Internet of Things (IoT) Devices

The rise of IoT devices has added new sources of digital evidence to forensic investigations. IoT devices, such as smart home appliances, wearables, fitness trackers, and even connected cars, can record valuable data that may be relevant to a case. As these devices become more integrated into daily life, they have the potential to provide a detailed picture of a suspect's activities and behaviors.

Key Evidence Sources in IoT Devices:

- **Smartphones and Wearables**: Fitness trackers, smartwatches, and other wearables collect data related to the user's health, location, and activities. This data can reveal information about a suspect's whereabouts, physical state, and interactions during the time of an incident.
- **Smart Home Devices**: Devices such as smart thermostats, security cameras, and voice assistants (e.g., Amazon Echo, Google Home) can provide evidence of a suspect's presence or actions in the home. Smart home devices often record audio, video, or sensor data, which can be crucial in criminal investigations.
- **Connected Vehicles**: Modern vehicles are equipped with GPS systems and onboard diagnostic (OBD) devices that can provide valuable data, including

location, speed, and even engine performance metrics. Investigators can extract and analyze this data to corroborate a suspect's alibi or trace their movements.

While IoT devices offer valuable evidence, they also present challenges related to privacy, data security, and the sheer volume of data collected. Investigators must be able to identify which data is relevant and ensure that it is properly collected and preserved for analysis.

Digital evidence can be found in a wide variety of devices and systems. From personal computers and mobile devices to cloud storage, networked systems, and IoT devices, each source offers unique insights that can help investigators piece together critical information. By understanding the various sources of digital evidence, investigators can ensure they properly collect, preserve, and analyze data that may prove vital to solving cases. As technology continues to evolve, so too must the skills and methods of digital forensic experts in order to keep pace with new sources of evidence.

2.3 Volatile vs. Non-Volatile Data

In digital forensics, understanding the difference between volatile and non-volatile data is essential to effectively conducting investigations. These two categories of data represent different characteristics in terms of how they are stored, accessed, and preserved, which is crucial when investigating digital evidence. Knowing how to identify and handle each type of data properly can significantly impact the success of an investigation, as well as the legal admissibility of the evidence.

1. Volatile Data

Volatile data refers to information that is temporarily stored in a computer or electronic device's memory and is lost once the power is turned off. This type of data is typically stored in RAM (Random Access Memory) or cache memory, which are designed for fast access but are not permanent. As a result, volatile data is highly susceptible to being erased or overwritten if the device is powered down, making it critical for forensic investigators to capture this data as soon as possible after an incident.

Key Characteristics of Volatile Data:

- **Temporary Storage**: Volatile data exists only as long as the device remains powered on. When the device is turned off or loses power, this data is lost.

- **Fast Access and Processing**: Volatile data is typically used by the operating system and applications to store temporary information, such as running processes, application states, and active user sessions.
- **Ephemeral Nature**: Because volatile data is lost once the device loses power, its preservation is time-sensitive, requiring immediate action by digital forensic investigators.

Examples of Volatile Data:

- **RAM Contents**: The contents of a device's RAM include active processes, running applications, and open files. This data can contain crucial evidence, such as the location of malware or temporary files.
- **CPU Cache**: The CPU cache stores frequently accessed data and instructions to improve system performance. In an investigation, it might contain fragments of data, passwords, or other relevant information.
- **Running Processes**: Information about programs that are actively running on the device, such as processes in the task manager on Windows or activity in the terminal on Unix-based systems, can provide insight into what the device was doing at the time of an incident.
- **Network Connections**: Information about current network activity, such as active network connections, IP addresses, ports, and protocols in use, is stored temporarily and may be lost after the system is powered down or rebooted.

Forensic Significance of Volatile Data: Volatile data can be a goldmine in digital forensics, as it often provides real-time evidence about the device's operation, activities, and any malicious behavior at the time of the incident. For example:

- **Tracking Malicious Activity**: A forensic investigator may examine volatile data to capture traces of malicious software, such as rootkits, Trojans, or active ransomware. By analyzing active processes, they can identify unauthorized programs or users.
- **User Activity and Session Information**: Volatile data can reveal details about the user's session, including logged-in users, open files, or recently executed commands, which can help piece together a timeline of events.
- **Memory Dumps**: In the case of a suspected cyberattack or data breach, investigators might perform a memory dump to capture the exact contents of RAM. This can reveal encryption keys, passwords, or other sensitive data that was in use during the incident.

Challenges with Volatile Data:

- **Ephemeral Nature**: The primary challenge with volatile data is its transient nature. Once the system is powered off, this data is lost, making it crucial to capture this information before any system shutdowns or reboots.
- **Difficulty in Extraction**: Unlike non-volatile data, which can be more easily extracted from storage devices, volatile data often requires specialized tools and techniques to capture, especially on live systems or running devices.

2. Non-Volatile Data

Non-volatile data, in contrast, is data that is persistently stored on a device's hard drive, solid-state drive (SSD), or other long-term storage media. This data remains intact even when the device is powered off or rebooted. Non-volatile data is typically stored in the form of files, system logs, databases, and other information that the device relies on for normal operation.

Key Characteristics of Non-Volatile Data:

- **Permanent Storage**: Non-volatile data is stored on a device's permanent storage medium, such as HDDs, SSDs, or optical drives. This data remains on the device until it is deliberately deleted, overwritten, or corrupted.
- **Slower Access and Processing**: Non-volatile storage is designed for durability and long-term retention, but it is typically slower to read from or write to compared to volatile memory (RAM).
- **Persistence**: The data stored on hard drives or SSDs remains intact even if the device loses power, making it crucial for investigators to recover evidence from these devices during digital forensics examinations.

Examples of Non-Volatile Data:

- **Files and Documents**: User-created files (e.g., text documents, spreadsheets, images) stored on a device's hard drive or SSD are a primary source of non-volatile data. These files are typically stored persistently and can be recovered during an investigation.
- **System Files and Logs**: The operating system generates system logs that record system events, errors, and user activity. These logs can offer valuable evidence regarding what happened on the device, such as login attempts, application launches, and potential system breaches.
- **Databases**: Databases containing structured data, such as customer information, transaction records, or corporate files, are stored on non-volatile storage devices.

They can be recovered to trace transactions or communications that are crucial to a case.

- **Emails and Communication Data**: Email inboxes, archives, and other communication records that are stored on servers or local hard drives are part of non-volatile data. This data can be preserved even after the device is powered off and can provide critical evidence in cases involving fraud, harassment, or cybercrime.
- **Application Data**: Some applications store user data and preferences in configuration files or local databases. Examples include web browser histories, application settings, and even offline data used by applications like email clients or cloud-based tools.

Forensic Significance of Non-Volatile Data: Non-volatile data is often the most important form of evidence in forensic investigations, as it contains a wealth of information that can corroborate timelines, verify alibis, or identify key actors in a case. Some key areas where non-volatile data is significant include:

- **Digital Documents and Files**: Investigators may examine file contents, metadata, and access history to determine how files were modified, who accessed them, and when they were used. For instance, in cases of intellectual property theft or document tampering, analyzing file metadata and versions can be critical.
- **System Activity Logs**: System logs provide a history of events that occurred on the device, including user logins, file access, error messages, and security alerts. These logs can help investigators understand the sequence of actions leading up to or following an incident.
- **Deleted Data Recovery**: Even when files are deleted from non-volatile storage, they may not be immediately wiped from the device. Using forensic tools, investigators can often recover these deleted files, which may contain critical evidence.

Timeline Reconstruction: Non-volatile data can help investigators construct an accurate timeline of events. Files, logs, and databases stored on non-volatile devices allow forensic experts to establish when certain actions occurred, helping to verify or challenge a suspect's account of events.

Challenges with Non-Volatile Data:

- **Data Overwriting**: Non-volatile data can be overwritten when new data is saved to the same location, making it difficult to recover deleted or altered files.

Specialized forensic tools are often required to recover overwritten data or to search for "slack space" where remnants of deleted files may remain.

- **Encryption**: Many modern devices employ encryption methods to protect non-volatile data. While encryption offers enhanced security, it can pose significant challenges to forensic investigators, requiring them to bypass encryption techniques or obtain passwords or decryption keys.

The distinction between volatile and non-volatile data is crucial in digital forensics, as it dictates the approach to evidence collection, analysis, and preservation. Volatile data, because of its temporary nature, must be captured quickly and requires specialized techniques to extract and analyze, often in a live environment. On the other hand, non-volatile data is more permanent and typically involves recovery from storage devices like hard drives or cloud systems. Understanding both types of data and their forensic significance helps investigators prioritize their efforts and ensures that critical evidence is not lost or overlooked during the investigation.

2.4 Understanding Metadata

Metadata is often referred to as "data about data," and it plays a critical role in digital forensics investigations. In the context of digital evidence, metadata provides additional information about a file or piece of data, offering insights into how, when, and by whom it was created, accessed, modified, or deleted. This auxiliary data is often stored alongside the actual content of a file, but it is not always immediately visible to end users. Forensic investigators rely heavily on metadata to establish timelines, verify authenticity, and track changes to digital files, making it a key tool in any digital investigation.

This section explores the concept of metadata, its types, how it is used in forensic investigations, and the challenges associated with analyzing and interpreting it.

1. What is Metadata?

Metadata is information that describes, explains, or otherwise provides context for the primary data or content. In digital forensics, metadata refers to the embedded details within a file or a piece of data, often including technical information about the file's origin, structure, modifications, and interactions with the operating system. It provides a way for forensic investigators to understand more about the history of a file or document, even if the original content has been altered or deleted.

While metadata doesn't always provide direct content (such as text or images), it can reveal crucial forensic details. For example, metadata can tell an investigator when a file was created, who created it, whether it was altered, and by whom. This type of information is vital in validating evidence, verifying timelines, and establishing facts.

2. Types of Metadata

There are several types of metadata, each providing different layers of information about the file. Some of the most common types encountered in digital forensics investigations include:

Descriptive Metadata: Descriptive metadata provides basic information about the file's content. It helps in identifying, searching, and locating a file. For example:

- **File name**: The name given to the file at creation.
- **Title and Author**: For documents, metadata can include the title of the file, the author's name, and other user-defined attributes.
- **Keywords/Tags**: Files often include metadata that categorizes content or associates it with specific terms or tags to make searching easier.

Structural Metadata: Structural metadata describes the organization and structure of the file, which helps users or systems understand how the content is arranged or formatted. Examples include:

- **File format/type**: Information on the type of file (e.g., PDF, JPEG, DOCX) and associated properties that define its structure.
- **Version control**: Data about file versions, including information about changes made between versions, can be tracked through structural metadata.
- **File size and encoding**: The size of the file, its encoding format, or even the number of pages or images it contains.

Administrative Metadata: Administrative metadata refers to the data necessary for managing the file's lifecycle. It provides details on how a file was created, stored, and modified. Examples of administrative metadata include:

- **Date and time stamps**: The creation, last modified, and last accessed timestamps are critical. These show when the file was created and when it was last edited or viewed, which can help investigators establish timelines.
- **Access Control and Permissions**: Metadata can also include information about who can access, modify, or delete the file. This is particularly important in legal

contexts, as it helps to establish who had control over the file at specific points in time.

Provenance Metadata: Provenance metadata tracks the history of the file's origin and movement. It records details on where the file came from, how it was transferred, and any changes it underwent. This metadata can include:

- **Creator/Author information**: The name of the individual who created the file.
- **File transfers**: Information about when and how the file was transferred between devices or systems.
- **File modifications**: History of edits or alterations to the file, including when these changes were made and by whom.

Embedded Metadata: Many modern file types (e.g., images, audio files, or videos) contain embedded metadata that describes the content and context of the file. Examples include:

- **EXIF Data (Exchangeable Image File Format):** Found in image files like JPEGs, EXIF data can include the camera model, date and time of capture, geolocation (GPS coordinates), and settings used for the photo (e.g., aperture, shutter speed).
- **Audio and Video Metadata**: Media files often include information about the creation time, resolution, and editing history. This can be useful for tracking the authenticity and timeline of media content.

3. Importance of Metadata in Digital Forensics

Metadata plays a pivotal role in digital forensics for several reasons, including its ability to:

- **Establish Timelines**: Metadata, such as creation, modification, and access timestamps, is invaluable in constructing an accurate timeline of events during an investigation. For instance, if a document was modified just hours before a crime or was accessed by a particular user, this data can directly connect the file to the case.
- **Authenticate Evidence**: Metadata is crucial for verifying the authenticity of a file. For example, metadata can be examined to determine if a document was tampered with or forged. Investigators can use metadata to check for inconsistencies between the file's properties and its expected behavior.
- **Trace Activity and Identify Involvement**: By examining metadata, investigators can trace who interacted with a file or system, when, and in what manner. This can

help establish a chain of custody, revealing the roles played by various individuals or systems in the creation or alteration of evidence.

- **Provide Context for Digital Evidence**: When investigators encounter digital evidence, metadata provides additional context that helps to interpret the content. For example, metadata associated with an email can include information about when and where it was sent, the sender and recipient, and the devices used.

4. Challenges of Metadata in Digital Forensics

Despite its usefulness, there are several challenges associated with metadata analysis in digital forensics:

Metadata Manipulation and Forgery: One of the primary challenges investigators face is the possibility of metadata manipulation. Users or attackers may modify metadata to hide evidence or mislead investigators. For example, an attacker could change a document's timestamps to make it appear as though it was created at a different time. Advanced forensic tools and techniques are needed to detect such tampering and verify the authenticity of metadata.

File System Limitations: Different file systems (e.g., FAT, NTFS, HFS+) store metadata in varying formats, which can make it difficult to extract and interpret metadata consistently across devices. Additionally, older file systems may not store as much metadata, which can limit the amount of forensic information available.

Incomplete or Lost Metadata: In some cases, metadata may be corrupted, deleted, or overwritten during system operations. This can result in missing information or the loss of critical timestamps or file access history, which may hinder investigators' ability to construct accurate timelines or verify evidence.

Privacy Concerns: Metadata can sometimes reveal personal or sensitive information, such as location data (from GPS-enabled devices) or personal interactions (from emails or social media). While this can be helpful for investigators, it also raises privacy concerns, particularly in cases involving innocent parties who are not directly involved in the case.

Volume of Data: In many digital forensics investigations, investigators must analyze a large volume of data, including files, emails, logs, and other sources. This can make it difficult to process and examine every piece of metadata effectively, and important details may be overlooked.

5. Tools for Extracting and Analyzing Metadata

Forensic investigators use specialized software tools to extract, view, and analyze metadata from digital files. These tools include:

- **FTK Imager**: A forensic imaging tool that can capture and analyze disk images, including metadata associated with files.
- **EnCase Forensic**: A powerful tool used to collect and analyze digital evidence, including metadata, from a wide variety of sources.
- **ExifTool**: A popular tool for extracting metadata from images, audio files, and videos, including EXIF data.
- **X1 Social Discovery**: A tool used to examine metadata in social media content and other web-based communications.
- **Autopsy**: An open-source forensic tool that helps investigators analyze disk images, uncover hidden metadata, and perform other forensic tasks.

These tools are designed to handle large volumes of data and provide forensic investigators with the necessary capabilities to identify, recover, and interpret metadata in a way that is admissible in court.

Metadata is an essential component of digital forensics, providing crucial context, authenticity checks, and valuable insights into the history of a file or system. By examining metadata, investigators can uncover details about when and how evidence was created, who interacted with it, and whether it has been altered. However, challenges such as manipulation, incomplete metadata, and privacy concerns make the proper handling and analysis of metadata a complex and delicate process. With the right tools and techniques, investigators can effectively leverage metadata to strengthen their cases and uncover the truth behind digital evidence.

2.5 The Lifecycle of E-Evidence

The lifecycle of e-evidence refers to the series of stages that digital evidence undergoes, from its creation or discovery to its eventual presentation in a legal context. Each stage of the lifecycle is critical for ensuring the integrity, authenticity, and admissibility of digital evidence in a court of law. Understanding this lifecycle is essential for digital forensic investigators, as it ensures that evidence is handled properly, reducing the risk of tampering or loss of crucial information.

This section will explore the stages of the e-evidence lifecycle, highlight the best practices for managing evidence at each stage, and discuss how each phase contributes to the overall integrity of the forensic investigation.

1. Creation and Identification of E-Evidence

The lifecycle of e-evidence begins with the creation or discovery of digital data that could be relevant to an investigation. This data could be anything from emails, text messages, and files to logs, network traffic, or records stored on a cloud server. E-evidence can originate from a variety of sources, including personal devices (smartphones, laptops), corporate systems (servers, databases), or digital communications (social media, emails).

Key Activities:

- **Creation of Data**: E-evidence may be created intentionally (e.g., a document or file) or unintentionally (e.g., system logs, browser history). Investigators often focus on digital traces left behind during the commission of a crime, as these can provide key insights.
- **Identification of Evidence**: Once potential e-evidence is identified, it must be classified and categorized. Investigators will assess whether the digital data is relevant and significant to the case at hand. This process involves evaluating the nature of the data and its potential connection to the crime being investigated.

Best Practices:

- Use tools and techniques to locate relevant digital traces from diverse sources (e.g., file systems, email servers, cloud storage, external devices).
- Ensure proper documentation of the identification process to maintain a clear chain of custody.

2. Collection and Acquisition of E-Evidence

After identifying potential e-evidence, the next stage involves collecting and acquiring the data. During this phase, forensic investigators use specialized techniques and tools to capture a copy of the digital evidence without altering or compromising it. This is a critical step because the integrity of the evidence must be preserved to ensure that it can be used in court.

Key Activities:

- **Data Acquisition**: Forensic investigators collect copies of the identified digital evidence, typically creating exact, bit-for-bit copies of hard drives, storage devices, or entire systems. This process may involve using forensic imaging tools to preserve the original evidence in a forensically sound manner.
- **Documenting the Collection Process**: Every action taken during the collection phase is meticulously documented. This includes noting the date, time, and methods used to acquire the evidence, as well as any individuals involved in the collection process.
- **Seizing Physical Devices**: In cases where e-evidence exists on physical devices (e.g., smartphones, computers), investigators may need to seize the devices for further analysis, following proper legal protocols.

Best Practices:

- Use write blockers or similar tools to ensure that evidence is not modified during collection.
- Maintain a strict chain of custody to document who collected the evidence and where it was stored at each stage.

3. Preservation and Storage of E-Evidence

Once e-evidence has been collected, it must be preserved to maintain its integrity for further analysis. This involves securely storing the evidence to prevent tampering, alteration, or degradation. Preservation ensures that the evidence can be reliably used later in the investigation or in court proceedings.

Key Activities:

- **Preservation of Original Evidence**: The original copies of the evidence must be secured in a controlled environment, such as an evidence locker or a secure server. The goal is to ensure that the original data is protected from unauthorized access or accidental modification.
- **Use of Forensic Images**: In most cases, investigators will work with forensic images (copies) of the evidence rather than the original data. This helps ensure that the original data is untouched and preserved while allowing investigators to conduct their analysis on a duplicate.
- **Storage Methods**: The evidence should be stored in an environment with controlled access to prevent tampering. Digital evidence may be stored in secure, encrypted drives or servers that require authentication for access.

Best Practices:

- Ensure that all devices and storage locations used for evidence storage are encrypted and securely locked.
- Maintain detailed records of the storage location and access history to ensure the chain of custody is upheld.

4. Analysis of E-Evidence

The analysis stage is where forensic investigators begin to examine the preserved e-evidence to extract relevant information, identify key facts, and piece together a timeline of events. This stage involves applying various forensic tools and methodologies to the evidence to uncover any hidden or obfuscated data.

Key Activities:

- **Data Extraction**: Using specialized forensic software, investigators extract and decode relevant data from the acquired digital evidence. This may involve recovering deleted files, decrypting encrypted data, or analyzing system logs and communications.
- **Data Interpretation**: Once extracted, the data must be interpreted to provide meaningful insights. This could involve identifying files or communications related to the crime, understanding patterns of behavior, or reconstructing timelines of actions.
- **Verification and Validation**: Forensic investigators must ensure that the extracted data is authentic and reliable. They may use hash values (e.g., MD5, SHA-1) to verify that the digital evidence has not been altered during the analysis phase.

Best Practices:

- Use industry-standard forensic tools that allow for repeatable, reliable, and verifiable results.
- Ensure proper handling of data, including the use of hashes to verify that files remain unchanged during the analysis process.

5. Presentation of E-Evidence

The final stage of the e-evidence lifecycle involves presenting the findings from the analysis in a manner that is understandable and legally acceptable in a court of law. The presentation must be clear, concise, and supported by documentation that demonstrates the integrity and authenticity of the evidence.

Key Activities:

- **Report Generation**: Investigators prepare detailed reports that summarize the findings of the analysis, outlining the evidence that was discovered and its relevance to the case. The report should include technical details of the evidence recovery process, including tools used, methodologies applied, and any challenges encountered.
- **Expert Testimony**: In many cases, digital forensic experts will be called to testify in court about the findings and the methodology used to obtain and analyze the evidence. The forensic expert may explain how the evidence was collected, preserved, and analyzed in a way that ensures its reliability and credibility.
- **Chain of Custody Documentation**: The chain of custody documentation must be provided to demonstrate that the evidence has been properly handled at every stage of its lifecycle, from collection through to presentation.

Best Practices:

- Present findings in a clear, non-technical manner that is easily understandable to the court and other stakeholders.
- Provide visual aids, such as graphs, charts, or screenshots, to help explain technical details and evidence recovery processes.

6. Disposal of E-Evidence

In some cases, e-evidence may need to be disposed of once the investigation is complete, or the case is closed. Proper disposal of e-evidence is essential to prevent unauthorized access or misuse. If the evidence is no longer needed, it must be securely wiped or destroyed.

Key Activities:

- **Secure Deletion**: Digital evidence should be securely wiped from storage devices using specialized tools that ensure data is unrecoverable. This process is especially important for devices that may contain sensitive personal or confidential information.

- **Destruction of Physical Media**: If the evidence is stored on physical devices (e.g., hard drives), these should be physically destroyed to prevent any possibility of data recovery.

Best Practices:

- Use government-approved methods for secure deletion and destruction to meet legal and regulatory requirements.

The lifecycle of e-evidence is a comprehensive process that spans from the creation and identification of digital data to its eventual destruction. Each stage of this lifecycle plays a critical role in ensuring that digital evidence remains credible, verifiable, and legally admissible. Forensic investigators must adhere to best practices throughout the process, including meticulous documentation, secure handling, and the use of appropriate tools, to maintain the integrity of the evidence. By following a systematic approach to managing e-evidence, investigators can effectively support legal proceedings, ensuring that digital evidence plays its proper role in the pursuit of justice.

3. Legal Frameworks and Ethical Considerations

Digital forensics operates at the crossroads of technology and law, making it essential to navigate the legal and ethical dimensions of the field with precision. This chapter explores the critical legal frameworks that govern the collection, analysis, and presentation of digital evidence, including laws on privacy, data protection, and evidence admissibility. Equally important, it examines the ethical responsibilities of forensic practitioners, from safeguarding individual rights to ensuring the integrity of investigations. By understanding these frameworks, you'll be better equipped to handle digital evidence in a manner that is both legally sound and ethically responsible.

3.1 Laws Governing Digital Evidence (GDPR, HIPAA, etc.)

In the realm of digital forensics, the handling, acquisition, and presentation of digital evidence are governed by various laws and regulations. These laws are designed to protect individuals' privacy and ensure that evidence is obtained, processed, and used in a manner that respects legal rights and adheres to ethical standards. Given the sensitive nature of digital data, the legal landscape surrounding digital evidence is complex and varies by jurisdiction, sector, and the type of information involved.

This section explores some of the most important laws that govern digital evidence, including the General Data Protection Regulation (GDPR), the Health Insurance Portability and Accountability Act (HIPAA), and others. It will also discuss the role these regulations play in digital forensics investigations and how they impact the collection, storage, and use of e-evidence.

1. General Data Protection Regulation (GDPR)

The General Data Protection Regulation (GDPR) is a comprehensive data protection law that came into effect in May 2018 in the European Union (EU). GDPR was designed to strengthen data privacy and protection for individuals within the EU and the European Economic Area (EEA). Given the global nature of the internet and digital communications, GDPR has a significant impact on digital forensics, especially in cases where data crosses international borders.

Key Provisions:

- **Data Protection by Design and by Default**: GDPR mandates that personal data is protected from the outset when developing systems or conducting investigations, including the secure collection, storage, and processing of data.
- **Rights of Data Subjects**: Individuals (referred to as "data subjects") have specific rights under GDPR, including the right to access their personal data, the right to correct inaccurate data, and the right to request data deletion (the "right to be forgotten"). Digital forensic investigators must navigate these rights carefully when collecting evidence.
- **Data Minimization and Purpose Limitation**: GDPR requires that only the data necessary for the investigation is collected and that the data is used exclusively for the purpose for which it was gathered. Investigators must ensure that personal data is not unnecessarily accessed or used in ways that violate the regulation.
- **Data Breaches and Notifications**: In the event of a data breach, GDPR mandates that data controllers report the breach within 72 hours. Forensic investigators must be aware of this requirement, especially when dealing with breaches involving personal data.

Impact on Digital Forensics:

- Forensic investigators operating within or outside the EU must be careful not to violate GDPR by collecting more data than necessary or by improperly handling personal data. When dealing with e-evidence that includes personal or sensitive data, investigators must ensure that they have appropriate legal grounds for accessing and processing that data.
- GDPR also has implications for cross-border data transfers. Digital evidence stored in cloud environments or external servers must be handled in compliance with international data protection laws, which may require specific safeguards when transferring evidence to or from outside the EU.

2. Health Insurance Portability and Accountability Act (HIPAA)

The Health Insurance Portability and Accountability Act (HIPAA) is a U.S. law designed to protect the privacy and security of individuals' health information. HIPAA sets strict standards for how healthcare organizations and their partners handle, store, and transmit protected health information (PHI), including in digital formats. HIPAA applies to a wide range of entities, including healthcare providers, insurers, and contractors that have access to health-related data.

Key Provisions:

- **Privacy Rule**: The HIPAA Privacy Rule regulates how PHI can be used and disclosed. It grants patients the right to access and control their health information and imposes restrictions on how it can be shared or accessed by unauthorized parties.
- **Security Rule**: The Security Rule establishes standards for safeguarding electronic PHI (ePHI) through physical, technical, and administrative measures. Forensic investigators working with ePHI must follow these security standards when collecting, storing, or analyzing evidence.
- **Breach Notification Rule**: HIPAA requires that healthcare entities notify individuals of a breach of their health information. In a digital forensics context, if ePHI is compromised or improperly accessed during an investigation, investigators must follow specific breach notification procedures.

Impact on Digital Forensics:

- Forensic investigators dealing with healthcare-related e-evidence must adhere to HIPAA's standards to ensure compliance with privacy and security requirements. They must take extra precautions to protect ePHI from unauthorized access during the investigation.
- Investigators may also be required to work with healthcare organizations to ensure that data is accessed only for legitimate purposes and that individuals' privacy rights are respected throughout the investigation.

3. Computer Fraud and Abuse Act (CFAA)

The Computer Fraud and Abuse Act (CFAA) is a U.S. federal law that criminalizes unauthorized access to computer systems and data. It is one of the most significant laws concerning computer crime and the protection of digital evidence in the United States.

Key Provisions:

- **Unauthorized Access and Hacking**: The CFAA makes it illegal to access computer systems, networks, or devices without authorization, including through hacking, phishing, or other means of bypassing security controls.
- **Fraudulent Activities**: The act also criminalizes using computer systems to commit fraud, identity theft, and other crimes. This is relevant to digital forensics because it often involves examining computer systems to detect unauthorized access or fraudulent activity.
- **Computer-Related Offenses**: The CFAA covers a wide range of offenses, including the distribution of malware, denial-of-service (DoS) attacks, and the theft

of data from computer systems. Forensic investigators may need to trace such activities during their investigations.

Impact on Digital Forensics:

- Forensic investigators must comply with the CFAA when accessing systems and devices for evidence. They must ensure that they are authorized to examine specific systems and obtain data lawfully.
- Investigators must be familiar with the provisions of the CFAA when investigating computer-related crimes, as digital evidence may be used to prove unauthorized access or fraud.

4. Electronic Communications Privacy Act (ECPA)

The Electronic Communications Privacy Act (ECPA) is a U.S. federal law that protects the privacy of electronic communications, including emails, telephone conversations, and other forms of digital communication. The act was established to safeguard individuals' communications against unauthorized surveillance and interception.

Key Provisions:

- **Wiretap Act**: The ECPA's Wiretap Act prohibits the interception of live communications, such as phone calls or real-time messaging, without consent. This is especially important for investigators conducting surveillance or monitoring communications.
- **Stored Communications Act (SCA):** The SCA protects stored communications, such as emails, text messages, and cloud-based data, from unauthorized access. It regulates how law enforcement and investigators can access such communications.
- **Pen Registers and Trap and Trace Devices**: The ECPA also governs the use of pen registers and trap-and-trace devices, which are used to record the sending and receiving of electronic communications.

Impact on Digital Forensics:

- Investigators must be cautious when accessing electronic communications or stored data to ensure they are not violating the privacy protections established by the ECPA.

- When dealing with cloud-based or email communications, investigators need to ensure that they follow proper legal procedures to obtain access to such data, including obtaining appropriate warrants or subpoenas where required.

5. Digital Millennium Copyright Act (DMCA)

The Digital Millennium Copyright Act (DMCA) is a U.S. law that aims to protect copyrighted material in the digital environment. It prohibits the unauthorized distribution and reproduction of copyrighted content, and it regulates the use of digital rights management (DRM) technology.

Key Provisions:

- **Anti-Circumvention Provisions**: The DMCA prohibits circumventing encryption or other protective technologies that safeguard digital content. This includes hacking or decrypting protected files without authorization.
- **Safe Harbor Provisions**: The DMCA includes "safe harbor" provisions that protect internet service providers (ISPs) and platforms from liability for user-generated content, as long as they act promptly to remove infringing material once notified.

Impact on Digital Forensics:

- Digital forensics investigators must be mindful of the DMCA when collecting and analyzing digital evidence that may be copyrighted. They must ensure that they are not violating copyright protections when accessing or handling content during their investigations.

The legal landscape governing digital evidence is multifaceted and constantly evolving. Laws like GDPR, HIPAA, CFAA, and ECPA, along with various national and international regulations, play a significant role in shaping the way digital evidence is handled during investigations. Forensic investigators must be aware of these legal frameworks to ensure that they comply with privacy and data protection laws, while also ensuring that the evidence they collect, store, and present in court remains admissible and valid. Understanding the nuances of these laws is essential for maintaining the integrity of digital forensics investigations and ensuring that justice is served while protecting individuals' rights.

3.2 Admissibility of E-Evidence in Court

The admissibility of e-evidence in court refers to whether digital evidence can be presented as valid and reliable during legal proceedings. Digital evidence, ranging from emails and text messages to files, logs, and data from mobile devices, is increasingly pivotal in investigations and court cases. However, not all e-evidence is automatically accepted in court. To be deemed admissible, e-evidence must meet specific legal standards and requirements that ensure its integrity, authenticity, and relevance to the case at hand.

This section will explore the key factors influencing the admissibility of digital evidence in court, the legal standards applied, and best practices for ensuring that e-evidence is both legally sound and effective in supporting the claims of a party involved in litigation.

1. Legal Standards for Admissibility of E-Evidence

There are several key legal standards that determine whether digital evidence can be introduced in court. These standards are designed to ensure that the evidence is not tampered with, is authentic, and is relevant to the case. The following are some of the most common standards for evaluating the admissibility of e-evidence:

Federal Rules of Evidence (FRE) (U.S.): In the United States, the Federal Rules of Evidence provide a framework for the admissibility of evidence in federal court. Specifically, Rule 901 of the FRE requires that evidence must be authenticated before it is admitted into court. This includes demonstrating that the e-evidence is what it purports to be, such as showing that an email, for example, was sent from a particular email address at a specific time.

Authentication: Under Rule 901, digital evidence must be shown to be what it claims to be, usually through corroborating evidence or testimony that can demonstrate the chain of custody, origin, or creation of the data. In the case of digital evidence, this can be done through metadata, digital signatures, hash values, or witness testimony from the person who collected the evidence.

The Best Evidence Rule: According to this rule, the best available evidence should be presented in court. For example, if an electronic document is in dispute, the original file should be presented. In cases involving digital data, this often means presenting the original electronic file, or an exact copy, rather than a printout or non-digital representation of the evidence.

Hearsay Rule: In many legal systems, hearsay is defined as a statement made outside of the court proceedings that is presented to prove the truth of the matter asserted.

However, in the context of e-evidence, certain digital communications (such as emails or text messages) may be admissible as exceptions to the hearsay rule. For instance, an email sent by a defendant may be allowed in court to prove the defendant's intentions or actions, provided it meets authentication requirements.

2. Chain of Custody and Integrity of Evidence

One of the critical concerns regarding the admissibility of digital evidence is ensuring that it has not been altered, tampered with, or compromised during the investigation or before it is presented in court. To establish the integrity of the evidence, forensic investigators must maintain a meticulous record of the chain of custody, which documents every instance of handling, storage, and transfer of the evidence.

Key Considerations for Chain of Custody in E-Evidence:

- **Documentation**: Every time digital evidence is accessed, collected, analyzed, or transferred, detailed records must be kept. This includes noting the time and date, the person handling the evidence, the method of transfer or storage, and any actions performed on the evidence. These records help demonstrate the evidence's authenticity.
- **Use of Hash Values**: Hash values (such as MD5, SHA-1, or SHA-256) are cryptographic algorithms that generate unique values for data. These hash values are calculated at the time of evidence collection and again after the analysis to ensure that the data has not been altered. Any change in the hash value would indicate that the evidence has been tampered with.

Secure Storage: Digital evidence must be stored in a secure manner to prevent unauthorized access or tampering. This may include using encrypted storage devices, physical locks, or secure cloud environments. Investigators must also restrict access to authorized personnel only and ensure that logs of who accessed the evidence are kept. Best Practices for Maintaining Chain of Custody:

- Use forensic tools that document every step in the collection and analysis process automatically.
- Securely store digital evidence in locked, encrypted locations with restricted access.
- Use write-blockers when collecting data from hard drives or other devices to prevent accidental modification of the original evidence.

3. Relevance and Admissibility Criteria

For e-evidence to be admissible, it must not only be authentic and untampered with, but also relevant to the case. In most legal systems, evidence must meet two major criteria to be admitted into court:

Relevance: The evidence must directly relate to the case, helping to establish the facts, prove or disprove a claim, or support the arguments of one of the parties involved. For instance, emails or text messages showing a defendant's intent may be relevant to a case involving fraud or harassment.

Probative Value vs. Prejudicial Impact: Even if evidence is relevant, it may be excluded if its prejudicial impact outweighs its probative value. For example, an email containing offensive language might be relevant to the case but could be considered inadmissible if it risks unfairly prejudicing the jury or the court.

Example of Relevance in E-Evidence:

Mobile Device Data: If a suspect's mobile phone records reveal location data that places them at the scene of a crime, this digital evidence may be admissible to establish their presence at the crime scene.

4. Digital Evidence and International Jurisdiction

In cases involving cross-border digital evidence, issues regarding jurisdiction can complicate the admissibility of e-evidence. Different countries have varying laws governing the collection and use of digital evidence, particularly when data is stored outside the jurisdiction where the investigation is taking place. For example, data stored on a server in another country might be subject to that country's laws, and law enforcement may need to obtain permission or cooperation from foreign authorities to access it.

Key Considerations for International Jurisdiction:

- **Mutual Legal Assistance Treaties (MLATs):** Many countries have agreements in place to assist one another in criminal investigations. These treaties can help ensure that digital evidence is handled and presented in a way that complies with both jurisdictions' legal requirements.
- **Data Localization Laws**: Some countries have data protection laws that require data to be stored within their borders, making it more difficult for investigators from other jurisdictions to access it.

5. Expert Testimony and Interpretation of E-Evidence

To ensure that e-evidence is understood in court, expert witnesses in digital forensics are often called upon to testify. These experts provide the court with technical insights into how digital evidence was collected, analyzed, and interpreted. Their testimony may address the methodology used in acquiring digital evidence, the tools and techniques employed, and how the evidence supports the claims in the case.

Key Roles of Expert Testimony:

- **Authentication of Evidence**: Experts can explain how digital evidence was authenticated and demonstrate the reliability of forensic tools used in the investigation.
- **Clarification of Complex Technical Details**: Given the technical nature of digital evidence, an expert can break down complex concepts, such as file systems, encryption, or metadata, in a manner that is understandable to a judge or jury.
- **Analysis of Digital Evidence**: Experts can provide their opinion on the findings derived from digital evidence, such as identifying the source of an email, proving the date and time of a transaction, or identifying patterns in data.

The admissibility of e-evidence in court is contingent upon several key factors, including authenticity, integrity, relevance, and the proper handling of evidence. Legal standards such as the Federal Rules of Evidence, the Best Evidence Rule, and the concept of hearsay must be considered when presenting digital evidence in court. A clear chain of custody, adherence to privacy and data protection laws, and expert testimony are critical to ensuring that e-evidence is deemed reliable and credible by the court. As digital evidence plays an increasingly pivotal role in modern investigations and litigation, forensic investigators must be well-versed in the legal requirements and best practices that govern its use to ensure its successful presentation in legal proceedings.

3.3 Cross-Border Investigations and Jurisdiction

In the globalized digital age, cross-border investigations and jurisdictional issues have become increasingly critical in the field of digital forensics. Digital evidence is often stored, transmitted, and accessed across international boundaries, making it more complex to collect and use this evidence in legal proceedings. Jurisdictional challenges arise when investigators must navigate different legal systems, conflicting laws, and data privacy regulations, all of which may differ from one country to another. This section explores the challenges and solutions related to cross-border digital investigations and how jurisdiction impacts the collection, storage, and admissibility of digital evidence.

1. The Challenge of Cross-Border Digital Evidence

The widespread use of cloud computing, international data storage, and the free flow of digital communications means that evidence in a criminal or civil case may be stored in different countries or on servers located far from the jurisdiction in which an investigation is taking place. This presents a unique set of challenges for law enforcement and forensic investigators.

Key Challenges in Cross-Border Investigations:

- **Conflicting National Laws**: Different countries have varying laws regarding data privacy, data protection, and the legal processes required to obtain digital evidence. For example, some countries have stringent data protection laws that may prevent law enforcement from accessing certain types of data without following specific legal procedures, while others may have more lenient laws for collecting evidence.
- **Data Sovereignty**: Many countries assert that data stored on servers within their borders should be subject to their jurisdiction and laws. This principle of data sovereignty can limit the ability of foreign investigators to access digital evidence stored in another country, particularly if that data is protected by local laws.
- **Privacy Concerns**: As concerns about privacy continue to grow, governments have enacted laws such as the General Data Protection Regulation (GDPR) in the European Union, which restricts the processing and movement of personal data across borders. These laws protect the rights of individuals and often require investigators to obtain specific permissions before accessing personal or sensitive data stored abroad.

Examples of Cross-Border Challenges:

- **Data Access**: A law enforcement agency in the U.S. seeking access to data stored in a server in the EU may face difficulties due to GDPR's strict regulations. Similarly, a request to access data from a server located in a jurisdiction that has very strict privacy laws (such as certain Asian or Middle Eastern countries) may be denied or delayed.
- **Extradition Issues**: In some cases, criminal investigations might require obtaining physical devices or servers located outside the jurisdiction of the investigating

country. Countries may refuse to cooperate if they believe the investigation violates their laws or sovereignty.

2. International Cooperation and Legal Frameworks

To mitigate the challenges of cross-border digital investigations, international cooperation is crucial. Over the years, multiple treaties, agreements, and conventions have been established to facilitate the exchange of digital evidence and provide a legal framework for international investigations.

Key Legal Frameworks for Cross-Border Investigations:

Mutual Legal Assistance Treaties (MLATs): MLATs are agreements between two or more countries that define the process for requesting assistance in obtaining evidence located within their jurisdictions. MLATs are commonly used to facilitate the exchange of digital evidence in criminal investigations. However, the process can be slow, as it often requires diplomatic channels, formal requests, and compliance with both countries' laws. Additionally, MLATs may not cover all forms of digital evidence, particularly data stored in the cloud or on platforms based in multiple countries.

Challenges of MLATs: MLATs can be slow and cumbersome, as they require requests to go through diplomatic and legal channels. This can delay investigations, particularly when urgent access to data is required. Moreover, some countries may be unwilling to grant requests due to concerns over privacy, national security, or legal differences.

The Council of Europe's Convention on Cybercrime (Budapest Convention): The Budapest Convention, adopted in 2001, is the first international treaty aimed at addressing crimes committed over the internet and computer networks. The convention provides a framework for international cooperation in investigating and prosecuting cybercrimes, including digital forensics, and facilitates the exchange of evidence across borders. It promotes harmonized laws between participating countries and offers a more efficient mechanism for cross-border investigations than traditional MLATs.

Key Provisions of the Budapest Convention:

- It enables the swift exchange of information and evidence related to cybercrimes between parties to the treaty.
- It establishes standards for the preservation of digital evidence to ensure it is not lost or tampered with during international investigations.

- It addresses issues like the interception of communications, search and seizure of electronic evidence, and the safeguarding of individuals' rights to privacy.

Limitations of the Budapest Convention: While the Budapest Convention has been a significant step in international cooperation on cybercrime, not all countries are signatories. Some countries, particularly those with more authoritarian regimes, may resist adopting the convention due to concerns over sovereignty, privacy, and control over their own legal processes.

The General Data Protection Regulation (GDPR): The GDPR, which came into effect in 2018, significantly impacts international investigations involving the transfer and processing of personal data across borders. It has specific rules governing the transfer of data to non-EU countries, which may limit the ability of foreign investigators to access evidence stored in the EU.

Impact on Digital Forensics: Investigators seeking to collect digital evidence from the EU or involving EU citizens must ensure that their actions comply with GDPR requirements. Data protection mechanisms must be in place, and personal data must be handled in accordance with privacy laws to avoid violations.

3. Jurisdictional Issues in Cross-Border Investigations

Jurisdiction refers to the legal authority of a court or agency to exercise its power over individuals, cases, or evidence. Jurisdictional issues arise when digital evidence is located in one country, but the investigation is conducted in another. These issues can be particularly challenging because digital evidence often crosses borders easily, making it unclear which country's laws apply.

Key Jurisdictional Issues in Cross-Border Digital Forensics:

Determining Applicable Law: One of the most challenging aspects of cross-border digital investigations is determining which country's laws apply. This is particularly important when an investigator needs to access evidence stored in a foreign country or investigate a crime that occurred in multiple jurisdictions. The law of the country where the data is stored, the law of the country where the investigation is taking place, and the laws that govern the internet and data transmission may all need to be considered.

Extraterritorial Application of Laws: Some countries, particularly the U.S., have laws that can apply extraterritorially. For example, the Computer Fraud and Abuse Act (CFAA) in the U.S. can be applied to unauthorized access of systems, even if the system is located outside the U.S. Similarly, the U.S. CLOUD Act allows the U.S. government to access data stored by American companies, even if the data is stored abroad, as long as the data pertains to a U.S. investigation. This extraterritorial application can raise significant conflicts with the laws of the country where the data is stored.

Data Encryption and Privacy: Encryption technologies and privacy regulations (such as GDPR or the Privacy Shield Framework) often complicate jurisdictional issues in cross-border investigations. Encrypted data may be inaccessible to foreign investigators unless they obtain the cooperation of the service provider or company storing the data. This can create delays or even prevent access to critical evidence.

4. Best Practices for Cross-Border Digital Investigations

To navigate the complexities of cross-border investigations and jurisdictional issues, forensic investigators must adopt several best practices:

- **Coordinate with International Partners**: Investigators should work with law enforcement agencies in other countries and leverage international agreements (such as MLATs or the Budapest Convention) to ensure that data is collected in compliance with local laws.
- **Ensure Data Preservation**: Given the complexities of international data access, investigators must take steps to preserve digital evidence as soon as it is identified. This might include ensuring that data is not overwritten, encrypted, or destroyed before international cooperation or legal processes are completed.
- **Seek Legal Counsel**: Due to the intricate legal nature of cross-border investigations, it is essential to consult with legal experts familiar with international data protection and privacy laws. Legal counsel can help navigate jurisdictional conflicts and ensure compliance with local regulations.
- **Use Secure Channels for Data Transfer**: When transferring data across borders, it is critical to use secure and legally approved channels to maintain the integrity of the evidence and avoid legal challenges related to data privacy.

Cross-border digital investigations present significant challenges, primarily due to the complexities of jurisdiction, differing national laws, data sovereignty issues, and the need for international cooperation. To address these challenges, investigators must stay informed about international agreements such as MLATs, the Budapest Convention, and relevant data protection laws. By understanding the legal frameworks governing digital evidence across borders and adhering to best practices for evidence collection, preservation, and transfer, forensic investigators can overcome jurisdictional hurdles and ensure that critical digital evidence is used effectively in court. As technology continues to advance and the internet further connects global networks, the importance of international cooperation in digital forensics will only continue to grow.

3.4 Ethical Principles in Digital Forensics

Digital forensics is a discipline grounded in the meticulous examination and analysis of electronic data, often in the context of criminal investigations, civil litigation, or organizational matters. Given the sensitive nature of the evidence involved, ethical considerations are paramount to ensuring that investigations are conducted with integrity, transparency, and respect for individuals' rights. Ethical principles in digital forensics help guide practitioners in making responsible decisions, safeguarding the privacy and confidentiality of individuals, and ensuring the reliability of their findings.

This section explores the core ethical principles that govern digital forensics, focusing on maintaining objectivity, privacy, and the legal integrity of the investigative process.

1. Respect for Privacy and Confidentiality

One of the most fundamental ethical principles in digital forensics is the respect for privacy and confidentiality. Digital evidence can include highly sensitive and personal information, such as private emails, medical records, financial data, or personal communications. Investigators must be diligent in ensuring that they do not unnecessarily violate an individual's privacy while conducting their analysis.

Key Considerations:

- **Minimizing Data Exposure**: Investigators must avoid accessing or disclosing data that is irrelevant to the investigation. For instance, if an investigator is analyzing a suspect's computer for evidence of a cybercrime, they should refrain from browsing through personal files unrelated to the case, such as family photos or private documents.
- **Confidentiality Agreements**: Forensic professionals are often required to sign confidentiality agreements, especially when dealing with private corporations or legal matters. These agreements help protect sensitive information from being disclosed or misused outside of the investigation.
- **Handling Sensitive Data**: When handling digital evidence containing sensitive information (such as financial data, medical records, or trade secrets), forensic investigators must take extra precautions. This includes securely storing the data,

limiting access to authorized personnel, and using encryption to protect the data from unauthorized access during the investigation.

Example of Privacy Violation:

In cases of corporate investigations, an investigator might uncover an employee's personal social media activity during a forensic analysis of their company-issued laptop. It is ethically inappropriate to delve into personal areas of the employee's life if it is not directly relevant to the case.

2. Integrity and Objectivity in Analysis

Ethical digital forensics professionals must remain impartial, objective, and accurate in their analysis and reporting of evidence. Bias, whether intentional or inadvertent, can undermine the credibility of the investigation and may result in false conclusions. Investigators must present their findings based on the facts and evidence, without attempting to manipulate or alter the outcome of the investigation to support a particular narrative.

Key Considerations:

- **Avoiding Bias**: Investigators should approach each case without preconceived notions or biases. They must avoid letting personal opinions, organizational pressure, or external influence sway the outcome of their analysis.
- **Accurate Representation of Findings**: The forensic process involves creating an unbiased record of what the evidence reveals. Digital forensic experts are expected to ensure their findings are based solely on the data recovered, including analysis results, metadata, and digital artifacts, without personal interpretation.
- **Transparency**: The methodology, tools, and processes used to conduct the forensic analysis should be transparent and well-documented. This ensures that findings can be verified and repeated by others if needed, adding to the credibility of the analysis.

Example of Objectivity:

In a criminal case, a forensic expert finds evidence that could exonerate a defendant but also discovers evidence that could implicate the defendant. The ethical obligation is to report both sets of findings impartially, rather than focusing only on the evidence that aligns with one side's argument.

3. Chain of Custody and Evidence Integrity

Maintaining the integrity of digital evidence is one of the most important ethical duties in digital forensics. The chain of custody refers to the documentation of the handling, transfer, and storage of digital evidence from the moment it is collected until it is presented in court. This record ensures that the evidence remains untampered with and can be proven to be authentic.

Key Considerations:

- **Proper Handling of Evidence**: Digital evidence must be collected, stored, and transported with utmost care. Any mishandling, such as failure to use write-blockers or improper storage of devices, can lead to accusations of tampering or contamination.
- **Documenting Every Step**: Every instance of evidence handling should be recorded in a chain of custody log, including the names of those who accessed or handled the evidence, the dates and times of access, and the reason for the action taken. This ensures that the evidence remains credible and defensible in court.
- **Securing Evidence**: Digital evidence should be stored in secure environments to prevent unauthorized access or tampering. Investigators must ensure that digital devices are placed in tamper-evident bags, and that digital files are stored in encrypted, access-controlled systems.

Example of Chain of Custody Violation:

If an investigator collects a hard drive from a crime scene and fails to properly document the chain of custody, it could open the door for defense attorneys to challenge the credibility of the evidence, potentially leading to it being excluded from court proceedings.

4. Compliance with Legal and Regulatory Standards

Ethical digital forensics requires strict adherence to local, national, and international laws and regulations governing evidence collection, data privacy, and information security. Violating legal standards not only damages the credibility of an investigation but can also lead to serious legal repercussions for investigators and their organizations.

Key Considerations:

- **Adherence to Laws**: Digital forensics professionals must understand and comply with the laws that govern digital evidence in their jurisdiction, including data protection and privacy laws (such as GDPR, HIPAA, etc.). For example, accessing a suspect's personal data without proper authorization can violate constitutional rights or laws related to data privacy.

- **Obtaining Legal Authorization**: Before conducting any forensic analysis, investigators must ensure they have the appropriate legal authority, such as a warrant or consent, especially when it comes to accessing personal data stored on private devices or cloud accounts.
- **Following Due Process**: Digital forensics professionals must ensure that every step of the investigation complies with legal and ethical standards, ensuring that evidence is admissible in court and that individuals' rights are protected.

Example of Legal Violation:

An investigator accesses a suspect's private email account without a warrant, violating their privacy rights and potentially undermining the entire investigation.

5. Transparency and Accountability

Transparency and accountability are central ethical principles in digital forensics. Investigators must be transparent about their methods, the tools they use, and the findings they uncover. They must also be prepared to defend their work, answer questions about their process, and ensure that their findings are open to scrutiny.

Key Considerations:

- **Clear Documentation**: Every step taken during the forensic process, from evidence collection to analysis and reporting, should be clearly documented. This ensures that others, including defense attorneys or independent auditors, can verify the work and understand how conclusions were reached.
- **Peer Review and Collaboration**: Forensic investigators should be open to peer review and collaboration. This allows for other experts to evaluate and validate the methods, tools, and results of an investigation, improving the overall accuracy and credibility of the findings.
- **Defending Findings in Court**: Forensic professionals may be required to testify in court. During such testimony, they must be able to explain their methodology, tools, and findings clearly and without bias, while also being open to cross-examination and scrutiny.

Example of Transparency:

If a digital forensic investigator is called to testify about the tools used in the investigation, they must be able to clearly explain how the tools work, why they were chosen, and how they were used to ensure the integrity of the data.

Ethical principles are the foundation of effective, credible, and responsible digital forensics. By upholding standards of privacy, integrity, objectivity, and transparency, digital forensic professionals can ensure that their work remains valid and admissible in court. Compliance with legal requirements, safeguarding evidence, and respecting individual rights are not only ethical imperatives but also essential to the credibility and success of the investigative process. As technology continues to evolve and digital evidence becomes more pervasive, maintaining a strong ethical framework is critical to the fair and just application of digital forensics in modern society.

3.5 Protecting Privacy During Investigations

Protecting privacy during digital forensics investigations is not just an ethical imperative; it is a legal and professional responsibility that ensures the integrity of the investigation and the rights of individuals. As investigators examine digital evidence, they often encounter sensitive personal information that is unrelated to the investigation. The challenge lies in safeguarding that privacy while still fulfilling the requirements of the case. This section will delve into the importance of privacy protection during digital forensics investigations and provide strategies for ensuring that privacy is maintained throughout the investigative process.

1. The Importance of Privacy Protection

In digital forensics, privacy protection is vital due to the sensitive nature of the data involved. With the increasing volume of personal information stored on electronic devices, such as social media accounts, emails, photographs, banking information, and health records, investigators must take care to respect the privacy rights of individuals while still conducting thorough and accurate investigations.

Key Reasons for Protecting Privacy in Digital Forensics:

- **Legal Requirements**: Many jurisdictions have stringent data protection and privacy laws (such as GDPR, HIPAA, or the Privacy Act) that impose strict conditions on how personal data is collected, accessed, and processed. Unauthorized access to personal data could result in severe legal consequences, including penalties for violation of privacy laws.

- **Preventing Unwarranted Exposure**: Digital evidence often contains data that is irrelevant to the investigation but could be damaging to individuals if exposed. For instance, investigating a cybercrime might uncover private conversations, financial transactions, or personal correspondence that have no bearing on the case but could harm a person's reputation or violate their right to privacy.
- **Public Trust**: Maintaining privacy during investigations helps preserve public trust in digital forensics. The perception that investigators respect privacy strengthens confidence in the forensic process and ensures that investigations are seen as fair and unbiased.

2. Strategies for Protecting Privacy During Investigations

To protect privacy while conducting digital forensics investigations, forensic experts must adopt specific strategies and best practices designed to minimize exposure of irrelevant personal data and safeguard the privacy of individuals involved.

Key Strategies for Protecting Privacy:

Data Minimization: One of the core principles of privacy protection is data minimization, which involves only collecting, accessing, and analyzing data that is directly relevant to the investigation. For example, if an investigator is examining a suspect's computer for evidence of a hacking incident, they should avoid examining personal files, such as family photos or personal emails, unless those files are explicitly related to the crime under investigation.

Example: If investigators are looking for evidence related to a financial fraud case, they should focus on relevant financial records and communications, avoiding the extraction of unrelated personal data, such as contacts or private messages.

Use of Forensic Tools with Privacy Controls: Modern forensic tools allow investigators to selectively analyze data by filtering out irrelevant content or restricting the scope of analysis to specific file types. These tools can help investigators isolate the information they need without overstepping privacy boundaries.

Example: Many forensic tools offer options to bypass or limit access to sensitive files, such as personal documents, photos, and social media accounts, unless they are clearly relevant to the investigation.

Data Redaction: In some cases, investigators may be required to redact or anonymize personal data that is not pertinent to the investigation. This can include deleting personal identifiers (e.g., names, addresses, contact details) from reports or evidence before sharing with other parties or the court. By doing this, forensic investigators protect individuals' privacy while ensuring the integrity of the evidence.

Example: If an investigator extracts chat logs from a messaging application, they may redact the names and personal details of individuals involved in conversations that are unrelated to the investigation.

Use of Write Blockers: A write blocker is a forensic tool that prevents any modification of the original data during the evidence collection process. By ensuring that data cannot be altered, write blockers help preserve the integrity of the original evidence. This is particularly important when working with personal devices like smartphones or computers, where private data may exist alongside evidence relevant to the case.

Example: During a search of a suspect's hard drive, investigators can use write blockers to ensure that no new data is added or old data is modified, thereby safeguarding personal information from unnecessary exposure.

Access Control and Chain of Custody: Limiting access to digital evidence ensures that only authorized personnel can view, analyze, and handle sensitive data. Proper access control prevents unauthorized individuals from viewing or tampering with private information. Additionally, maintaining a strict chain of custody ensures that all actions taken with the evidence are recorded and transparent, which can help mitigate privacy violations.

Example: A forensic examiner working on a case might restrict access to personal documents on a suspect's computer to just the core investigation team, ensuring that sensitive information is not exposed to others working on the case.

3. Legal and Ethical Guidelines for Privacy Protection

Digital forensics professionals must also be guided by both legal and ethical standards when it comes to privacy. Privacy laws and ethical guidelines offer clear rules for the protection of individuals' rights during digital investigations.

Key Legal and Ethical Guidelines:

- **General Data Protection Regulation (GDPR):** In the European Union, the GDPR provides a robust framework for data privacy and security. It mandates that individuals have control over their personal data and establishes rules for how data should be handled during investigations. Digital forensics professionals must ensure that any personal data collected during investigations complies with GDPR principles, such as data minimization and purpose limitation.

- **Example**: When collecting data from cloud servers or other data storage locations in the EU, forensic investigators must ensure that personal data is only accessed for lawful, specific purposes and that individuals' privacy rights are respected.

- **The Fourth Amendment (U.S.):** In the U.S., the Fourth Amendment protects individuals from unreasonable searches and seizures, including digital searches. Forensic investigators must obtain proper warrants before accessing private devices or data, ensuring that the search does not violate individuals' constitutional rights.
- **Example**: Before extracting data from a smartphone, a forensic investigator must have a warrant or explicit consent, ensuring that the individual's privacy rights are not infringed upon.

- **Ethical Guidelines from Professional Organizations**: Several professional organizations, such as the International Society of Forensic Computer Examiners (ISFCE) and Association of Digital Forensics, Security, and Law (ADFSL), offer ethical guidelines for digital forensics practitioners. These guidelines emphasize the importance of conducting investigations with respect for privacy and confidentiality, avoiding unnecessary exposure of personal data, and maintaining objectivity and impartiality.
- **Example**: The ISFCE Code of Ethics stresses the importance of forensic professionals acting in the best interest of justice, while respecting the privacy of individuals involved in the investigation.

4. Privacy Risks in Cloud and Mobile Forensics

As cloud computing and mobile devices become central to many investigations, new privacy concerns have emerged. Cloud services store vast amounts of personal and business data in remote data centers, often across multiple countries. Similarly, mobile devices contain a wealth of personal information, including geolocation data, contact lists, and communication records, all of which can be privacy-sensitive.

Cloud Forensics and Privacy:

- Investigators must be cautious when accessing cloud-based data, as it may be stored across various jurisdictions. Different countries have different data privacy regulations, and accessing data stored outside of the investigator's jurisdiction could violate privacy laws.

- **Example**: When conducting a forensic examination of cloud-based data, investigators must ensure they comply with the privacy laws of the country where the data is stored and seek appropriate consent or legal authorization.

Mobile Forensics and Privacy:

- Mobile devices pose unique privacy challenges due to their personal nature and the variety of data they contain. Investigators must ensure they access only relevant data, such as text messages related to the investigation, and avoid exposing sensitive personal information like photos or contact lists.
- **Example**: In mobile forensics, investigators should use selective extraction techniques to only pull relevant data, such as call logs or messages related to the investigation, while leaving other personal data untouched.

5. Balancing Privacy with Investigative Needs

While privacy protection is essential, investigators must also ensure that they collect and analyze all the relevant data necessary for the investigation. Striking a balance between privacy and the need for a thorough investigation is a delicate task that requires careful consideration.

Key Balance Strategies:

- **Clear Objectives**: Investigators should clearly define the scope of the investigation and focus on collecting only the data necessary to support the case. This helps minimize the risk of inadvertently accessing private data.
- **Supervision and Oversight**: In some cases, it may be beneficial to involve a neutral third party, such as a privacy officer or legal counsel, to oversee the investigation and ensure that privacy protection is maintained throughout the process.

Protecting privacy during digital forensics investigations is both a legal and ethical obligation. As digital evidence increasingly plays a role in legal cases, the need to balance thorough investigative work with respect for individuals' privacy has never been greater. By adhering to privacy protection strategies, legal guidelines, and ethical standards, digital forensic professionals can ensure that investigations remain fair, just, and respectful of the rights of all individuals involved. As technology continues to advance, privacy concerns will evolve, and digital forensic experts must stay vigilant to adapt to new challenges and continue safeguarding privacy while conducting their work.

4. Tools of the Trade: Software and Hardware Essentials

Behind every successful digital forensic investigation lies a powerful arsenal of tools designed to uncover the truth hidden in data. This chapter introduces you to the essential software and hardware that form the backbone of forensic work, from industry-standard programs like EnCase and FTK to specialized hardware such as write blockers and forensic workstations. You'll explore the features, applications, and limitations of these tools, along with the distinction between open-source and commercial solutions. By understanding and mastering these tools, you'll gain the technical edge needed to collect, analyze, and preserve evidence effectively.

4.1 Overview of Forensic Software (e.g., EnCase, FTK, Autopsy)

Forensic software plays a pivotal role in digital investigations, enabling forensic professionals to collect, analyze, and report on digital evidence in a methodical and legally defensible manner. These software tools are designed to perform specific tasks such as acquiring data from digital devices, creating forensic images of data, recovering deleted files, and analyzing complex data sets. In this section, we will explore some of the most widely used forensic software tools in the industry: EnCase, FTK, and Autopsy, providing an overview of their capabilities, key features, and applications in modern digital forensics.

1. EnCase Forensic

EnCase is one of the most renowned and widely used forensic software solutions in the field of digital forensics. Developed by OpenText, EnCase has long been a favorite of law enforcement, corporate security teams, and forensic investigators due to its comprehensive toolset and powerful capabilities.

Key Features of EnCase:

- **Data Acquisition**: EnCase allows investigators to create bit-for-bit forensic images of hard drives, mobile devices, and other digital storage media, ensuring that the original data remains unaltered and can be used in court as evidence.

- **Advanced File Analysis**: EnCase provides tools for deep file analysis, including the ability to recover deleted files, analyze file systems, and view metadata. Its powerful search and filtering capabilities enable investigators to quickly find relevant evidence.
- **Chain of Custody Management**: EnCase includes features to track and document the chain of custody of digital evidence, which is essential for maintaining the integrity of the evidence throughout the investigative process.
- **Reporting**: EnCase has built-in reporting tools that automatically generate comprehensive reports of forensic findings, which can be used in legal proceedings.
- **Multi-Platform Support**: EnCase supports a wide range of platforms, including Windows, Mac OS, and Linux, making it suitable for a diverse array of forensic investigations.
- **Use Cases**: EnCase is often used in complex criminal investigations, corporate security breaches, and litigation support, especially when large volumes of data need to be analyzed and when high standards of admissibility in court are required.

2. FTK (Forensic Toolkit)

Developed by AccessData, FTK is another leading forensic software tool used for data acquisition, analysis, and reporting. FTK is particularly known for its speed and ability to handle large data sets, which makes it an ideal choice for investigators dealing with large-scale or time-sensitive cases.

Key Features of FTK:

- **Data Imaging and Acquisition**: Like EnCase, FTK allows investigators to perform bit-level imaging of digital devices, ensuring that all evidence is preserved in its original form.
- **Fast File Search and Analysis**: FTK's proprietary indexing technology enables investigators to quickly search through large volumes of data to identify relevant evidence. This includes searching for specific keywords, file types, or file metadata.
- **Email and Database Analysis**: FTK includes specialized features for analyzing email data, including recovery of deleted emails and the extraction of email headers and attachments. Additionally, FTK can analyze data stored in databases, making it an invaluable tool for cases involving enterprise systems or online platforms.

- **Visualization Tools**: FTK has a powerful suite of visualization tools that help investigators identify patterns and relationships in data. This includes timeline views, graphical representations of evidence, and case analysis dashboards.
- **Reporting**: FTK generates detailed forensic reports that can be easily shared with stakeholders or used in court. Reports can be customized to include specific findings or evidence to align with case needs.
- **Use Cases**: FTK is often used in criminal investigations, financial fraud cases, and corporate investigations, particularly when dealing with large or complicated datasets. Its strong indexing and search capabilities make it a go-to choice for investigators who need to sift through vast amounts of data quickly.

3. Autopsy

Autopsy is an open-source, free forensic tool developed by Basis Technology. Despite being free, it is widely respected in the digital forensics community for its ability to handle a range of investigative tasks, from data acquisition to in-depth analysis. Autopsy's extensible nature makes it popular among both small-scale investigations and larger law enforcement agencies.

Key Features of Autopsy:

- **File System Analysis**: Autopsy supports a wide range of file systems, including FAT, NTFS, exFAT, and HFS+, which are commonly found in personal computers and mobile devices. It helps investigators explore file systems, view files and directories, and recover deleted files.
- **Keyword Search and Indexing**: Autopsy provides a powerful search function that allows investigators to perform keyword searches and index data for quick analysis. This is helpful for identifying critical evidence based on search terms or phrases.
- **Timeline Analysis**: Autopsy includes timeline analysis features that help investigators visualize the sequence of events surrounding the evidence. This is particularly useful in criminal investigations, where knowing the timing of actions is crucial.
- **Data Carving**: Autopsy is equipped with data carving capabilities, which allow investigators to recover fragmented files, even if the original file system structure is damaged or deleted.
- **Multi-Platform Support**: Autopsy is compatible with multiple operating systems, including Windows, Linux, and macOS, making it a versatile tool for investigators working in diverse environments.

- **Extensibility via Modules**: One of the most notable features of Autopsy is its extensibility. It can be enhanced with third-party modules that add support for additional types of analysis, such as mobile forensics or cloud evidence extraction.
- **Use Cases**: Autopsy is commonly used by law enforcement agencies, especially in situations where budget constraints limit the use of proprietary software. It is also employed by academic researchers, small businesses, and independent investigators due to its open-source nature and flexibility.

4. Comparison of EnCase, FTK, and Autopsy

When evaluating forensic software, it's important to understand the unique features, strengths, and weaknesses of each tool to choose the best one for a particular investigation.

- **EnCase vs. FTK**: EnCase and FTK are both commercial tools known for their comprehensive capabilities and support for large-scale investigations. However, EnCase is often considered more user-friendly and versatile, especially when dealing with complex cases, while FTK is preferred for its fast indexing and search capabilities, making it ideal for sifting through large datasets quickly.
- **EnCase vs. Autopsy**: EnCase is a more robust, enterprise-level tool with advanced reporting, better legal compliance features, and stronger support for diverse platforms. In contrast, Autopsy, while powerful, is better suited for smaller investigations or those working within budget constraints. Autopsy's open-source nature makes it an excellent option for users who want to customize their toolset.
- **FTK vs. Autopsy**: FTK is a commercial tool with high-end features for enterprise and large-scale investigations, while Autopsy, being free, is a popular choice for smaller cases or academic settings. FTK's performance with large datasets and its comprehensive email and database analysis features make it a strong contender in the professional space, while Autopsy excels as a cost-effective tool for basic forensic needs.

The choice of forensic software plays a crucial role in the success of a digital investigation. EnCase, FTK, and Autopsy each bring unique features to the table, with EnCase and FTK being comprehensive commercial tools favored by large agencies and enterprises, while Autopsy provides a free and flexible alternative for smaller cases. Regardless of the tool chosen, the core goals of forensic software remain the same: to help investigators efficiently collect, analyze, and present digital evidence in a legally defensible manner while maintaining the integrity and privacy of the data involved. Understanding the capabilities and limitations of each software tool is key to choosing the right solution for any digital forensic investigation.

4.2 Hardware Tools for Data Recovery and Analysis

Hardware tools play an indispensable role in digital forensics, providing the physical means to extract, preserve, and analyze data from a variety of digital devices. These tools are essential in cases where traditional software solutions cannot be used, or when physical damage to a device has occurred, requiring specialized equipment to recover lost or inaccessible data. In this section, we will explore the types of hardware tools commonly used in digital forensics, focusing on their functionality and how they complement software-based forensic methods.

1. Write Blockers

A write blocker is one of the most important tools in digital forensics, as it prevents any modification to the original data during the acquisition process. This is crucial for maintaining the integrity and admissibility of evidence, ensuring that forensic investigators collect a bit-for-bit copy of data without altering the original storage medium.

Key Features:

- **Data Preservation**: Write blockers allow forensic professionals to access and copy data from hard drives, flash drives, and other storage devices without the risk of overwriting or altering the original data. This ensures that the evidence remains intact and untainted for use in court.
- **Types of Write Blockers**: Write blockers come in both hardware and software forms. Hardware write blockers physically attach between the forensic workstation and the target drive, while software-based write blockers work within the operating system to prevent write operations. Hardware write blockers are generally considered more reliable because they offer protection at a low level, irrespective of the OS.
- **Applications**: Write blockers are used extensively during evidence acquisition, especially when copying data from suspect devices, ensuring that investigators do not inadvertently alter any critical evidence. They are used in computer forensics, mobile forensics, and other digital investigations where data integrity is paramount.

Examples:

- **Tableau Forensic Write Blocker**: Known for its reliability, this hardware tool is widely used for creating forensic images from hard drives and other digital media.

- **Logicube Forensic Write Blocker**: Another leading tool in the industry that supports a variety of storage devices, including SATA, IDE, and SAS.

2. Forensic Duplicators

A forensic duplicator is a specialized piece of hardware designed to create exact, bit-for-bit copies of digital storage devices. These duplicators are critical in ensuring that investigators work with a clone of the data, not the original device, thus preserving the integrity of the original evidence.

Key Features:

- **Bit-for-Bit Copying**: Forensic duplicators create exact copies of hard drives, USB drives, memory cards, and other storage media. The duplication process captures every bit of data, including deleted files, hidden files, and unallocated space, ensuring that no evidence is missed.
- **Write-Protected Duplications**: Many forensic duplicators are paired with write blockers, ensuring that the original media cannot be altered while a copy is being made. This is a crucial feature for maintaining the integrity of evidence.
- **Speed and Efficiency**: Forensic duplicators are optimized for high-speed duplication, allowing investigators to quickly copy large amounts of data while preserving the original media's state.
- **Applications**: These tools are used primarily in the acquisition phase of an investigation. They are used by investigators to create forensic images from suspect devices or digital storage media, which are then analyzed using software tools in later stages of the investigation.

Examples:

- **Logicube Forensic Duplicator**: This tool supports a wide variety of drives and is known for its ability to create multiple simultaneous duplications, speeding up the data acquisition process.
- **DigiQuest Forensic Duplicator**: Another commonly used duplicator that features high-speed duplication and write-blocking capabilities.

3. Data Recovery Hardware Devices

Data recovery hardware devices are used in situations where physical damage to a storage device prevents normal access to data. These tools can help recover data from damaged or corrupted hard drives, solid-state drives (SSDs), and other types of storage media, ensuring that forensic investigators can still access critical evidence.

Key Features:

- **Physical Repair**: Data recovery hardware can include specialized devices that allow forensic investigators to repair or rebuild damaged storage devices. For instance, they can help recover data from drives with damaged read/write heads, motor issues, or corrupted circuits.
- **Component-Level Recovery**: These devices can allow investigators to work with the internal components of storage devices. For instance, in cases where the physical interface of a hard drive is damaged, forensic technicians may use a specialized recovery tool to access the internal chips or platters of a drive.
- **Recovery from Dead Drives**: Some data recovery tools enable the recovery of data from drives that are not powering on, using techniques such as low-level recovery or interfacing with the drive's internal electronics to bypass failures.
- **Applications**: Data recovery hardware tools are used when a storage device is physically damaged, such as when it suffers from a head crash, water or fire damage, or when it is otherwise non-functional. These tools allow forensic investigators to recover data from these damaged devices, enabling them to proceed with their investigation even when a device has been physically compromised.

Examples:

- **DeepSpar Disk Imager**: A hardware tool specifically designed for recovering data from damaged or malfunctioning hard drives. It can recover data even from drives that fail to boot or are otherwise non-functional.
- **Atola Insight Forensic**: A high-performance tool that offers both imaging and data recovery capabilities for damaged drives, particularly useful in cases where the device cannot be accessed using regular forensic software.

4. Forensic SATA/IDE Adapters

Forensic SATA/IDE adapters are used to connect hard drives to forensic workstations. These adapters support various drive types, including SATA, IDE (PATA), SAS, and even older formats, making them essential for investigators working with a range of devices.

Key Features:

- **Device Connectivity**: These adapters allow forensic investigators to connect a variety of storage devices to a forensic workstation. Whether working with an old IDE hard drive, a modern SATA SSD, or a server-class SAS drive, these adapters provide the necessary interface.
- **Data Integrity**: Many forensic adapters come with built-in write blockers, ensuring that data is not altered while being examined. This is critical for maintaining the integrity of the original evidence.
- **Compatibility**: Forensic SATA/IDE adapters support different storage protocols, enabling investigators to interface with a variety of devices without the need for multiple specialized cables.
- **Applications**: These adapters are used during evidence acquisition, allowing investigators to connect a range of storage devices to forensic systems to clone or analyze the data. They are essential when dealing with devices that require specific connectors that the standard forensic workstation does not have.

Examples:

- **CRU DataPort Forensic Adapter**: A well-known forensic adapter that allows investigators to interface with various drives and comes with a built-in write blocker.
- **Acelab Forensic Adapters**: These adapters provide flexibility in connecting a wide range of storage devices, supporting both SATA and IDE connections.

5. Portable Forensic Workstations

A portable forensic workstation is a mobile device that combines all the essential tools for data acquisition, analysis, and reporting in a single, portable setup. These workstations are often ruggedized to withstand the demands of fieldwork, such as remote or outdoor investigations, and are equipped with powerful forensic tools for on-site data analysis.

Key Features:

- **All-in-One Forensic Solution**: Portable workstations typically include forensic imaging software, write blockers, adapters, and other hardware components necessary for a comprehensive investigation in the field.
- **Rugged Design**: These systems are often designed to be durable, with shockproof, dustproof, and waterproof features that make them suitable for use in challenging environments.
- **High-Performance Components**: Despite their portability, these workstations are equipped with powerful CPUs, large storage capacity, and advanced forensic

software, ensuring investigators can perform detailed analysis even in remote locations.

- **Applications**: Portable forensic workstations are used in field investigations where it is not feasible to transport evidence back to a forensic lab. They allow investigators to collect, analyze, and report on digital evidence on-site, reducing the time between evidence acquisition and analysis.

Examples:

- **BlackBag Forensic Portable Workstation**: A portable solution designed specifically for mobile forensic investigations. It is equipped with the necessary tools for on-site imaging, analysis, and reporting.
- **Toughbook Forensic Workstations**: Panasonic's Toughbook laptops are often used as portable forensic workstations due to their rugged design and powerful computing capabilities, combined with forensic software packages.

Hardware tools for data recovery and analysis are integral to successful digital forensic investigations. Write blockers, forensic duplicators, data recovery devices, SATA/IDE adapters, and portable workstations all play critical roles in the evidence collection and analysis process. By using these hardware tools in conjunction with software-based forensic tools, investigators can ensure the accuracy, integrity, and admissibility of the data they recover. As digital devices continue to evolve and become more complex, the demand for specialized forensic hardware will continue to grow, ensuring that investigators can meet the challenges posed by modern technology in their efforts to uncover the truth.

4.3 Open-Source vs. Commercial Tools

In the field of digital forensics, the choice of tools significantly influences the effectiveness, efficiency, and cost of an investigation. Two primary categories of forensic tools are widely used: open-source tools and commercial tools. Each has its distinct advantages and limitations, and the decision to use one over the other often depends on the specific needs of the investigation, the budget available, and the investigator's expertise. In this section, we will explore the differences between open-source and commercial tools, providing a comparison of their key features, strengths, weaknesses, and common applications in digital forensics.

1. Open-Source Forensic Tools

Open-source forensic tools are freely available to the public and can be modified, shared, and distributed under an open-source license. These tools are typically developed and maintained by the community, including academic researchers, independent professionals, and volunteers. Open-source tools are often valued for their transparency, flexibility, and cost-effectiveness.

Key Features of Open-Source Tools:

- **Cost-Free**: The most significant advantage of open-source tools is that they are typically free to use. This makes them highly attractive for law enforcement agencies, small organizations, and independent investigators with limited budgets.
- **Transparency**: Open-source software comes with access to the source code, which means that users can inspect, modify, and adapt the code to suit specific needs. This level of transparency ensures that there are no hidden functionalities or malicious code in the software, increasing trust in the tools.
- **Community Support**: Open-source tools often benefit from strong community support, with forums, documentation, and collaborative contributions providing a wealth of resources. This community-driven approach can lead to rapid improvements and updates based on the needs of the users.
- **Flexibility and Customization**: Since users can modify the source code, open-source tools offer greater flexibility for customization. Investigators can adapt the tools to meet the specific requirements of a case or integrate them with other systems.
- **Regular Updates**: Open-source tools are frequently updated by developers and contributors, ensuring that they remain compatible with the latest operating systems, hardware, and file systems.

Common Open-Source Forensic Tools:

- **Autopsy**: One of the most widely used open-source forensic platforms, Autopsy is a digital forensics tool that supports file system analysis, data carving, timeline analysis, and metadata extraction. It is particularly popular for its extensibility and the availability of third-party modules.
- **The Sleuth Kit (TSK):** TSK is a collection of command-line tools that allow investigators to analyze disk images, recover deleted files, and explore file systems. It is the underlying engine that powers Autopsy.
- **Wireshark**: Wireshark is a well-known open-source tool for network forensics. It is used to capture and analyze network traffic, helping investigators identify suspicious activity or trace digital footprints.

- **Volatility**: Volatility is a framework for memory forensics, enabling investigators to analyze volatile data from RAM and uncover evidence of malware, rootkits, and other hidden processes.

Applications of Open-Source Tools:

- **Budget-Constrained Investigations**: Open-source tools are an excellent choice for law enforcement agencies, small businesses, or independent investigators who may have limited financial resources but still require robust forensic capabilities.
- **Educational and Research Purposes**: Due to their availability and transparency, open-source tools are often used in academic research, training programs, and forensics courses to teach new professionals the basics of digital forensics.
- **Customizable Forensic Workflows**: Open-source tools are frequently used in environments where investigators need to customize their forensic workflows to meet specific case requirements.

2. Commercial Forensic Tools

Commercial forensic tools are proprietary software products developed and sold by private companies. These tools are designed for professional and enterprise-level use, offering advanced features, technical support, and comprehensive capabilities for complex investigations. While commercial tools come with a cost, they are often preferred in high-stakes investigations, such as corporate security breaches, high-profile criminal cases, and large-scale forensic operations.

Key Features of Commercial Tools:

- **Advanced Capabilities**: Commercial tools tend to offer a broader and more sophisticated range of features compared to open-source tools. They are designed to handle a wide variety of cases, from basic data acquisition to complex data analysis, including cloud forensics, mobile forensics, malware analysis, and encrypted data decryption.
- **Technical Support and Training**: One of the primary advantages of commercial tools is the dedicated technical support and training that accompany them. Companies offering commercial forensic software often provide expert assistance, troubleshooting, and updates to ensure smooth operations in complex or high-pressure investigations.
- **User-Friendly Interface**: Commercial forensic tools often come with polished, user-friendly interfaces that make them easier to navigate for investigators, reducing the learning curve and increasing productivity. These tools are often

designed with law enforcement and corporate users in mind, who may not have specialized technical backgrounds.

- **Integrated Solutions**: Many commercial forensic tools provide a fully integrated solution, meaning that the software includes everything needed for the entire forensic process, from data acquisition to reporting. This integration simplifies workflows and reduces the need for multiple standalone tools.
- **Legal and Compliance Features:** Commercial forensic tools often include features to assist investigators with maintaining legal compliance, such as chain of custody management, audit trails, and reporting templates designed for court presentation.

Common Commercial Forensic Tools:

- **EnCase Forensic**: EnCase is one of the leading commercial forensic tools, known for its comprehensive capabilities in data acquisition, analysis, and reporting. It supports a wide range of devices, including desktops, mobile phones, and cloud environments.
- **FTK (Forensic Toolkit):** FTK, developed by AccessData, is a powerful forensic tool that excels in data indexing, analysis, and reporting. It is particularly strong in handling large volumes of data and email analysis.
- **X1 Social Discovery**: A tool designed for social media forensics, X1 Social Discovery allows investigators to collect and analyze data from social media platforms and web-based communications, which is critical in modern investigations.
- **Cellebrite UFED**: Cellebrite's Universal Forensic Extraction Device (UFED) is a leader in mobile forensics, enabling the extraction of data from a wide range of mobile devices, including encrypted and password-protected smartphones.

Applications of Commercial Tools:

- **High-Profile Criminal Investigations**: Commercial tools are typically used in law enforcement and government agencies where advanced features, high levels of support, and reliable results are required for complex investigations such as cybercrime, terrorism, or fraud.
- **Corporate Security and Incident Response**: Large corporations often use commercial forensic tools to respond to data breaches, investigate insider threats, and perform e-discovery during legal proceedings. The comprehensive features and integration with other security systems make commercial tools ideal for enterprise use.

- **Mobile and Cloud Forensics**: With the increasing use of mobile devices and cloud services, commercial tools like Cellebrite UFED and EnCase have developed specialized features for handling mobile and cloud forensics, addressing the unique challenges posed by these environments.

The choice between open-source and commercial tools ultimately depends on the specific needs of the investigator, the complexity of the case, and the available resources. Open-source tools offer flexibility, transparency, and cost-effectiveness, making them ideal for budget-conscious investigators, educational purposes, and smaller-scale cases. However, they may lack the advanced features and professional support offered by commercial tools, which are designed for complex, large-scale investigations that require sophisticated capabilities, robust support, and integration with other forensic tools. Both types of tools play important roles in the field of digital forensics, and many investigators find that a hybrid approach, using both open-source and commercial solutions, provides the best balance of cost and functionality.

4.4 Building a Digital Forensics Toolkit

A well-equipped digital forensics toolkit is crucial for any investigator tasked with examining digital evidence. The complexity of modern technology, with its diverse devices, file systems, and types of data, requires investigators to have a broad set of tools at their disposal. Building a comprehensive forensics toolkit involves selecting the right mix of hardware, software, and procedures to ensure that the digital evidence is preserved, analyzed, and presented correctly. This section will discuss the essential components of a digital forensics toolkit, providing a framework for building a toolkit that meets the demands of various investigations.

1. Hardware Components of a Forensic Toolkit

Hardware tools play a foundational role in digital forensics by facilitating data acquisition, recovery, and preservation. Below are the key hardware tools that should be included in any forensic investigator's toolkit:

1.1 Write Blockers

Write blockers are essential to ensure that the original evidence is not altered during the acquisition process. These devices allow for read-only access to the storage device, protecting the integrity of the data. Whether the evidence is stored on a hard drive, USB stick, or memory card, write blockers ensure that no changes are made to the device, which is critical for preserving the chain of custody and ensuring that the evidence is admissible in court.

- **Types**: Write blockers are available as hardware devices that physically sit between the target media and the forensic workstation. Some software-based write blockers can also be used, but hardware write blockers are preferred due to their reliability.
- **Recommended Brands**: Tableau Forensic Write Blocker, Logicube WriteBlocker.

1.2 Forensic Duplicators

Forensic duplicators are used to create exact bit-for-bit copies of digital media. This is a critical step in digital forensics as investigators typically work with duplicates of the original data to avoid any chance of altering the evidence. The duplicator will capture not only the active data but also any deleted, hidden, or unallocated data.

- **Key Features**: Many duplicators support multiple drive types (SATA, IDE, SAS), can clone drives simultaneously, and come equipped with write-blocking capabilities to ensure that no data is written during the duplication process.
- **Recommended Brands**: Logicube Forensic Duplicator, DeepSpar Disk Imager.

1.3 Data Recovery Tools

Sometimes, evidence is not readily accessible due to corruption, damage, or issues with the device. Specialized data recovery hardware can assist in retrieving this information, even from physically damaged drives. Data recovery tools range from basic recovery kits for logical errors to sophisticated systems for recovering data from severely damaged hard drives or SSDs.

- **Applications**: These tools are typically used in cases where drives have been physically damaged or have failed to boot due to hardware issues.
- **Recommended Brands**: DeepSpar, Atola Insight Forensic.

1.4 Forensic Adapters and Cables

Forensic adapters and cables are required to connect various storage devices to a forensic workstation. These adapters enable the investigator to connect devices such as old IDE hard drives, SATA drives, or even mobile device storage to a modern workstation for analysis.

- **Application**: Forensic adapters ensure that investigators can connect various devices without having to rely on the original hardware.
- **Recommended Brands**: CRU DataPort Forensic Adapter, Acelab Forensic Adapters.

1.5 Portable Forensic Workstations

Forensic investigators often need to work in the field or in environments where access to a traditional forensic lab setup is not available. A portable forensic workstation offers a mobile, rugged solution that integrates multiple forensic tools in one device, including the capability for data acquisition, analysis, and reporting.

- **Key Features**: These workstations typically include high-powered laptops or tablets with embedded forensic software, write blockers, and forensic duplicators.
- **Recommended Brands**: Panasonic Toughbook, BlackBag Forensic Workstation.

2. Software Components of a Forensic Toolkit

Software is equally crucial to the digital forensics process, assisting investigators in analyzing and interpreting data. A good digital forensics toolkit includes a variety of software tools tailored to specific tasks, from data imaging and analysis to network forensics and mobile device extraction. Here are the essential software tools:

2.1 Forensic Imaging Software

Forensic imaging software creates a bit-for-bit copy of the data stored on digital media. It ensures that every file, deleted file, and unallocated space is copied, preserving the integrity of the original data. The imaging process often includes hashing algorithms to verify that the duplicate is an exact replica of the original device.

- **Recommended Software**: FTK Imager, EnCase Forensic, Guymager (open-source).

2.2 Data Analysis Tools

Data analysis software is essential for examining the contents of disk images and identifying valuable evidence. These tools allow investigators to search for keywords, identify file signatures, recover deleted files, and conduct timeline analyses. They also support advanced features like carving data from unallocated space and creating visual representations of the data.

- **Recommended Software**: Autopsy (open-source), X1 Social Discovery (for social media), ProDiscover Forensic.

2.3 Mobile Forensics Tools

Given the rise in mobile device usage, mobile forensics tools are essential for extracting and analyzing data from smartphones, tablets, and other mobile devices. These tools can recover data such as contacts, messages, emails, GPS data, and app data, including deleted information, from both Android and iOS devices.

- **Recommended Software**: Cellebrite UFED, XRY, Oxygen Forensic Detective.

2.4 Network Forensics Tools

Network forensics involves the monitoring and analysis of network traffic to identify suspicious activity or trace digital footprints. Network forensics tools help investigators capture and analyze data packets in real time, identifying cyberattacks, unauthorized access, or other malicious behavior.

- **Recommended Software**: Wireshark (open-source), Network Miner, X1 Search (for network data and cloud environments).

2.5 Hashing and File Integrity Software

Hashing software is used to generate unique cryptographic hashes (e.g., MD5, SHA-1) for files, drives, and disk images. This ensures that digital evidence has not been tampered with and provides a way to verify the integrity of data during the collection, transfer, and analysis stages.

- **Recommended Software**: FTK Imager (built-in hashing), HashMyFiles (free tool), Veracrypt (encryption and verification).

3. Key Considerations When Building a Toolkit

When building a digital forensics toolkit, there are several key considerations that must be taken into account:

3.1 Types of Investigations

The nature of the investigations you plan to handle should heavily influence the tools you select. For example:

- **Mobile Forensics**: If you expect to work frequently with mobile devices, tools like Cellebrite UFED or XRY should be prioritized.
- **Network Forensics**: If your cases often involve analyzing network traffic, software like Wireshark and Network Miner will be crucial.
- **General Forensics**: For broader digital forensics, tools like FTK Imager and Autopsy will provide robust imaging and analysis capabilities.

3.2 Budget

The budget available for your toolkit will also affect your choices. Open-source software can be very effective, especially in cases where funding is limited. However, for complex or high-profile investigations, commercial tools may be necessary for their advanced features, comprehensive support, and integration capabilities.

3.3 Training and Support

Commercial tools often come with professional support and training, which can be invaluable in complex investigations. If you opt for open-source tools, be prepared to invest time in training and community support.

3.4 Legal Compliance and Chain of Custody

Ensuring the integrity of evidence is essential in digital forensics, and your toolkit should include tools that help maintain proper documentation, auditing, and reporting to protect the chain of custody. Commercial tools often have built-in features to assist with this, while open-source tools may require more manual tracking.

3.5 Scalability and Integration

Your toolkit should be scalable to handle a growing volume of data and evolving technologies. It should also integrate well with other tools and systems used within your organization or investigative team to streamline workflows.

Building an effective digital forensics toolkit involves a careful selection of both hardware and software tools tailored to the specific needs of your investigations. By understanding the essential components of a forensic toolkit, such as write blockers, forensic duplicators, analysis software, and mobile forensics tools, you can ensure that you are well-equipped to handle a variety of forensic challenges. Whether you choose open-source tools, commercial tools, or a combination of both, your toolkit must provide the functionality, reliability, and support necessary to handle the ever-evolving landscape of digital forensics.

4.5 Keeping Up with Technological Advances

Digital forensics is an ever-evolving field, driven by rapid advancements in technology. As new devices, software, and communication methods emerge, forensic investigators must constantly update their skills, tools, and knowledge to remain effective. The landscape of digital forensics is shaped by a combination of innovation in digital technologies and new challenges that arise from these innovations. This section explores how digital forensics professionals can keep up with technological advances, ensuring their practices are up to date and relevant.

1. Understanding the Impact of Emerging Technologies

Emerging technologies continually reshape the landscape of digital forensics by introducing new forms of evidence, increasing complexity in data storage, and creating new avenues for cybercrimes. These technological advancements often result in both opportunities and challenges for forensic investigators.

1.1 Internet of Things (IoT)

The rise of IoT devices, including smart home systems, wearable devices, and connected vehicles, has dramatically increased the amount of digital evidence that can be collected in an investigation. These devices continuously collect and transmit data, from location tracking and health information to voice recordings and video surveillance.

- **Challenges**: IoT devices often store data in proprietary formats, creating difficulties in data extraction and analysis. Additionally, the sheer volume of data generated by IoT devices can overwhelm traditional forensic tools.
- **Opportunities**: The wealth of evidence that can be obtained from IoT devices opens new investigative possibilities, especially in cases involving surveillance, location tracking, or personal activity.

1.2 Cloud Computing and Virtual Environments

Cloud computing has transformed how data is stored, accessed, and shared, presenting both opportunities and obstacles for forensic investigators. Data is often dispersed across multiple locations, including public and private cloud services, making it more difficult to pinpoint the exact location of evidence. Virtual environments, including virtual machines and containers, further complicate investigations due to the complexity and flexibility they offer in handling data.

- **Challenges**: Investigators face hurdles in accessing data stored in the cloud, as it requires cooperation from service providers and navigating data sovereignty issues. Furthermore, virtual machines and containers can hide or obscure the true location of digital evidence.
- **Opportunities**: Cloud forensics tools are becoming more advanced, allowing investigators to access and analyze data from cloud environments more effectively. Virtualization also enables investigators to replicate environments, preserving evidence in a controlled, isolated setup for analysis.

1.3 Cryptography and Encryption

As cybercriminals increasingly rely on encryption and cryptographic technologies to safeguard their communications and data, digital forensics experts are faced with the ongoing challenge of decrypting or bypassing these protections. Cryptography, including end-to-end encryption in messaging apps and encrypted disk storage, plays a significant role in modern cybercrime investigations.

- **Challenges**: Decrypting encrypted data remains one of the most difficult aspects of modern forensics. Cryptographic techniques are constantly evolving, making it harder for investigators to keep pace.
- **Opportunities**: As encryption methods evolve, forensic professionals can leverage new decryption techniques and tools to break these protections. Additionally, some tools are incorporating machine learning and AI algorithms to assist with cracking encryption or identifying weaknesses in cryptographic systems.

1.4 Artificial Intelligence (AI) and Machine Learning (ML)

Artificial intelligence (AI) and machine learning (ML) technologies are making their way into the digital forensics world, both as tools for investigators and as challenges posed by cybercriminals. AI and ML algorithms can be used to automate data analysis, detect anomalies, and uncover hidden patterns within vast datasets, significantly improving the speed and accuracy of forensic investigations.

- **Challenges**: The growing use of AI by cybercriminals, such as for creating sophisticated malware or launching targeted attacks, presents a new challenge in digital forensics. Investigators must stay ahead of these developments by continually enhancing their knowledge of AI-driven criminal activities.
- **Opportunities**: AI-powered forensic tools can be used to streamline evidence review and automate routine tasks like data indexing, reducing the time investigators spend on repetitive tasks and allowing them to focus on higher-priority work.

1.5 Blockchain Technology

Blockchain technology, which underpins cryptocurrencies like Bitcoin, is increasingly being considered for applications beyond digital currency. Blockchain can be used for secure data storage, transaction tracking, and ensuring data integrity. Forensics professionals must adapt to handle investigations involving blockchain-based evidence, such as transactions in cryptocurrencies or smart contracts.

- **Challenges**: Blockchain presents a unique challenge in that the decentralized nature of the technology means investigators may have difficulty accessing evidence without cooperation from blockchain networks or key players in the cryptocurrency ecosystem.
- **Opportunities**: Investigators can leverage blockchain forensically to trace cryptocurrency transactions, identify patterns of behavior, and track assets across multiple transactions, opening new investigative pathways in cybercrime cases.

2. Training and Continuing Education

Given the rapid pace of technological advancement, it is essential for digital forensics professionals to invest in continuous learning and skill development. Without staying current on the latest technologies, tools, and methods, forensic experts risk becoming obsolete in an increasingly high-tech world.

2.1 Attending Conferences and Workshops

Industry conferences, seminars, and workshops provide excellent opportunities for forensic professionals to stay up to date with the latest advancements in the field. These events offer networking opportunities, hands-on experience with new tools, and sessions led by industry leaders discussing emerging trends and best practices.

Notable Conferences: DEF CON, SANS Digital Forensics and Incident Response Summit, and the International Conference on Digital Forensics & Cyber Crime (ICDF2C) are examples of gatherings where professionals can engage with the latest trends and innovations in the field.

2.2 Certification Programs

Certification programs are designed to ensure that forensic investigators maintain a high level of competence and expertise. These programs cover a range of topics, including the use of advanced forensic tools, knowledge of legal standards, and the ability to handle complex cases involving emerging technologies.

Examples of Certifications:

- **Certified Computer Examiner (CCE):** This certification focuses on computer and network forensics.
- **Certified Forensic Computer Examiner (CFCE):** Offered by the International Association of Computer Investigative Specialists (IACIS), this certification is widely recognized in the industry.
- **Certified Ethical Hacker (CEH):** A valuable certification for understanding cybersecurity and forensics from an attacker's perspective.

2.3 Self-Directed Learning

Forensic professionals can stay ahead of the curve by self-learning, through online courses, webinars, research papers, and technical blogs. Self-directed learning provides flexibility and allows individuals to focus on areas of interest or areas where new technology is emerging, such as mobile forensics or cloud security.

- **Online Learning Platforms**: Platforms like Coursera, Udemy, and Pluralsight offer courses in digital forensics and cybersecurity, covering new tools and techniques as they arise.

3. Collaborating with Technology Experts and Developers

As technology continues to evolve, collaborating with developers and tech experts becomes increasingly important for staying informed about upcoming changes. Working alongside software developers or cybersecurity experts can help forensic investigators understand the underlying principles of new technologies and gain early insights into potential challenges.

3.1 Building Partnerships

Digital forensics investigators should establish relationships with software vendors, researchers, and industry leaders who are on the cutting edge of technology. Collaboration with cybersecurity companies, law enforcement agencies, and academic institutions can provide access to early-stage tools and research, which is invaluable for staying ahead of technological shifts.

3.2 Contributing to Open-Source Communities

Many of the most advanced forensic tools and techniques have emerged from the open-source community. Contributing to or collaborating with these communities not only helps to shape the tools but also provides forensic professionals with the latest developments in forensic technology. It also allows investigators to share knowledge, discuss challenges, and contribute to the development of new solutions.

Keeping up with technological advances in digital forensics is an ongoing challenge, but it is also an opportunity for forensic professionals to grow and adapt. Emerging technologies such as IoT, blockchain, AI, and encryption continually shape the digital forensics landscape, requiring investigators to update their skill sets, tools, and methods to keep pace. By attending conferences, pursuing certifications, engaging in self-learning, collaborating with experts, and contributing to open-source communities, forensic professionals can remain at the forefront of their field. With these strategies in place, digital forensics investigators can navigate the complexities of modern investigations and continue to deliver results in an ever-changing digital world.

5. Data Acquisition and Preservation

In digital forensics, the first and most crucial step is the proper acquisition and preservation of evidence. This chapter covers the critical processes involved in securing data without altering or damaging it, ensuring its integrity for later analysis. You'll learn about forensic imaging techniques, including the use of write blockers, disk cloning, and capturing volatile data from live systems. The importance of maintaining a clear chain of custody will also be highlighted, emphasizing the role of documentation in preserving the credibility of the evidence. With these methods, you'll gain the skills necessary to collect data securely and preserve it for accurate, admissible analysis.

5.1 Imaging Techniques: Cloning and Copying

Imaging is one of the most critical steps in the digital forensics process. It ensures that a precise, bit-by-bit copy of the original digital evidence is created, preserving the integrity of the data and allowing investigators to perform analysis without altering the original media. There are two primary imaging techniques used in digital forensics: cloning and copying. Both methods have their specific use cases, advantages, and challenges. Understanding the differences between them and knowing when to use each is essential for any forensic investigator.

1. The Concept of Imaging in Digital Forensics

In the context of digital forensics, "imaging" refers to the process of creating an exact copy of a digital storage medium—such as a hard drive, flash drive, or memory card. This copy, often referred to as a "forensic image," preserves the full content of the device, including files, metadata, hidden data, unallocated space, and even deleted files. Imaging is crucial because it allows investigators to examine and analyze the data without jeopardizing the integrity of the original evidence.

Imaging also enables forensic professionals to work on a duplicate of the data while maintaining the chain of custody and ensuring that any changes to the original device are avoided. This process is foundational for preserving the reliability and admissibility of evidence in court.

2. Cloning: Creating a Bit-for-Bit Duplicate

Cloning refers to the process of creating an exact, bit-for-bit copy of the original storage device. This process typically involves duplicating every sector, including active data, deleted files, and unallocated space, ensuring that no data is overlooked. Cloning tools capture all of the data from the source device in its exact state, which can be particularly important when the goal is to preserve the integrity of the device for potential future legal or investigative use.

How Cloning Works:

- **Bit-for-Bit Copying**: A clone is a direct replica of the original device, and every byte of data, including unused or deleted data, is copied exactly. This process involves capturing all physical and logical sectors of the device, including metadata and unallocated space.
- **Software Tools**: Forensic duplicators or imaging software like FTK Imager, Guymager, or hardware devices like the Tableau Forensic Duplicator are commonly used for cloning. These tools ensure the forensic image maintains the original's integrity by verifying the hash values during the process.

Advantages of Cloning:

- **Exact Replication**: The cloned image is a true, exact copy of the original, preserving the entire structure of the data, which is vital in complex investigations.
- **Complete Data Capture**: Cloning captures all data, including files that have been deleted but are still recoverable or that exist in unallocated space, which is important in certain criminal investigations (e.g., fraud or hidden data).
- **Chain of Custody**: Since a cloned image is a complete duplicate of the original media, it allows the forensic team to preserve the chain of custody and ensures that investigators only work with the clone, not the original evidence.

Disadvantages of Cloning:

- **Time-Consuming**: Cloning a device, especially a large one, can be a time-consuming process due to the sheer volume of data involved. This can be particularly challenging if investigators are working with multiple devices.
- **Large Storage Requirements**: Cloning creates an identical copy of the original data, which can require significant amounts of storage space, especially when dealing with large drives or high-capacity devices.

3. Copying: Logical Extraction of Files and Data

In contrast to cloning, copying refers to extracting only the logical data from the storage device, such as files, folders, or partitions, while leaving out unallocated space and other data that is not actively in use. This process focuses on copying the contents of the device, typically excluding deleted files, unallocated space, or other hidden data that might not be visible in the normal file structure.

How Copying Works:

- **File System-Level Copying**: Copying typically focuses on the active data, which is readily accessible from the file system. Investigators may extract specific files or folders from a device using specialized software tools.
- **Data Recovery Tools**: Tools like FTK Imager, EnCase, and X1 Search are used to perform logical extractions of the data. These tools often allow the investigator to select specific types of evidence (such as emails or documents) to extract from the device.

Advantages of Copying:

- **Faster Process**: Copying is faster than cloning because it focuses on active data rather than performing a bit-for-bit duplication. This is especially useful when dealing with large drives or when time is a critical factor.
- **Smaller File Size**: Since only the accessible data is copied, the resulting image will be much smaller than a cloned image, reducing the storage space required.
- **Targeted Evidence Collection**: Copying allows investigators to focus on specific files or types of data, making it ideal for cases where only certain information is required or when resources are limited.

Disadvantages of Copying:

- **Loss of Data**: The biggest drawback of copying is that it does not capture deleted files or unallocated space. Investigators may miss crucial evidence stored outside the active file system, such as hidden files, system logs, or files that were recently deleted.
- **Risk of Missing Evidence**: In some cases, particularly with cases involving sophisticated attempts to hide evidence, copying alone may not be sufficient to uncover all the information that exists on the device.

4. When to Use Cloning vs. Copying

The decision to clone or copy a device in digital forensics depends on the type of investigation and the data required. Below are some general guidelines for determining when to use each method:

When to Use Cloning:

- **Comprehensive Investigations**: Cloning is appropriate when investigators need a complete and comprehensive picture of the data on a device, including hidden or deleted files. It is especially useful for complex investigations where the entirety of the device's data is relevant.
- **Critical Cases**: Cloning is ideal for cases that involve serious criminal activities, such as cybercrime, fraud, or terrorism, where even seemingly insignificant data could be critical.
- **Forensic Analysis in Court**: When the chain of custody and data integrity need to be rigorously maintained for legal purposes, cloning ensures that the original evidence is untouched and preserved.
- **Data Recovery**: If a device is suspected to have damaged or inaccessible sectors, cloning allows investigators to attempt recovery of data that may not be directly accessible through logical extraction.

When to Use Copying:

- **Targeted Investigations**: If an investigator is only interested in specific files or types of data, copying can be a quicker, more efficient option.
- **Limited Resources**: When time or storage space is a concern, copying the relevant files rather than cloning the entire device can save both time and disk space.
- **Routine Investigations**: For cases involving easily accessible, unencrypted data, copying may be sufficient to gather the necessary evidence without the need for a full clone.

Both cloning and copying are fundamental techniques in digital forensics, but each serves distinct purposes. Cloning is the preferred method when it is essential to preserve the integrity and completeness of the original device, especially when dealing with complex or high-stakes investigations. Copying, on the other hand, offers a more efficient way to extract specific data from a device when time, resources, or the scope of the investigation require a more focused approach. By understanding the strengths and limitations of each imaging technique, forensic investigators can make informed decisions about which method to use in any given situation, ensuring that digital evidence is preserved, analyzed, and presented effectively.

5.2 Ensuring Chain of Custody

In digital forensics, chain of custody is a critical concept that ensures the integrity, reliability, and credibility of digital evidence throughout the entire investigative process. It refers to the documentation, tracking, and management of evidence from the moment it is collected until it is presented in court, ensuring that it has not been tampered with or altered at any point. The chain of custody is fundamental for upholding the admissibility of evidence in court and protecting the rights of all parties involved in the investigation.

This section discusses the importance of the chain of custody in digital forensics, best practices for maintaining it, and the challenges investigators may face in preserving the integrity of digital evidence.

1. The Importance of Chain of Custody in Digital Forensics

The chain of custody provides a clear and verifiable record of who has handled the evidence, when, and under what circumstances. It ensures that the evidence has been securely maintained, preventing allegations of tampering or mishandling. A properly documented chain of custody can be the difference between the acceptance and rejection of evidence in a court of law.

1.1 Legal Relevance

In criminal investigations, the admissibility of digital evidence hinges on proving that the evidence presented in court is identical to the evidence originally collected. Any breaks or inconsistencies in the chain of custody can cast doubt on the authenticity and integrity of the evidence, potentially leading to its exclusion in court. Therefore, investigators must be diligent in documenting each step of the evidence handling process.

1.2 Preventing Tampering

Digital evidence is vulnerable to tampering, whether intentional or accidental. Unlike physical evidence, digital data can be altered, deleted, or corrupted with relative ease, particularly when it is transferred, copied, or accessed. Ensuring a proper chain of custody is crucial for preventing unauthorized access, accidental modifications, or malicious tampering with digital evidence. By maintaining a secure and documented chain of custody, investigators help prevent challenges to the credibility of the evidence.

2. Best Practices for Maintaining Chain of Custody

Maintaining an unbroken chain of custody requires strict protocols and adherence to best practices from the moment evidence is collected until it is presented in court. The following best practices help ensure that the integrity of digital evidence is preserved throughout the investigative process.

2.1 Proper Documentation

Every piece of digital evidence must be thoroughly documented, starting with its initial acquisition. Key details to record include:

- **Time and date of collection**: When was the evidence acquired? This establishes a clear timeline.
- **Name of the individual who collected the evidence**: Identifies the person responsible for acquiring the evidence.
- **Description of the evidence**: Clearly identify the device or media from which the evidence was extracted, including serial numbers, make, model, and any distinguishing features.
- **Condition of the evidence**: Document the state of the evidence at the time of collection, including whether it was powered on or off, or if it showed signs of damage or tampering.
- **Forensic tools and methods used**: Record the software and techniques used to acquire and preserve the evidence, ensuring a transparent process.

Every transfer of the evidence between individuals, agencies, or locations must also be documented. This includes when evidence is handed over for analysis, when it is stored, and when it is transferred to another department, ensuring an accurate and transparent record.

2.2 Use of Evidence Bags and Tamper-Evident Packaging

To ensure that digital evidence is not tampered with or altered, it should be stored in tamper-evident packaging, such as evidence bags, sealed containers, or evidence lockers. These types of packaging make it immediately apparent if the evidence has been accessed or modified. Tamper-evident seals should be applied to any external storage devices or physical media containing digital evidence (e.g., hard drives, USB sticks).

2.3 Hashing

One of the most effective ways to ensure the integrity of digital evidence is through hashing. A cryptographic hash function, such as MD5, SHA-1, or SHA-256, produces a unique string of characters (hash value) for any given file or dataset. By generating a hash of the original digital evidence and comparing it to the hash of the evidence at later stages of analysis, investigators can verify that no alterations have occurred.

For example, when an image is taken of a device's hard drive, a hash value is calculated and recorded. During subsequent handling, the evidence is re-hashed at every step (such as during duplication, transfer, and storage), ensuring that the hash value remains unchanged and confirming that the evidence is identical to the original.

2.4 Secure Storage

Once digital evidence is collected, it must be securely stored in a controlled environment. The storage system should have restricted access to ensure that only authorized personnel can handle or view the evidence. Physical and digital access controls, such as locked cabinets, secure rooms, and access logs, should be implemented to prevent unauthorized access. Moreover, evidence storage should be clearly marked and identifiable.

For digital evidence, the storage system should be isolated from any external networks or internet connections to prevent malware infections or accidental overwriting. If the evidence is stored on external hard drives or servers, encryption should be applied to prevent unauthorized access in case the storage device is lost or stolen.

2.5 Transfer and Handling Protocols

Any transfer of digital evidence—whether between individuals, agencies, or locations—should be performed according to established handling protocols. Evidence should be transported in secure, tamper-evident packaging, and each transfer must be documented in the chain of custody log. At every stage, a clear record of who has had access to the evidence and when should be maintained.

2.6 Role of Digital Forensic Software Tools

Forensic software tools used for imaging or analyzing digital evidence should be configured to create a log of all actions performed on the evidence. This log should detail every step taken, including when the image was created, what actions were performed on it, and who was involved. This helps to ensure transparency and can be referenced in court to demonstrate that the evidence was handled according to proper protocols.

3. Chain of Custody Challenges in Digital Forensics

While maintaining an unbroken chain of custody is essential, digital forensics investigators often face challenges in ensuring the integrity of evidence throughout the process. Some of the common challenges include:

3.1 Digital Evidence is Fragile

Unlike physical evidence, which can remain intact for long periods of time, digital evidence is inherently more fragile. It can be accidentally overwritten, corrupted, or compromised due to technical failures or improper handling. For example, a device's contents may be inadvertently altered when investigators attempt to open files or run diagnostic software. To counter this risk, investigators must employ forensic imaging techniques that avoid making changes to the original evidence.

3.2 The Complexity of Multiple Devices

In many cases, digital evidence may come from multiple devices, such as smartphones, laptops, tablets, servers, and cloud storage. Keeping track of numerous pieces of evidence requires even more meticulous documentation, as each device needs to be treated as a separate piece of evidence with its own chain of custody. This complexity can introduce errors in tracking and handling, especially when evidence is spread across different locations or agencies.

3.3 Data Volatility

Digital evidence is often stored in volatile memory, such as RAM, which can be wiped or overwritten when the device is powered off or restarted. Investigators need to be cautious in preserving volatile data, capturing it before shutting down or rebooting devices. Failure to properly preserve volatile data could result in the loss of crucial evidence, especially in cases involving malware or cyberattacks.

3.4 Cross-Border Issues

In international investigations, digital evidence may be subject to different legal requirements and chain of custody protocols. Evidence may need to cross borders, making it difficult to ensure that it remains secure and uncontaminated throughout the process. Investigators must navigate international treaties and legal frameworks (such as the Budapest Convention) to ensure that proper procedures are followed.

Ensuring the chain of custody in digital forensics is a vital step in maintaining the integrity and credibility of digital evidence. By adhering to best practices for documentation, handling, storage, and transportation, forensic investigators can guarantee that the evidence remains admissible in court. Despite the challenges posed by digital evidence's fragility and complexity, the use of forensic tools, proper procedures, and vigilance ensures that digital evidence can be protected and preserved throughout the investigative process. Properly maintaining the chain of custody not only safeguards the integrity of evidence but also strengthens the legitimacy of the entire forensic investigation.

5.3 Write Blockers and Their Importance

In digital forensics, ensuring the integrity of evidence is paramount. One of the most effective tools to maintain this integrity during data acquisition and analysis is the write blocker. A write blocker is a hardware or software device that prevents any data from being written to a storage device during the forensic examination process. This tool is vital for preserving the original state of digital evidence and ensures that investigators can perform their work without inadvertently altering or corrupting the data. In this section, we will explore the concept of write blockers, their different types, and their critical role in forensic investigations.

1. The Role of Write Blockers in Digital Forensics

The primary function of a write blocker is to prevent any changes—intentional or accidental—to the data on the storage medium. When a forensic investigator is working with digital evidence, it is crucial that the original data remains unaltered. Even minor changes, such as the modification of file timestamps or the creation of hidden files, can jeopardize the credibility and admissibility of the evidence in court. Write blockers ensure that, during the investigation, the original data on a hard drive, USB flash drive, or other storage device remains unchanged.

1.1 Preserving Evidence Integrity

In any forensic investigation, the chain of custody and the integrity of the evidence are crucial. A write blocker ensures that data is not modified during the forensic acquisition process, which is vital for maintaining the integrity of the evidence. This tool prevents data from being written to or modified on the original storage device, thus ensuring that the evidence remains in its original, unaltered state. This is essential for both the credibility of the forensic process and the admissibility of the evidence in court.

1.2 Avoiding Accidental Changes

Forensic investigators may inadvertently alter data when they interact with storage devices during analysis. For example, opening a file on a hard drive or transferring data may cause hidden files to be modified or system logs to be updated. A write blocker prevents these changes, even if the investigator inadvertently attempts to access or alter files, thereby ensuring that the evidence is untouched.

2. Types of Write Blockers

Write blockers come in two main categories: hardware write blockers and software write blockers. Both types serve the same core function of preventing data writing to a storage device but differ in how they are implemented and the level of control they offer.

2.1 Hardware Write Blockers

Hardware write blockers are external devices that physically connect to the storage media (e.g., a hard drive, solid-state drive, or USB flash drive). The device sits between the storage media and the computer, acting as a protective barrier that blocks any write commands sent from the computer to the storage device. When the storage device is connected to the write blocker, data can be read but not written to the device, preserving its integrity.

How It Works: A hardware write blocker is inserted between the storage device and the computer. It intercepts any attempt by the operating system to send write commands to the device and prevents these commands from reaching the storage device. The write blocker allows the device to be read normally but prevents any writing, thus ensuring the device's contents remain unchanged.

Advantages: Hardware write blockers are often more reliable and secure because they physically prevent any write commands from reaching the storage device. They also provide an additional layer of protection because they do not rely on the operating system or software, reducing the risk of software bugs or vulnerabilities.

Examples: Some commonly used hardware write blockers include the Tableau Forensic Duplicator, Logicube Forensic Drive Blocker, and Wiebetech Forensic UltraDock. These devices typically offer multiple ports for various storage media types and include LED indicators to show the status of the write block.

2.2 Software Write Blockers

Software write blockers are programs that run on the forensic workstation and control access to the storage device. Unlike hardware write blockers, software write blockers are typically used when dealing with virtual environments or when a hardware device is not available. These software tools modify the system's behavior to prevent writes to the connected device.

How It Works: Software write blockers work by intercepting any system-level write requests to the storage device and blocking them before they reach the device. While they cannot physically block write access like hardware blockers, they rely on the operating system to enforce this protection.

Advantages: Software write blockers are more flexible and can be used in situations where hardware write blockers are impractical or unavailable. They are useful for analyzing devices where hardware interfaces may not be compatible or when working with virtualized systems.

Examples: Some well-known software write blockers include WriteBlocker, FTK Imager, and X1 Social Discovery. These tools allow investigators to safely access storage devices by preventing any changes to the original data.

3. Importance of Write Blockers in Digital Forensics

3.1 Ensuring Admissibility in Court

In legal proceedings, digital evidence must be handled with the utmost care to ensure its admissibility in court. Any modification of the original data can lead to questions about its authenticity, potentially resulting in the exclusion of the evidence. A write blocker ensures that no data is altered, guaranteeing that the evidence remains pristine and credible. This is crucial for maintaining the integrity of the forensic investigation and for upholding the legal standards required in a court of law.

3.2 Maintaining the Chain of Custody

The chain of custody is a fundamental principle in forensic investigations, ensuring that the evidence is handled, stored, and transferred securely. By using a write blocker, forensic investigators can confidently maintain an unbroken chain of custody. This tool acts as a safeguard that prevents accidental data modification during acquisition and analysis, ensuring that the evidence remains untouched throughout the investigation process.

3.3 Preventing Malicious or Accidental Alterations

Write blockers prevent both accidental and malicious modifications of digital evidence. Forensic investigations often involve handling devices with sensitive or potentially malicious data. Without a write blocker, an investigator may inadvertently alter or overwrite important information. Write blockers mitigate this risk by providing a safeguard against such alterations, ensuring the authenticity of the evidence.

3.4 Supporting Data Recovery

In many forensic cases, investigators need to recover data from damaged or degraded storage devices. Write blockers ensure that during the recovery process, no changes are made to the original device. By preserving the integrity of the evidence, investigators can perform recovery techniques with confidence, knowing that the device remains in its original state.

Write blockers are indispensable tools in digital forensics, providing the necessary protection to ensure the integrity and reliability of digital evidence. Whether in the form of hardware or software, write blockers prevent any accidental or intentional alterations to data, safeguarding the evidence for analysis and legal proceedings. By maintaining an intact chain of custody and ensuring the authenticity of the evidence, write blockers play a pivotal role in upholding the standards of digital forensic investigations. As digital evidence continues to be critical in criminal investigations and legal proceedings, understanding the importance and proper use of write blockers is essential for every digital forensic professional.

5.4 Live vs. Dead Acquisition

In digital forensics, data acquisition refers to the process of collecting digital evidence from a storage device, such as a hard drive, mobile phone, or server. One of the most critical decisions that forensic investigators must make during the acquisition process is whether to conduct a live acquisition or a dead acquisition. These two methods are used to gather data from a device, but they differ significantly in terms of timing, approach, and the type of data they capture. Understanding the differences between live and dead acquisition is crucial for ensuring that evidence is collected correctly, remains admissible in court, and is preserved in its most relevant form.

In this section, we will explore the key differences between live and dead acquisition, discuss the advantages and disadvantages of each method, and examine when each method is appropriate in digital forensic investigations.

1. Live Acquisition

Live acquisition refers to the process of collecting data from a device that is powered on and actively running. In live acquisition, forensic investigators make a bit-for-bit copy of the device's active data, including the contents of volatile memory (such as RAM), running processes, system logs, network connections, and any open files. This method is often used when investigators need to capture evidence that is in a dynamic state and may be lost once the device is powered off.

1.1 Advantages of Live Acquisition

Captures Volatile Data: The most significant advantage of live acquisition is the ability to capture volatile data, which would be lost if the device were powered down. Volatile data includes data in RAM, system caches, running processes, network connections, and other temporary data. For example, if the device is running malware or participating in an ongoing cyberattack, capturing the data in RAM can provide crucial evidence that may otherwise be lost.

Preserves Active State of the Device: Live acquisition allows forensic investigators to capture the device in its active, running state, which can be important in certain investigations. It can provide real-time data, such as live logs of system activity or active network connections, that offer insights into the device's current use or behavior.

Important for Time-Sensitive Investigations: In some cases, time-sensitive data may be actively being transferred, altered, or stored on the device. A live acquisition allows the investigator to capture that data before it is deleted, overwritten, or transferred to another location.

1.2 Disadvantages of Live Acquisition

Risk of Data Alteration: Since live acquisition involves working with an active device, there is a risk of altering or modifying the evidence during the process. Even small actions, such as opening files or interacting with the device's operating system, can change data, potentially compromising the integrity of the evidence.

Potential for Malware Execution: In cases where the device is infected with malware, conducting a live acquisition can cause the malware to execute or propagate, potentially damaging or altering the data. This poses a significant risk, especially in cases involving cybercrime or active security threats.

Limited by Device Performance: Live acquisition can be slower compared to dead acquisition, particularly when dealing with large amounts of data or complex systems. The forensic investigator must also ensure that the system does not crash or experience performance issues during the acquisition process.

Requires Advanced Tools and Techniques: Live acquisition often requires specialized forensic tools and techniques that can safely capture volatile data without altering the system or introducing risks. This requires skilled investigators and careful planning to ensure that the acquisition is performed correctly.

2. Dead Acquisition

Dead acquisition, on the other hand, refers to the process of collecting data from a device that is powered off or otherwise non-operational. In dead acquisition, the investigator may physically remove the storage media (such as a hard drive, SSD, or memory card) from the device and create an image of the storage device directly, without interacting with the device's operating system. This method typically focuses on capturing non-volatile data, such as files, folders, system partitions, and the device's file system.

2.1 Advantages of Dead Acquisition

No Risk of Altering Evidence: Since the device is powered off during a dead acquisition, there is no risk of altering the data or interacting with active processes. This makes it a safer method when working with physical evidence, as no system processes or files are inadvertently modified.

Capture All Non-Volatile Data: Dead acquisition focuses on non-volatile data, such as the file system, system files, and data stored on disk. This data typically remains intact even if the device is powered off, making it an excellent method for collecting static information such as files, logs, and other artifacts.

Simpler Process: Dead acquisition is often easier to conduct compared to live acquisition because the investigator does not have to worry about managing volatile data or dealing with active system processes. Once the device is powered down, the investigator can safely create a bit-for-bit copy of the storage media, which is often the goal of the acquisition.

Fewer Risks of Malware Propagation: Since the device is powered off, there is little to no risk of triggering malware or security issues during the acquisition process. This is particularly important when dealing with devices suspected of being infected with malicious software.

2.2 Disadvantages of Dead Acquisition

Cannot Capture Volatile Data: The primary drawback of dead acquisition is that it cannot capture volatile data, which is critical in certain investigations. Data stored in RAM, running processes, and other temporary states are lost when the device is powered down. This means that any evidence related to real-time activities (such as running programs, network connections, or encryption keys) may not be captured.

Potential for Data Loss During Shutdown: In some cases, shutting down a device may result in data being lost, especially if the device is in the process of writing data to storage or if there are unsaved changes. Additionally, some devices or operating systems may perform automatic disk encryption or other security measures upon shutdown, which could complicate the acquisition process.

Limited Insight into Active System State: Since dead acquisition focuses on static data, it does not provide any insight into the device's active state. This may limit the ability of investigators to understand the real-time behavior or usage of the device, which can be crucial in cases involving cybercrime, fraud, or security breaches.

3. Choosing Between Live and Dead Acquisition

The decision to perform a live or dead acquisition depends on the specifics of the case, the type of evidence sought, and the device's state at the time of acquisition.

3.1 When to Use Live Acquisition

When Volatile Data Is Critical: If the investigation involves capturing volatile data (e.g., RAM, running processes, network activity, or system logs), live acquisition is the best choice. This is particularly relevant in cases of active cybercrimes, malware analysis, or real-time communications, where the data may be in use or modified during the investigation.

When Time-Sensitive Evidence Is Present: If the investigator needs to capture data before it is lost or overwritten (for example, in cases where data is being actively transmitted or altered), live acquisition may be necessary to preserve this fleeting information.

3.2 When to Use Dead Acquisition

When Volatile Data Is Not Needed: If the investigation is focused on non-volatile data—such as files, folders, and system information—dead acquisition is typically preferred. This method ensures that the evidence is preserved without the risk of alteration.

When Security and Integrity Are Top Priorities: Dead acquisition is ideal when it is important to ensure the integrity of the evidence and avoid any risk of malware execution or data modification. This is particularly true when handling sensitive devices or systems that could be compromised by running processes or malware.

Both live and dead acquisition methods play crucial roles in digital forensics, and each method offers distinct advantages and disadvantages depending on the type of data being sought and the circumstances of the investigation. Live acquisition is essential when capturing volatile data or real-time system activity, while dead acquisition provides a safer, less intrusive approach for obtaining non-volatile data without the risk of altering the evidence.

Forensic investigators must carefully evaluate the specifics of each case to determine the best approach to data acquisition, balancing the need for comprehensive evidence collection with the need to preserve the integrity of the data and avoid potential risks. Understanding when and how to use live or dead acquisition methods is fundamental for ensuring that digital evidence is properly handled and remains admissible in court.

5.5 Safeguarding Evidence from Tampering

In digital forensics, safeguarding evidence from tampering is one of the most critical aspects of the investigative process. As digital evidence can be easily altered, deleted, or corrupted, ensuring its integrity throughout the collection, analysis, and presentation phases is essential. Any tampering with evidence—whether intentional or accidental—can lead to the inadmissibility of the evidence in court, undermine the credibility of the investigation, and even lead to the dismissal of cases. This section explores various techniques and best practices for safeguarding digital evidence from tampering, focusing on methods that ensure the evidence remains unaltered from the moment it is collected until it is presented in court.

1. Establishing Chain of Custody

The chain of custody refers to the chronological documentation of evidence handling. It tracks every individual who has had access to the evidence, the actions they performed with it, and the location where it was stored. This documentation is vital for ensuring that digital evidence has not been tampered with during its lifecycle. A break in the chain of custody can cast doubt on the integrity of the evidence.

1.1 Importance of Chain of Custody

Ensures Integrity: The chain of custody provides an unbroken record of who accessed the evidence and when, ensuring that no one has tampered with the evidence during the investigation.

Legal Admissibility: A properly maintained chain of custody is essential for ensuring that evidence remains admissible in court. Courts require that evidence be handled securely and without tampering; otherwise, it may be challenged by defense attorneys.

Preventing Evidence Alteration: By maintaining a documented and controlled process for the handling of evidence, investigators can ensure that the digital evidence remains in the same state as when it was first collected.

1.2 Best Practices for Maintaining Chain of Custody

Use Detailed Logs: Maintain detailed records of when and by whom the evidence was collected, transferred, stored, and analyzed. Each transaction should be signed by the individual responsible for it.

Label Evidence Clearly: Every piece of evidence should be clearly labeled with unique identifiers to track it easily through the forensic process.

Secure Storage: Physical and digital storage locations should be secure, with restricted access to prevent unauthorized individuals from tampering with the evidence.

2. Write Blockers and Preventing Evidence Alteration

As mentioned previously, write blockers are essential in safeguarding digital evidence. Write blockers are devices or software tools that prevent any data from being written to a storage device during the forensic acquisition process. When an investigator copies data from a digital device, a write blocker ensures that no inadvertent changes, such as file overwriting or system alterations, occur on the original storage media.

2.1 The Role of Write Blockers

Prevent Accidental Modification: Write blockers prevent changes to the original data, safeguarding it from accidental modification. Even small actions, like reading a file, could trigger changes such as updating timestamps or system files, but a write blocker ensures that no data can be written to the storage medium.

Ensure Integrity in Court: Evidence collected using write blockers is less likely to be contested in court since the original device is not modified during the collection process.

2.2 Types of Write Blockers

Hardware Write Blockers: These devices physically prevent any data from being written to a storage medium when it is connected to a computer.

Software Write Blockers: These tools are software applications that prevent write commands from reaching the storage device.

3. Digital Evidence Encryption

Encryption is an essential tool for safeguarding digital evidence, especially in cases where sensitive data is involved. Encryption ensures that even if evidence is stolen or tampered with, it remains unreadable without the proper decryption key. Encryption should be used both for evidence at rest (i.e., when it is stored) and during the transfer process to prevent unauthorized access.

3.1 Importance of Encryption

Protects Confidentiality: Encryption ensures that sensitive evidence, such as personal data or confidential communications, remains secure.

Prevents Data Leakage: If digital evidence is intercepted or accessed by unauthorized individuals, encryption renders the data useless without the decryption key.

3.2 Best Practices for Encryption

Use Strong Encryption Standards: Use industry-standard encryption protocols, such as AES (Advanced Encryption Standard) with a secure key length (e.g., 256-bit), to ensure that evidence is well protected.

Secure Key Management: The encryption keys themselves should be stored securely and only accessible to authorized personnel. The compromise of encryption keys can lead to a complete breach of evidence security.

4. Forensic Imaging and Hashing

Forensic imaging involves creating an exact, bit-for-bit copy of the digital evidence. This is essential for ensuring the original device is preserved in its unaltered state while providing investigators with a working copy of the data to analyze.

4.1 Importance of Forensic Imaging

Creates an Exact Replica: Forensic images capture all data, including deleted files and hidden information. This process ensures that investigators can analyze the evidence without altering the original data.

Prevents Data Loss: By working with a forensic image rather than the original storage device, investigators can conduct in-depth analysis without risking damage or corruption to the evidence.

4.2 Hashing to Ensure Integrity

A hash value is a unique, fixed-length string generated from the contents of the digital evidence. It serves as a fingerprint of the data and is used to ensure that the evidence has not been altered.

Verification with Hashing: After creating a forensic image, investigators generate a hash value of the image and compare it to the hash value of the original device. If the values match, it proves that the image is an exact replica of the original, preserving its integrity.

MD5, SHA-1, and SHA-256: Common hash algorithms used in digital forensics include MD5, SHA-1, and SHA-256. While MD5 and SHA-1 are commonly used, SHA-256 is preferred for its higher security.

5. Secure Storage and Handling of Evidence

Once digital evidence is collected, it must be securely stored to prevent tampering. Proper storage and handling procedures should be followed to ensure that evidence remains intact and tamper-free throughout the investigation.

5.1 Secure Physical Storage

Locked Storage: Digital evidence should be stored in a secure, locked location with access controlled to prevent unauthorized access. This can include physical security such as safes or locked cabinets.

Access Logs: Every individual who handles the evidence should be logged to maintain the chain of custody and ensure that only authorized personnel can access the evidence.

5.2 Secure Digital Storage

Encryption of Evidence: As mentioned earlier, encrypted digital storage ensures that evidence remains secure. Using encrypted disks, USB drives, or cloud storage services ensures that even if unauthorized individuals gain access to the storage medium, the data will be unreadable.

Cloud Storage with Access Control: When storing digital evidence in the cloud, ensure that robust access controls and encryption protocols are in place. Only authorized users should have access to the evidence, and all access should be logged and monitored.

6. Audit Trails and Monitoring

Audit trails are essential for monitoring any actions taken on digital evidence. Every interaction with evidence—from data collection to analysis—should be logged to ensure that any tampering or unauthorized access can be detected quickly.

6.1 Importance of Audit Trails

Real-Time Monitoring: Real-time logging allows investigators to monitor access to evidence, providing an early warning of any potential tampering.

Accountability: Audit trails ensure that all personnel handling evidence are held accountable for their actions. These records can be reviewed to identify unauthorized or suspicious activity.

Safeguarding digital evidence from tampering is a fundamental aspect of digital forensics. By following best practices for maintaining the chain of custody, using write blockers, employing encryption techniques, creating forensic images, and securely handling evidence, investigators can ensure that digital evidence remains intact and credible throughout the investigation process. The integrity of the evidence is critical for both the success of the investigation and its admissibility in court, making it essential that forensic professionals adopt strict measures to prevent tampering and preserve the authenticity of the evidence at all stages.

6. File Systems and Data Storage

Understanding how data is stored and organized on digital devices is key to successfully uncovering hidden or deleted evidence. In this chapter, you'll explore the inner workings of file systems, from common types like NTFS, FAT, and EXT to more complex structures used in modern computing. You'll learn how data is allocated, managed, and retrieved by operating systems, and discover how to track and recover files, even when they've been deleted or corrupted. This chapter will also cover the forensic significance of partition tables, unallocated space, and other storage artefacts that hold critical evidence for investigators.

6.1 Anatomy of File Systems (FAT, NTFS, EXT, etc.)

File systems are the backbone of data storage on computers and other digital devices. They define how data is organized, stored, accessed, and managed on storage media, such as hard drives, solid-state drives, and external storage devices. Understanding the anatomy of file systems is essential for digital forensic investigators, as each file system handles data differently, and specific artifacts can be found within these systems that may be critical to an investigation.

In this section, we will explore the anatomy of common file systems—such as FAT (File Allocation Table), NTFS (New Technology File System), and EXT (Extended File System)—and examine their structure, features, and significance in digital forensics.

1. FAT (File Allocation Table) File System

FAT is one of the oldest and most widely used file systems, initially developed by Microsoft for use with MS-DOS. Over time, FAT has evolved into several versions, including FAT12, FAT16, and FAT32. Despite being an older file system, FAT is still commonly used in flash drives, memory cards, and other portable storage devices because of its simplicity and broad compatibility.

1.1 Structure of FAT

The key components of the FAT file system include:

- **Boot Sector**: This contains the file system's metadata, including information about the partition size, file system type, and the location of the FAT.

- **FAT Table**: The File Allocation Table itself contains a map of clusters (the smallest unit of storage) on the disk. Each entry in the table corresponds to a cluster, and it indicates whether the cluster is free, used, or the end of a file.
- **Data Area**: This is where the actual file data is stored. The data area is divided into clusters, and the size of each cluster depends on the total size of the volume.
- **Root Directory**: This directory contains the names and metadata of files and directories on the disk, including file names, extensions, attributes, timestamps, and cluster pointers.

1.2 Forensic Relevance of FAT

- **Deleted File Recovery**: When files are deleted in a FAT file system, the directory entry is removed, and the file's clusters are marked as free, but the data often remains intact until overwritten. Forensic investigators can recover deleted files by examining the FAT table and checking for unused clusters that contain remnants of deleted data.
- **File Fragmentation**: FAT file systems tend to fragment files when there is insufficient contiguous space to store them. Forensic investigators may find evidence of fragmented files and be able to reconstruct them by piecing together clusters from different locations on the disk.

2. NTFS (New Technology File System)

NTFS is a more advanced and robust file system developed by Microsoft to address the limitations of FAT. It is the default file system for modern versions of Windows, supporting large volumes, file-level security, encryption, and more efficient storage mechanisms. NTFS is known for its reliability, scalability, and support for complex file attributes.

2.1 Structure of NTFS

The main components of an NTFS file system include:

- **Master Boot Record (MBR) or GPT**: The MBR (on smaller drives) or GUID Partition Table (GPT, used for larger drives) stores partitioning information and points to the partition containing the NTFS file system.
- **Boot Sector**: This contains the boot code necessary to start the operating system.
- **NTFS Volume Boot Record (VBR):** This sector contains metadata about the NTFS file system, including the size of the sectors and the number of clusters.
- **MFT (Master File Table):** The MFT is the heart of NTFS. It contains detailed information about every file and directory on the volume, including metadata such

as file names, timestamps, security attributes, file sizes, and pointers to the actual data clusters.

- **Data Run**: NTFS organizes data into clusters, and each data run in the MFT points to a specific sequence of clusters where the file's data is stored.
- **Log File**: NTFS uses a log file to track changes to the file system. It is useful for recovery after a system crash or power failure.

2.2 Forensic Relevance of NTFS

- **File and Directory Metadata**: NTFS stores rich metadata in the MFT, which can include information such as timestamps (created, modified, accessed) and security settings (permissions). Forensic investigators can extract this metadata to gather valuable evidence.
- **Alternate Data Streams (ADS):** NTFS supports alternate data streams, which allow multiple pieces of data to be stored within a single file. These streams are often used for hidden or malicious data. Forensic investigators must look for and recover ADS, as they may contain evidence of hidden files or covert activities.
- **Deleted Files and MFT Recovery**: When a file is deleted in NTFS, the MFT entry is marked as free, but the data remains on the disk until it is overwritten. Forensics can recover deleted files by scanning the MFT and looking for unallocated entries that reference deleted data.
- **File System Journaling**: NTFS uses journaling to track file system changes. This provides a valuable source of evidence, as it logs actions like file modifications and deletions.

3. EXT (Extended File System)

EXT is a family of file systems commonly used in Linux and other Unix-like operating systems. The most widely used versions are EXT2, EXT3, and EXT4, with EXT4 being the most current and popular in modern Linux distributions. Each iteration of EXT has improved on performance, scalability, and reliability.

3.1 Structure of EXT

The components of an EXT file system include:

- **Superblock**: The superblock contains metadata about the file system, including its size, block size, and free space. It also stores the location of key file system structures, such as the inode table.

- **Inode Table**: Each file and directory in EXT is represented by an inode. The inode contains metadata such as file ownership, permissions, size, timestamps, and pointers to data blocks.
- **Data Blocks**: These blocks store the actual data of files and directories. Data blocks are managed by inodes and are located in different areas on the disk.
- **Block Group Descriptor Table**: The file system is divided into block groups, and this table tracks the free and used blocks in each group.
- **Directory Entries**: These entries map file names to inodes. Each directory entry contains a file name and a reference to the associated inode.

3.2 Forensic Relevance of EXT

- **File System Journaling (EXT3/EXT4)**: EXT3 and EXT4 file systems support journaling, which logs changes made to the file system. In the case of a crash or improper shutdown, the journal can help forensic investigators recover file system state and identify recent changes.
- **File and Directory Metadata**: Like NTFS, EXT stores file metadata, including timestamps (creation, modification, access) and permissions. This can be used to establish timelines or verify the integrity of files.
- **Deleted Files**: When a file is deleted on an EXT file system, the inode and associated data blocks are freed, but the actual data may remain intact until it is overwritten. Forensics can recover deleted files by scanning for unreferenced inodes and examining the data blocks.
- **Hidden Data**: Similar to NTFS, EXT file systems can hide data through mechanisms like hard links (which create multiple directory entries for the same inode). Investigators must check for such hidden data to ensure they do not miss important evidence.

Understanding the anatomy of different file systems, such as FAT, NTFS, and EXT, is essential for forensic investigators. Each file system has unique features, structures, and characteristics that can provide valuable evidence in a digital investigation. By knowing how these file systems manage data and metadata, forensic investigators can identify artifacts, recover deleted files, and trace user actions—ultimately helping to solve crimes and uncover critical information. Familiarity with the anatomy of these file systems allows investigators to approach evidence collection with precision and ensure that digital evidence remains intact and usable in court.

6.2 Locating Deleted or Hidden Files

In digital forensics, one of the primary goals is to recover and analyze digital evidence, which often includes locating deleted or hidden files. Deleted files are not immediately erased from storage; instead, the operating system typically marks the space occupied by the files as "available" for new data. Similarly, hidden files are those intentionally concealed by users or malicious actors to avoid detection. Understanding how to locate these files is crucial for forensic investigators, as they may contain critical evidence related to criminal activity, breaches, or suspicious behavior.

This section will explore the techniques and tools used to locate deleted or hidden files on various file systems, including the processes involved in their recovery.

1. Deleted Files: Understanding the Process of Deletion

When a file is deleted, the operating system (OS) typically removes the reference to the file from the directory structure and marks the space the file occupies as free. However, the data itself is not immediately overwritten, and it remains on the storage medium until it is replaced by new data. Forensic investigators can often recover deleted files by searching for these remnants.

1.1 Common File Deletion Methods

Soft Deletion: When a file is deleted normally (for example, by pressing the delete key in Windows), the operating system marks the space it occupied as available but does not immediately overwrite it. The file's directory entry is removed, but the content is left intact, making recovery possible.

Hard Deletion: In some cases, files are deleted using secure deletion methods or third-party tools that overwrite the data multiple times. These methods make recovery more difficult, as the data is permanently erased from the storage device.

Deleted File Recovery: Tools such as Recuva, PhotoRec, and FTK Imager can be used to scan the free space on a drive to recover deleted files. These tools work by looking for unallocated clusters or sectors that were previously occupied by deleted files. By examining the structure of the file system, forensic investigators can often reconstruct the deleted data.

1.2 File System-Specific Considerations

Different file systems handle file deletion in different ways, affecting the ease of file recovery. Here are some specifics about how popular file systems manage deleted files:

FAT File System: In FAT, when a file is deleted, its directory entry is removed, and the corresponding clusters are marked as free in the File Allocation Table (FAT). The data itself remains in the clusters until they are overwritten. As FAT does not support journaling or advanced file recovery features, deleted files can be easily recovered with the right tools if the clusters have not been overwritten.

NTFS File System: NTFS handles deleted files more robustly, as it uses the Master File Table (MFT) to store metadata about each file. When a file is deleted, NTFS marks the MFT entry as free but does not overwrite the data immediately. Deleted files in NTFS can often be recovered by locating the unreferenced MFT entries and identifying the data blocks that were used by the file.

EXT File System: In EXT file systems, files are deleted when their corresponding inodes are freed. Like FAT, the data often remains on the disk until overwritten. EXT file systems (such as EXT3 and EXT4) support journaling, which can help in recovering data after a crash, but deleted files in these systems may be harder to recover if the file system has been written to heavily.

2. Locating Hidden Files

Hidden files are intentionally concealed from the user or the operating system, often to avoid detection. These files may be created by malware or by users attempting to hide sensitive information. In forensic investigations, identifying and recovering hidden files is critical to uncovering important evidence.

2.1 Methods for Hiding Files

Alternate Data Streams (ADS) in NTFS: NTFS supports a feature known as Alternate Data Streams (ADS), which allows multiple data streams to be associated with a single file. While the primary file is visible to the user, the alternate data streams can be used to store hidden files or data. This feature is often exploited by malware or malicious users to hide files in plain sight.

Forensic Techniques for Locating ADS: Tools like ADS Scanner or NTFSStreams can be used to search for hidden alternate data streams within NTFS file systems. These tools can detect streams attached to files that are not easily visible in the file system's standard directory listings.

Hidden Partitions: In some cases, users or criminals may hide entire partitions on a storage device. A partition may be marked as "hidden" through the operating system or by modifying the partition table. Tools such as Partition Find and Mount or TestDisk can help forensic investigators locate hidden partitions on a disk.

Steganography: Steganography is the practice of concealing information within other files, such as embedding a document or image within an audio or video file. Specialized steganalysis tools, such as StegExpose or Steghide, can help investigators detect and extract hidden data from files that appear to be normal.

File Attribute Modification: In many file systems, files can be hidden by setting certain attributes. For example, in Windows, a file can be marked with the "hidden" attribute, making it invisible to the user under standard file listings. In Linux systems, files can be hidden by prefixing them with a dot (e.g., .hiddenfile). Forensic investigators can list all files, including those with hidden attributes, by using specific commands or tools.

Windows Command Line: To reveal hidden files in Windows, investigators can use the dir /ah command, which shows hidden files marked with the "hidden" attribute.

Linux Command Line: In Linux, files prefixed with a dot (e.g., .config) can be revealed by using the ls -a command.

3. Advanced Techniques for Locating Deleted or Hidden Files

Forensic investigators often use specialized tools and techniques to locate deleted or hidden files. These methods go beyond simple recovery tools and often require expertise in the underlying file system structures.

3.1 File Carving

File carving is the process of searching for file fragments in unallocated space and reconstructing files based on their signatures. This technique is particularly useful for recovering files from fragmented or partially deleted data. Carving tools such as Scalpel, Foremost, and PhotoRec are commonly used in forensic investigations to extract data from sectors of the disk that are not actively in use.

3.2 Hex Editors

Hex editors allow forensic investigators to examine the raw contents of a storage device in hexadecimal format. By manually inspecting the data, investigators can locate remnants of deleted or hidden files, even when they are not associated with any directory entry or file system structure. This technique is particularly useful for locating files that have been fragmented or partially overwritten.

3.3 Searching Unallocated Space

When data is deleted, the corresponding file system structures (such as directory entries or MFT records) are typically removed, but the actual file data may remain in the unallocated space on the disk. Forensic investigators can scan unallocated sectors or clusters to locate data remnants from deleted or hidden files. Tools like EnCase, FTK Imager, and X1 Search can facilitate this process by searching free space for file signatures and potential data fragments.

Locating deleted or hidden files is a vital part of the digital forensics process, as these files can often contain critical evidence. By understanding how different file systems handle deleted data and employing various techniques such as file carving, ADS scanning, and partition recovery, forensic investigators can recover hidden or deleted files and analyze them for relevant information. With the right tools and expertise, investigators can successfully uncover even the most elusive pieces of digital evidence, helping to solve crimes, protect individuals, and secure systems.

6.3 Recovering Data from Damaged Storage

Data recovery from damaged storage devices is one of the most challenging and critical tasks in digital forensics. Storage media such as hard drives, solid-state drives (SSDs), flash drives, and optical media can become physically or logically damaged, making it difficult to retrieve data. However, forensic investigators must possess the knowledge, tools, and techniques to recover important evidence from these damaged devices. Whether it's the result of physical damage, accidental deletion, corruption, or system failure, recovering data from compromised storage is often essential for preserving the integrity of an investigation.

This section explores the methods, challenges, and best practices for recovering data from damaged storage devices, focusing on both physical and logical damage scenarios.

1. Types of Storage Damage

Before diving into the recovery techniques, it's essential to understand the different types of damage that storage devices can experience. These damages can be categorized into two main types: physical damage and logical damage.

1.1 Physical Damage Physical damage occurs when the storage device itself is compromised. This can result from factors like hardware failure, environmental damage, or mishandling. Some common examples of physical damage include:

- **Mechanical Failure (HDDs):** Hard Disk Drives (HDDs) contain moving parts such as platters and read/write heads. These can fail due to excessive wear, overheating, or impact. Physical damage can cause the read/write heads to come into contact with the platters, potentially resulting in scratches, data corruption, or loss.
- **Circuit Board Damage (HDDs and SSDs):** The circuit board of the drive, which handles data read/write operations, can be damaged by electrical surges, water exposure, or physical impact.
- **Wear and Tear (SSDs):** Solid-state drives (SSDs) have no moving parts, but they wear out over time due to the limited number of write cycles each cell can undergo. When an SSD reaches its wear threshold, it can lead to data loss or corruption.
- **Water, Fire, and Physical Impact**: External factors like water or fire damage, or simply dropping the device, can also cause irreparable damage to storage media, making recovery more challenging.

1.2 Logical Damage Logical damage refers to issues that affect the file system, partition structure, or data integrity without physically harming the device. This type of damage typically involves corruption or accidental deletion of data. Examples of logical damage include:

- **File System Corruption**: File systems, such as NTFS, FAT, or EXT, can become corrupted due to improper shutdowns, malware, software bugs, or user errors. Corruption can result in data becoming inaccessible or the system being unable to read the drive.
- **Accidental Deletion**: Files may be accidentally deleted by the user or through software malfunctions, but the data may still reside on the device and can be recovered if the space hasn't been overwritten.
- **Partition Table Corruption**: The partition table maps how data is stored on a device. If the partition table becomes corrupted or damaged, it may lead to the drive being unrecognized or data becoming inaccessible.
- **Bad Sectors or Blocks**: A storage medium may develop bad sectors or blocks, which are areas that are physically damaged but are still logical sectors on the disk. This can result in read/write failures or data corruption.

2. Data Recovery Techniques

2.1 Physical Damage Recovery

When physical damage occurs, data recovery often requires specialized equipment, environment-controlled clean rooms, and expert knowledge. Forensic investigators typically rely on professional data recovery services in these cases. However, there are some techniques and best practices that can be applied:

Disk Imaging in a Controlled Environment: If the drive is still functional but physically damaged (e.g., by a head crash), the first step is to create a bit-for-bit copy of the disk in a controlled environment. This image can be used for further analysis, reducing the risk of further damage during the recovery process. A disk imager tool like FTK Imager or dd in Linux is typically used for this purpose.

Use of Specialized Recovery Tools: For damaged hard drives (HDDs), specialized recovery tools can help recover data from mechanically failed drives. For example, tools like PC-3000 or DeepSpar Disk Imager are designed to work with damaged drives, allowing investigators to recover data from malfunctioning sectors or heads by bypassing damaged components or manually controlling the drive.

Head or Platter Replacement: In cases of severe physical damage to the read/write heads or platters of an HDD, it may be necessary to replace the damaged parts with those from a donor drive. This process must be done in a cleanroom environment to avoid introducing contaminants that could further damage the drive. This is typically only done by specialized recovery firms.

Flash-Based Storage Recovery (SSDs/USB): SSDs and USB flash drives are much more challenging to recover once physically damaged. However, techniques like replacing the damaged memory chip or using tools such as Chip-off Recovery (removing NAND chips from the damaged drive and reading them through specialized hardware) may allow investigators to recover data. These techniques often require expertise and precision.

2.2 Logical Damage Recovery

Recovering data from logical damage can be more straightforward compared to physical damage, though it still requires careful techniques and tools. Several methods can be used to recover logically damaged data:

File System Repair: For logical file system corruption, recovery tools like TestDisk or chkdsk (for NTFS and FAT systems) can be used to scan the file system for errors and repair logical structures. These tools can rebuild damaged partition tables, restore lost files, and fix corruption in directories or file metadata.

Data Carving: When a file system is too corrupted to allow access to the files, forensic investigators often use data carving techniques. This involves scanning the unallocated space of a disk for file signatures (such as the header and footer of a JPEG or PDF) and extracting these fragments. Tools like Scalpel or PhotoRec can be used for file carving.

Partition Recovery: If a partition table becomes corrupted or lost, recovery tools like TestDisk can help by scanning the raw disk for partition information. These tools look for signature patterns that match the partitions and attempt to reconstruct the original partition table, allowing access to the data.

File Recovery Software: Software like Recuva, R-Studio, or ProDiscover can scan storage devices for deleted or lost files. These tools look for unallocated space and perform low-level scans to recover files that were deleted or lost due to logical errors.

2.3 Handling Bad Sectors

When a storage device develops bad sectors, data recovery can become more complicated. However, there are ways to handle this issue:

Sector Remapping: Most modern storage devices (especially HDDs) have built-in mechanisms to remap bad sectors to spare sectors. In cases of minor damage, running a tool like chkdsk or using a low-level formatter may help the device remap bad sectors and make the drive usable again for data recovery.

Forensic Imaging: When bad sectors are present, creating an image of the disk can be challenging. Using tools like DeepSpar Disk Imager or FTK Imager can help by skipping over bad sectors or reading them multiple times to recover as much data as possible. It's crucial to preserve data integrity when dealing with damaged sectors to avoid further data loss.

3. Best Practices in Data Recovery from Damaged Storage

Forensic investigators should follow certain best practices to maximize the chances of successful data recovery and ensure that the integrity of the evidence is preserved throughout the process.

Avoid Using the Affected Device: To prevent further damage or overwriting of the data, the damaged storage device should not be used once it's discovered to be compromised. Instead, the focus should be on creating a bit-for-bit copy of the device (forensic image).

Make Multiple Copies: Whenever possible, create multiple copies of the recovered data to preserve evidence. Keep an original and at least one backup copy for analysis to avoid risking the loss of data during recovery.

Document the Process: Every step in the data recovery process should be documented meticulously. This includes the tools used, any attempts made to repair or recover data, and the methods employed. Proper documentation ensures the process is repeatable and verifiable in court.

Handle Physical Media Carefully: When dealing with physically damaged media, ensure that the storage device is handled with care. Avoid touching the surface of hard drives or storage chips to prevent introducing further damage.

Data recovery from damaged storage is a complex and delicate process that requires expertise, specialized tools, and an understanding of both physical and logical damage. While physical damage often necessitates professional intervention, logical damage can often be repaired using advanced recovery software and techniques. In either case, a systematic and methodical approach to recovery, combined with a focus on preserving evidence integrity, is crucial to ensuring that critical data is not lost.

6.4 Forensic Significance of Partition Tables

In digital forensics, partition tables hold critical forensic significance as they provide the foundational structure for how data is stored and organized on a storage device. These tables essentially define the boundaries of the partitions (logical sections) that make up a disk, specifying where data is located, how it is structured, and how to access it. Understanding the forensic significance of partition tables is vital for investigators, as these structures can provide vital clues in criminal investigations, data recovery, and incident response.

This section will explore the importance of partition tables in digital forensics, how they function, and the challenges forensic investigators may face when dealing with damaged or hidden partition tables.

1. What is a Partition Table?

A partition table is a data structure on a hard disk or storage device that maps out how the drive is divided into partitions. Each partition represents a logical division of the disk, containing its own file system and data. The partition table defines the size, location, and types of partitions on the device, and it is typically located at the beginning of the disk.

There are different partitioning schemes, with the most common being:

MBR (Master Boot Record): MBR is the older partitioning scheme used primarily in BIOS-based systems. The MBR contains the partition table, a bootloader, and other metadata about the disk. It can support up to four primary partitions or three primary partitions and one extended partition, which can further contain logical partitions.

GPT (GUID Partition Table): GPT is the newer, more robust partitioning scheme that replaced MBR in many modern systems. It is part of the UEFI (Unified Extensible Firmware Interface) standard and supports larger disk sizes and more partitions (up to 128 partitions in Windows). GPT is more resilient to data corruption and provides additional redundancy, as it stores a backup of the partition table at the end of the disk.

The partition table is essential for the operating system to recognize and access the data on the disk. Without a valid partition table, the data is usually inaccessible, and the storage device might be unrecognized or appear as unallocated space.

2. Forensic Relevance of Partition Tables

In the context of digital forensics, partition tables are crucial for several reasons. The following points highlight their forensic significance:

2.1 Identifying Data Layout and Structure

The partition table tells forensic investigators where to look for specific data on a disk. It defines where partitions begin and end, allowing investigators to access the exact location where files are stored. If a partition table is intact, it can be used to quickly identify the layout of the drive, helping investigators recover deleted or hidden data.

2.2 Recovering Data from Deleted or Lost Partitions

One of the most important roles of the partition table in digital forensics is in recovering data from deleted or lost partitions. If a partition is deleted, the partition table entry pointing to it is removed, but the data within the partition typically remains on the disk unless overwritten. Forensic investigators can use specialized tools to search for deleted partition structures and reconstruct the partition table.

Tools for Partition Table Recovery: Tools like TestDisk, GParted, and R-Studio can scan the raw sectors of a disk for remnants of partition information, allowing investigators to recover lost or deleted partitions. These tools typically use heuristics to locate partition signatures or entries and can even rebuild the partition table if it has been damaged or overwritten.

2.3 Detecting Hidden Partitions

In some cases, partitions may be intentionally hidden to evade detection. Malicious actors, for instance, may hide partitions to conceal illegal data or to protect information from being discovered by law enforcement. These hidden partitions often have no visible entry in the partition table or may be marked as inactive, making them difficult to detect.

Forensic Techniques for Detecting Hidden Partitions: Specialized tools, such as Partition Find and Mount or DiskInternals Partition Recovery, can help forensic investigators identify hidden partitions by scanning the raw disk for unallocated space that could potentially be used for hidden partitions. Some forensic investigators may also use hex editors to inspect the raw structure of a disk and identify anomalies in partition entries that might indicate the presence of hidden partitions.

2.4 Investigating Drive Tampering

In cases of drive tampering or manipulation, the partition table can provide clues as to whether the drive has been altered. For example, a drive with an altered partition table might indicate that partitions were resized or moved, potentially to cover up traces of activity or to conceal illicit data. Forensic investigators can examine the partition table for inconsistencies or evidence of tampering, such as unexpected changes in partition size, type, or flags.

Metadata and Forensic Artifacts: A partition table stores metadata about each partition, including its start and end locations, size, file system type, and attributes. By analyzing this metadata, investigators can uncover potential tampering and track the modification history of a disk. Additionally, the partition table may contain flags or indicators suggesting that the disk was part of a RAID array or had been encrypted, pointing investigators toward additional avenues of inquiry.

2.5 Locating System and Evidence Partitions

In some forensic investigations, the partition table can be useful for identifying partitions that contain system files or evidence. For example, a system partition may contain operating system files, logs, and other important data related to an ongoing investigation. A forensic investigator can analyze the partition table to locate these critical partitions and recover evidence that might be hidden within them.

System and Recovery Partitions: Many operating systems, particularly Windows, create recovery partitions that store system restore points, boot files, or backup data. These partitions can be crucial for investigators, as they may contain traces of system activity, user behavior, or remnants of deleted files. Forensic tools can be used to access these partitions and extract evidence.

3. Recovering and Analyzing Partition Tables

Forensic investigators often face situations where the partition table has been corrupted, deleted, or overwritten, making it challenging to access the data stored on a drive. However, there are various methods for recovering and analyzing partition tables.

3.1 Scanning for Partition Signatures

Partition tables are often built on standard structures that can be recognized by specialized software. Even if the partition table is missing or corrupted, many recovery tools are designed to scan the drive for known partition signatures (such as those used by MBR or GPT). By locating these signatures, forensic investigators can reconstruct a partition table, allowing access to the partitions and the data within.

3.2 Rebuilding the Partition Table

In cases of severe corruption or loss of the partition table, investigators may need to manually rebuild the partition table. This process typically involves scanning the raw disk for partition data and matching it to known partitioning formats. Tools like TestDisk and EaseUS Partition Master can help in this process, automating the recovery of partitions and the rebuilding of the partition table.

3.3 Using Hex Editors for Deep Analysis

Hex editors allow forensic investigators to examine the raw data of a storage device, including the partition table. By inspecting the raw sectors of a disk, investigators can identify remnants of partition information that can be used to manually reconstruct the partition table. This method requires a deep understanding of how partition tables are structured and is often used as a last resort when other recovery methods fail.

4. Challenges in Partition Table Forensics

While partition tables are crucial for digital forensics, they present several challenges, including:

Overwriting: If data in a partition is overwritten by new data, recovering the original partition may be impossible. The more the disk is written to, the lower the chances of recovery.

Encrypted Partitions: Some partitions may be encrypted to protect the data they contain. If investigators cannot obtain the encryption key, recovering the data in these partitions may be impossible.

Corruption: Partition tables can become corrupted due to physical damage, improper shutdowns, malware, or faulty software. Recovery from corruption may require significant expertise and specialized tools.

Partition tables hold significant forensic value as they provide vital information about the layout and structure of a storage device. Forensic investigators can use partition tables to identify, recover, and analyze data stored on a device, even when the partitions have been deleted, hidden, or damaged. Understanding partitioning schemes, recognizing the forensic importance of partition tables, and employing specialized tools and techniques are essential for digital forensics professionals when dealing with complex cases involving lost or hidden data.

6.5 Interpreting Storage Artefacts

In the field of digital forensics, storage artifacts refer to remnants or traces of data left behind on a storage device, even after the data has been deleted, overwritten, or corrupted. These artifacts can be invaluable in forensic investigations, providing crucial evidence for investigators looking to uncover deleted files, track user activity, or understand the history of interactions with the device. The interpretation of storage artifacts is a critical skill for forensic professionals, as it involves not only recovering these traces but also understanding their context and relevance to the investigation.

This section will delve into the significance of storage artifacts, common types of artifacts found on storage devices, and how forensic investigators interpret and analyze these artifacts to build a clearer picture of events on a device.

1. What Are Storage Artifacts?

Storage artifacts are any traces or remnants of data that remain on a storage device after the user believes it has been deleted or wiped. These artifacts include fragments of files, metadata, operating system logs, deleted file entries, or even data remnants left in unallocated space. Often, storage artifacts arise due to the way operating systems handle data deletion, data overwriting, and file system management.

When files are deleted, the operating system typically removes only the pointers to the data within the file system's allocation table. However, the actual data blocks associated with the file may not be overwritten immediately, making it possible for forensic investigators to recover the file or pieces of it. The presence of these artifacts can reveal significant information about the past activities and behaviors of the user on the device.

2. Types of Storage Artifacts

Several types of storage artifacts are commonly found on storage devices. These can be categorized into a few major types based on the type of data or location where the artifact resides:

2.1 Deleted Files and Partially Overwritten Data

When a file is deleted, the operating system typically marks the space occupied by the file as available for new data. However, the actual data remains on the storage device until it is overwritten. Forensic investigators can often recover deleted files by scanning for unallocated space or identifying file remnants that have not been overwritten.

File Carving: File carving is a technique used to recover deleted files or fragments by searching the raw disk sectors for known file signatures (headers and footers). This technique is useful when the file system is damaged or corrupted, and no directory entries remain.

Slack Space: Slack space refers to the unused space at the end of a cluster that may contain remnants of deleted data. Forensic investigators analyze slack space to retrieve partial or fragmented data that might remain after file deletion.

2.2 File System Metadata

File systems, such as NTFS, FAT, or EXT, store metadata about files, including file names, timestamps, permissions, and more. Even when a file is deleted, its metadata may still be present in the file system and provide valuable information to investigators.

File Names and Paths: Even after deletion, the file names and paths may remain in the file system's metadata or allocation table, helping forensic professionals identify files that were previously present on the device.

Timestamps: Metadata such as "last accessed," "last modified," and "created" timestamps are essential for understanding the activity surrounding a file. These timestamps can provide a timeline of events, indicating when a file was created, modified, or deleted.

2.3 System Logs and Temporary Files

Operating systems and applications often create logs and temporary files to track user activity and system operations. These files can serve as valuable forensic artifacts when investigating a device.

Event Logs: System logs, such as the Windows Event Log, record a history of system activities, including login attempts, file accesses, and application usage. These logs can help investigators reconstruct user actions and detect potential signs of malicious activity.

Temporary Files: Operating systems and applications often create temporary files that store data temporarily while a program is running. These files may contain valuable evidence, even after the associated program has closed. For example, web browsers often create temporary files and cache data that may contain remnants of previously visited websites or downloaded files.

2.4 Hidden and Encrypted Data

In some cases, storage artifacts can be deliberately hidden or encrypted to evade detection. Users or malicious actors may employ encryption or conceal data to protect sensitive information or hide evidence of illicit activity.

Hidden Files and Partitions: Files and partitions can be hidden through a variety of methods, such as using tools to mark the partition as inactive or using special attributes to make files invisible in the file system. Forensic investigators use specialized tools to uncover hidden files and identify hidden partitions.

Encrypted Files: Files may be encrypted using various encryption algorithms to protect their contents. While encrypted files are not inherently accessible without the key, investigators may be able to recover metadata associated with the encrypted files, such as file names, sizes, or modification timestamps, which can provide context to the investigation.

2.5 Unallocated Space and Free Space

Unallocated space refers to the areas of a storage device that are not currently assigned to any active file or partition. Free space refers to areas that were previously used by files but are no longer allocated to any data, either due to deletion or system activity. Both unallocated and free space are important areas to examine when searching for residual data.

Data Remnants: Even after a file is deleted, its data may remain in unallocated space until it is overwritten. Forensic investigators can recover data fragments from these areas using specialized recovery software and data carving techniques.

File System Residues: Some file systems, such as NTFS, leave behind remnants of deleted files or data structures in unallocated space, such as unused MFT (Master File Table) records or fragmented data clusters. Investigators can analyze this space to recover evidence that has been seemingly erased.

3. Interpreting and Analyzing Storage Artifacts

The interpretation of storage artifacts involves more than just recovering data; it requires understanding the context and significance of the recovered data within the scope of the investigation. Forensic investigators need to be skilled in analyzing these artifacts, which involves:

3.1 Contextualizing Data

When interpreting storage artifacts, it's crucial to place the data in the proper context. This includes understanding the file's creation, modification, and deletion timelines, which can provide insights into the user's actions and intentions. The use of metadata, timestamps, and system logs is essential to contextualize the recovered data.

Timestamp Analysis: The sequence of timestamps can help investigators build a timeline of user activity. For example, a file might show a creation timestamp, a modified timestamp, and an access timestamp. A discrepancy between these timestamps can indicate unusual activity, such as file tampering or unauthorized access.

3.2 Data Correlation

Forensic investigators should correlate storage artifacts with other evidence sources, such as network logs, email records, and user activity logs. Correlating artifacts from different sources can provide a clearer and more comprehensive picture of the user's behavior and intentions.

Cross-Referencing Evidence: By cross-referencing storage artifacts with network traffic logs, forensic investigators can establish connections between actions on the storage device and external activities, such as downloading files, browsing websites, or interacting with online services.

3.3 Investigating Hidden or Stealth Data

Forensic investigators must be especially vigilant when searching for hidden or encrypted data. Advanced techniques and tools can help uncover data that might be intentionally concealed or encrypted, providing crucial evidence that may otherwise remain undetected.

Encryption Cracking: In some cases, investigators may attempt to crack the encryption on a file or partition using brute-force methods or by attempting to exploit known vulnerabilities in the encryption algorithm. However, cracking encryption can be time-consuming and may not always be successful, depending on the strength of the encryption.

3.4 Examining Unallocated Space and Slack Space

Unallocated space and slack space can provide valuable insights into what files were previously stored on a device. Investigators should use specialized tools to analyze these areas and recover data remnants. The analysis of slack space, in particular, can reveal deleted fragments of files that were not completely overwritten.

Slack Space Analysis: Forensic tools like EnCase or Autopsy can analyze slack space to recover deleted data fragments. These fragments may provide incomplete or partial data, but they can still be useful for piecing together evidence.

4. Challenges in Interpreting Storage Artifacts

While storage artifacts can be incredibly valuable, there are several challenges that forensic investigators may face when interpreting them:

Data Overwriting: Once data is overwritten, it becomes significantly harder or even impossible to recover. The more times data is overwritten, the lower the chances of successful recovery.

Data Fragmentation: Files that are fragmented across different areas of the disk can be difficult to recover in their entirety. Data carving techniques may be required to piece together fragmented files.

Encryption: Encrypted data presents significant challenges, as without the decryption key, investigators cannot access the contents. The recovery of metadata associated with encrypted files may still provide useful insights, but decryption is often necessary to access the full evidence.

Interpreting storage artifacts is a critical aspect of digital forensics, requiring forensic investigators to recover and analyze residual data left behind on storage devices. By understanding the types of storage artifacts, using specialized tools to recover them, and contextualizing the recovered data within the broader scope of the investigation, forensic professionals can uncover important evidence that may have otherwise been overlooked. Despite the challenges, the ability to effectively interpret storage artifacts is an essential skill in digital forensic investigations.

7. Forensic Imaging and Analysis

Forensic imaging is one of the most critical steps in digital forensics, allowing investigators to create an exact, bit-by-bit copy of a device's storage for analysis. This chapter explores the process of forensic imaging, detailing best practices for capturing accurate, verifiable images while maintaining the integrity of the original data. You'll learn how to use specialized tools to create and validate forensic disk images, ensuring they are legally admissible. Additionally, the chapter covers the techniques for analyzing these images, from recovering deleted files to identifying hidden or encrypted data, and demonstrates how forensic investigators can extract valuable insights while preserving the original evidence.

7.1 Preparing for Imaging: Tools and Best Practices

In digital forensics, creating an exact, bit-by-bit copy of a storage device, commonly referred to as an imaging process, is one of the most important steps for preserving digital evidence. This forensic image serves as a working copy that can be analyzed without risking damage or alteration to the original data. The integrity of the forensic process depends on how well the imaging procedure is carried out. Thus, preparation is a critical step in ensuring that the evidence remains intact, accurate, and admissible in court. This chapter will explore the essential tools and best practices to follow when preparing for the imaging process, covering both the technical aspects and procedural considerations.

1. Importance of Forensic Imaging

Forensic imaging is crucial because it allows investigators to analyze a device's data without directly interacting with the original hardware, thus preventing data modification or destruction. The image must be an exact replica of the source device, including files, file system structures, unallocated space, metadata, and hidden or deleted files. By using a bit-by-bit copy (also known as a raw image), the forensic image captures all the data that could be relevant to an investigation, ensuring that no information is lost or altered.

Additionally, forensic imaging ensures that:

- **Chain of custody is maintained**: The process is done in a controlled environment to prevent any alteration of the original data.

- **Evidence is preserved for future analysis**: The image provides a copy that can be analyzed at a later date, even if the original device becomes unavailable or damaged.

2. Selecting the Right Imaging Tools

Choosing the right tools is one of the first and most crucial steps in preparing for a forensic imaging operation. The tools selected must provide an exact, verifiable copy of the source device and have features that align with the investigation's requirements.

2.1 Hardware Tools for Imaging

Hardware-based forensic tools can help investigators capture a reliable image of a storage device. These tools often offer features such as write-blocking, which ensures the integrity of the original data by preventing any changes to the source device during imaging.

Write-Blockers: These are essential tools in forensic imaging. They ensure that no data is written to the original device during imaging. Write-blockers can be hardware-based or software-based, but hardware-based write-blockers are generally more reliable and secure. Common brands include Tableau, Logicube, and WiebeTech.

Forensic Duplicators: These are specialized devices designed to create bit-for-bit copies of hard drives. Forensic duplicators allow investigators to create an image quickly and securely, often supporting multiple disk types and formats. Some duplicators include features that allow the creation of a hash value (a digital fingerprint) for the source and destination devices, verifying the integrity of the image.

2.2 Software Tools for Imaging

In addition to hardware tools, several software solutions allow forensic investigators to create forensic images. These tools are versatile, often providing advanced features such as image verification, compression, encryption, and support for various storage formats.

FTK Imager: This tool from AccessData is widely used in the forensic community for creating disk images, whether from hard drives, memory cards, or mobile devices. FTK Imager can capture an image in several formats (e.g., raw image, E01, AFF) and verify the image using hash algorithms.

dd: The Unix-based dd command is one of the most commonly used software tools for creating bit-by-bit disk images. It is highly flexible and efficient but requires familiarity with command-line interfaces. dd is suitable for both large and small-scale forensic investigations.

Guymager: A free and open-source disk imaging tool for Linux-based systems, Guymager is an excellent alternative for investigators working in an open-source environment. It allows the creation of forensic images in the raw, E01, and AFF formats.

X1 Forensic Imager: Another tool in the forensic community, X1 Forensic Imager, offers support for both imaging and file preview. It integrates image verification and supports multiple formats for image storage.

2.3 Image Storage Media

Once the forensic image is created, it must be stored securely to preserve its integrity. The storage media used to hold the image must have sufficient capacity to store the entire image file and, if necessary, any additional logs or supporting documentation.

External Hard Drives: Typically used for storing forensic images, external hard drives must be large enough to store the image while leaving space for logs, reports, and backups. They should also support write-blocking to prevent accidental modification of the image.

Network Attached Storage (NAS): In some environments, NAS can be used for storing forensic images. This is particularly useful in collaborative investigations where multiple users need to access the image over a network. However, network security and access control are critical to prevent unauthorized tampering with the evidence.

Solid-State Drives (SSDs): Although not as common as traditional hard drives, SSDs can be used to store forensic images, especially when higher read/write speeds are needed. However, due to wear leveling and data retention challenges in SSDs, additional caution is necessary when using them in digital forensics.

3. Forensic Imaging Best Practices

While selecting the right tools is essential, preparing for the imaging process also involves following a series of best practices to ensure the accuracy, integrity, and legal admissibility of the collected evidence.

3.1 Verify the Integrity of the Source Device

Before beginning the imaging process, it is essential to verify the integrity of the source device. Investigators should ensure that the device has not been tampered with or altered before imaging. This includes:

Documenting the device's state: Record the model, serial number, and any visible signs of tampering. Photographs of the device and its connections can provide useful documentation for later stages of the investigation.

Write protection: Implement write-blocking mechanisms to prevent any modification to the original device during the imaging process. The use of hardware-based write blockers is the most reliable method to ensure that no data is accidentally written to the source device.

3.2 Ensure Proper Documentation and Chain of Custody

The process of creating a forensic image must be documented thoroughly to maintain a proper chain of custody. This documentation ensures that the evidence can be traced back to its original source and helps establish the integrity of the collected data.

Chain of Custody Forms: These forms must accompany the forensic image and record all actions taken with the device, including when it was seized, by whom, and what tools were used in the imaging process. The goal is to prevent challenges to the image's authenticity in court.

Hashing: Before and after imaging, investigators should calculate and record hash values (e.g., MD5, SHA-1, SHA-256) for the source device and the forensic image. Hash values are unique digital fingerprints that ensure the image is an exact replica of the original data. Any modification to the data would result in a different hash value, immediately alerting the investigator to potential tampering.

3.3 Select the Appropriate Imaging Method

Different situations may require different imaging methods. The two most common types of imaging are:

Raw Imaging (DD Image): A raw disk image, also known as a bit-for-bit copy, captures the entire contents of the storage device, including both allocated and unallocated space. This type of image is the most accurate, providing a full snapshot of the device.

File System Imaging (E01, AFF, or Expert Witness Format): These formats capture a logical image of the disk, including the file system structures and files. File system images are useful when there is a need to recover specific files quickly, but they do not always capture the raw disk's full content (e.g., slack space, deleted files).

3.4 Prevent Overwriting or Corruption of Data

It is crucial to prevent any accidental overwriting or corruption of data during the imaging process. Investigators should avoid writing any data to the source drive, use tools that create verifiable images, and ensure the forensic copy is stored in a secure location.

3.5 Use Write Protection on the Destination Media

The storage device where the forensic image is stored should also be write-protected. This ensures that the image remains intact and free from any alterations after the imaging process. Write-protection is especially important when storing the image on external media or shared storage systems.

Preparing for imaging is a critical step in the digital forensics process that demands attention to detail, careful planning, and the use of reliable tools. Ensuring the integrity of the original device, selecting the proper imaging tools, adhering to best practices, and maintaining a clear chain of custody are all essential components of a successful forensic imaging process. By following these guidelines, forensic investigators can produce high-quality, legally defensible images that will serve as the foundation for a thorough and accurate investigation.

7.2 Creating Forensic Disk Images

Creating forensic disk images is a fundamental process in digital forensics, essential for preserving the integrity of digital evidence. This process involves producing a bit-by-bit copy of a storage device, which includes all data, both visible and hidden, on the device. By creating an exact replica of the original data, investigators can perform detailed analysis without risking alteration or corruption of the original evidence. This chapter will cover the key steps in creating forensic disk images, the various types of disk images, the best practices for ensuring image integrity, and the tools used in the process.

1. Understanding Forensic Disk Imaging

Forensic disk imaging is the process of making a precise, identical copy of a storage device (hard drive, SSD, memory card, etc.) to use for further analysis while ensuring that the original device remains untouched. The disk image captures everything from active files and system logs to unallocated space and deleted files that may contain valuable evidence.

Key Characteristics of Forensic Disk Images:

- **Bit-by-bit duplication**: A forensic disk image is an exact bit-for-bit copy of the source device, meaning that every bit of data is replicated, including hidden or deleted files that may not be visible through the operating system.
- **Integrity Verification**: Forensic disk images are accompanied by hash values (e.g., MD5, SHA-1, SHA-256), ensuring that the image is an exact replica of the source device and has not been tampered with during the imaging process.
- **Preservation of Evidence**: The image allows investigators to analyze the contents of the device without modifying the original, thus preserving the integrity of the evidence for later use in legal proceedings.

2. Types of Forensic Disk Images

Forensic investigators can create different types of disk images depending on the requirements of the investigation. The most common formats are raw images (bitstream copies), as well as file system-based formats.

2.1 Raw Disk Image (DD Image)

A raw disk image is a bit-by-bit copy of the entire storage device. This is the simplest and most universally accepted type of forensic image. It captures every bit of data, including:

- All files and directories.
- Deleted or unallocated space.
- Slack space (unused space within allocated clusters).
- Metadata and file system structures.

A raw image file is typically saved with the .dd extension and is a complete reflection of the original disk. The primary advantage of raw disk images is their comprehensive capture of all data. However, raw images can be large in size, especially for devices with large storage capacities.

2.2 Expert Witness Format (E01)

The Expert Witness Format (E01) is a proprietary disk image format that includes additional metadata, such as the creation date, imaging software used, and hash values. E01 images are widely used in forensic investigations because they support:

- **Compression**: Reducing the file size of the image.
- **Verification**: Storing hash values to verify the integrity of the image.
- **Encryption**: Protecting the image with a password for security.

While E01 files are useful for reducing storage space and enhancing security, they may not be as universally supported as raw disk images.

2.3 Advanced Forensic Format (AFF)

The Advanced Forensic Format (AFF) is an open-source disk image format designed to capture a full disk image while offering features like compression, encryption, and metadata storage. Like E01, AFF images support:

- Hashing to verify integrity.
- Compression for smaller image file sizes.
- Encryption for sensitive data protection.

AFF images are useful when dealing with large amounts of data and offer flexibility, but they might not have the same widespread compatibility as raw images.

3. Steps in Creating a Forensic Disk Image

The process of creating a forensic disk image is intricate and must follow a strict protocol to ensure the integrity and reliability of the evidence. Below are the key steps involved in creating a forensic disk image:

3.1 Preparing the Environment

Before creating a disk image, it is essential to prepare both the hardware and software tools. This includes ensuring the imaging device is functional and that the proper write-blocking methods are in place to avoid any accidental data modification on the source device.

- **Write Protection**: Ensure that write-blockers are in place. Write-blockers prevent any data from being written to the source device, thus preserving the integrity of the evidence.
- **Secure Storage**: Prepare a secure location for storing the forensic image. This may involve using an external hard drive, network-attached storage (NAS), or cloud storage, depending on the volume of data and the sensitivity of the case.
- **Documentation**: Prepare chain of custody forms and ensure that all the necessary documentation is in place. This includes recording the serial numbers of the devices involved, the imaging software used, and any hash values generated during the imaging process.

3.2 Connecting the Devices

Once the imaging environment is prepared, connect both the source device (the device to be imaged) and the destination media (where the image will be stored). The source device can be a hard drive, SSD, or any other type of storage, while the destination media should be large enough to accommodate the full disk image.

Write-Blocking: Ensure that write-blockers are connected between the source device and the system used for imaging. This step ensures that the original device is not altered during the imaging process.

3.3 Selecting Imaging Software

Choose appropriate software for the imaging process. Popular forensic tools include FTK Imager, EnCase, or open-source tools like dd. These tools support a variety of image formats, including raw images (DD), E01, and AFF.

- **FTK Imager**: A widely used software for creating forensic images, FTK Imager allows the creation of raw, E01, and AFF images, offering verification and hash generation features.
- **EnCase**: A comprehensive forensic tool used by law enforcement and forensic professionals, EnCase provides robust features for imaging and data analysis.
- **dd**: A command-line tool in Unix-based systems that allows the creation of bit-for-bit raw disk images. While powerful, dd requires expertise to ensure it is used correctly.

3.4 Imaging the Device

Start the imaging process by selecting the appropriate source and destination drives in the software. The imaging software will create an exact bit-for-bit copy of the source device, ensuring that every sector of the storage medium is captured.

Hashing: During the imaging process, the software generates a hash value for both the source device and the image being created. This hash value serves as a unique digital fingerprint, ensuring the integrity of the image. The hash value should be documented in the chain of custody forms and recorded for future verification.

Image Verification: Once the image is created, the software will automatically verify the integrity of the image by comparing the hash values of the original device and the image. This step ensures that the image is an exact replica and has not been altered during the process.

3.5 Storing and Securing the Image

After the image is created, store it in a secure location to preserve its integrity. This may involve creating multiple copies of the image and storing them in different physical or cloud-based locations to ensure redundancy.

- **Hash Verification**: After transferring the image to storage media, verify the hash values once again to ensure the integrity of the image remains intact.
- **Encryption and Compression**: If necessary, the image can be encrypted and/or compressed for secure storage. This is particularly important when dealing with sensitive data, such as personal information or confidential files.

3.6 Documentation and Chain of Custody

The final step is to document the entire process thoroughly. The chain of custody should include the following:

- Serial numbers and model details of the source and destination devices.
- Details of the imaging software used, including version numbers and configuration settings.
- Hash values of both the source device and the forensic image to verify integrity.
- Personnel involved in the imaging process, including their roles and signatures.

This documentation ensures that the forensic image can be proven to be an accurate and untampered copy of the original device, making it admissible in court.

4. Best Practices for Creating Forensic Disk Images

To ensure that the forensic disk image is both accurate and legally defensible, investigators should follow best practices, including:

- **Use of Write-Blocking Devices**: Always use a write-blocker to prevent any changes to the original device during imaging.
- **Verification and Hashing**: Always generate hash values for both the source device and the image to verify integrity.
- **Create Multiple Copies**: For redundancy, create multiple copies of the forensic image and store them in different secure locations.
- **Maintain Detailed Documentation**: Thorough documentation of every step, including hash values, software used, and chain of custody, is critical for legal defensibility.

Creating forensic disk images is a fundamental aspect of digital forensic investigations. It involves making an exact, bit-for-bit replica of a storage device while ensuring that the integrity of the original evidence is maintained. By following the proper steps and using the right tools, forensic professionals can ensure that the disk image is accurate, secure, and legally admissible. The use of proper documentation, hash values, and write-blocking devices are essential for ensuring the image's reliability in a court of law.

7.3 Analyzing Disk Images for Evidence

In digital forensics, once a forensic disk image has been created, the next crucial step is the analysis of the image for relevant evidence. Analyzing disk images involves carefully examining the bit-for-bit replica of the original device to uncover hidden, deleted, or encrypted data that may serve as evidence in an investigation. This process requires specialized software tools, a methodical approach, and a thorough understanding of file systems, metadata, and various types of digital artifacts.

This chapter explores the key steps involved in analyzing forensic disk images, the tools and techniques used for analysis, and best practices for ensuring that the process is thorough, accurate, and legally defensible.

1. Importance of Analyzing Disk Images

The analysis of disk images is essential because it allows investigators to examine the contents of a device without modifying the original evidence. By examining the image, investigators can recover deleted files, detect hidden data, trace user activities, and identify any potential artifacts that might support or contradict claims in a case. This process is crucial for both criminal and civil investigations, where digital evidence can play a pivotal role.

Key objectives of analyzing disk images include:

- **Recovering Deleted Files**: Files that have been deleted may still reside on the disk in unallocated space. Forensic analysis can often recover these files, which may contain crucial evidence.
- **Examining Metadata**: Metadata, such as timestamps, file sizes, and access logs, can provide valuable insight into the usage and manipulation of files.
- **Identifying Hidden or Encrypted Files**: Some files may be intentionally hidden or encrypted. Advanced forensic tools can help detect and decrypt these files.
- **Tracing User Activities**: Investigators can use disk images to trace the activities of a suspect, such as internet browsing history, email exchanges, and document modifications.

2. Preparing for Disk Image Analysis

Before starting the analysis process, investigators must ensure that they are in a secure and controlled environment to prevent accidental alteration of the evidence. The following steps should be followed:

2.1 Verifying the Integrity of the Disk Image

Before beginning any analysis, it's essential to verify that the disk image has not been altered since it was created. This is done by comparing the hash value of the disk image with the hash value recorded during the imaging process. If the hashes match, the image is verified as an exact, unaltered copy of the original device.

2.2 Setting Up the Analysis Environment

The analysis environment should include the necessary software tools, hardware, and secure storage systems to handle the disk image. It's also important to ensure that the environment is isolated from external networks to prevent any unauthorized access or modifications.

2.3 Documenting the Analysis Process

As with the imaging process, the analysis process must be documented meticulously. This documentation should include:

- The tools and techniques used in the analysis.
- The procedures followed to analyze and extract data.
- The personnel involved in the analysis.
- The timeline of events, including when the image was analyzed and any findings.

This documentation is crucial for maintaining the chain of custody and ensuring that the evidence remains legally admissible.

3. Tools and Techniques for Analyzing Disk Images

A variety of specialized forensic tools and software packages are available to aid in the analysis of disk images. These tools are designed to recover data, search for evidence, and generate reports based on findings.

3.1 File System Analysis

The file system is the structure that organizes and manages files on a storage device. Different operating systems use different file systems (e.g., NTFS, FAT32, EXT4), and each file system has its own methods for storing data. Forensic tools can be used to analyze these file systems for the following:

- **File Recovery**: Files that are deleted but not overwritten still reside in unallocated space. Forensic tools can search this space to recover these files.
- **File Metadata**: Metadata provides information about files, such as their creation, modification, and access times. Analyzing this metadata can provide insights into user actions and timelines.
- **File Integrity**: By examining the file system structure and the integrity of files, investigators can identify any suspicious or tampered files.

3.2 Searching for Artifacts

Artifacts are data remnants that remain after files have been deleted or modified. Forensic analysis can uncover various types of artifacts that can help build a case. Common artifacts include:

- **Web Browsing History**: Evidence of websites visited can be found in browser history, cache, and cookies. These artifacts can provide valuable information about a suspect's online activities.
- **Email and Messaging**: Emails and chat logs may still reside in unallocated space or hidden files. Analyzing these artifacts can provide critical communication records.
- **System Logs and Configurations**: System logs can provide insight into the device's usage, including login times, software installations, and system errors.

3.3 Recovering Deleted Files

Deleted files do not vanish immediately from a disk; instead, their entries in the file system are marked as deleted, and the space they occupy is designated as unallocated. Forensic software tools can scan the unallocated space for deleted files and attempt to recover them. Some of the techniques used in deleted file recovery include:

- **File Carving**: This process involves searching for file signatures and recovering files based on their known patterns or file headers. Carving is useful for recovering files that have been partially overwritten.
- **Slack Space Analysis**: Slack space refers to the unused space within a file's allocated cluster. Even when a file is deleted, it may still be recoverable in slack space.

3.4 Advanced Techniques for Encrypted and Hidden Data

Hidden or encrypted data may require more advanced techniques to uncover. Forensic tools can be used to detect and extract this data, depending on the encryption or hiding method used.

- **Encryption Detection**: If a disk or files are encrypted, forensic investigators may attempt to identify encryption methods and break the encryption (if possible). Tools like Passware or FTK Imager can assist in identifying encrypted files and attempting decryption.
- **Steganography Detection**: Steganography is the practice of hiding data within other files, such as embedding messages in image files. Specialized tools are used to detect and extract hidden data in such files.

3.5 Timeline Analysis

Another critical aspect of disk image analysis is timeline creation. Forensic investigators can piece together the sequence of events on the device by analyzing file timestamps, system logs, and other metadata. This can help establish a timeline of user activities, such as file modifications, deletions, and access times.

3.6 Keyword Searching

Forensic tools often include keyword searching capabilities, allowing investigators to search through the entire disk image for specific terms or phrases. This can be used to locate evidence related to the case, such as incriminating emails, documents, or communications.

4. Handling and Presenting Findings

Once the analysis is complete, investigators must compile their findings into a coherent and legally defensible report. This report should include:

- **Summary of Findings**: A clear and concise summary of the key evidence found in the disk image, including any recovered files, artifacts, or metadata.
- **Screenshots and Documentation**: Screenshots or other visual documentation of the evidence can be valuable for supporting the findings and making the analysis easier to understand for non-technical stakeholders.
- **Chain of Custody**: The report must include a section on the chain of custody, documenting the handling and storage of the disk image throughout the analysis process.
- **Testimony Readiness**: If necessary, investigators should be prepared to present their findings in court. The analysis must be thorough and defensible, with all actions clearly documented.

5. Best Practices for Analyzing Disk Images

To ensure the integrity and reliability of the analysis process, forensic investigators should adhere to the following best practices:

- **Work on Copies, Not the Original**: Always perform the analysis on a copy of the disk image, leaving the original image untouched to preserve its integrity.
- **Use Reliable Forensic Tools**: Employ industry-standard, well-validated forensic tools to perform the analysis. These tools must be capable of creating reports that are legally admissible.

- **Maintain Detailed Logs**: Keep detailed logs of all actions taken during the analysis. This helps to ensure transparency and provides documentation in case the process needs to be reviewed or challenged.
- **Document Findings and Methodology**: All findings should be carefully documented, along with the methodologies used in the analysis. This documentation ensures that the findings can be understood and trusted by others, including in a legal setting.

The analysis of forensic disk images is a vital aspect of digital forensics, enabling investigators to extract valuable evidence from storage devices. By using appropriate forensic tools and techniques, investigators can recover deleted files, detect hidden data, and trace user activities. However, the process requires careful planning, methodical execution, and strict adherence to best practices to ensure the integrity of the evidence and the legal admissibility of the findings. A thorough and well-documented analysis is essential for building a solid case, whether in criminal, civil, or corporate investigations.

7.4 Recovering Deleted Data

One of the most crucial tasks in digital forensics is recovering deleted data. Often, deleted files are not immediately removed from a storage device but are simply marked as deleted, allowing the possibility of recovery. Forensic investigators rely on various techniques to recover this data, especially when it has been erased or hidden by the user. The process of recovering deleted data is critical in many investigations, as deleted files may contain vital evidence that can establish timelines, confirm events, or provide links to suspects and victims.

This chapter will delve into the process of recovering deleted data from digital devices, explaining the techniques, tools, and challenges involved, as well as the importance of data recovery in the broader context of digital forensics.

1. Understanding Deleted Data

When a file is deleted from a system, the operating system does not typically erase the file's contents immediately. Instead, it marks the space occupied by the file as "available" for reuse, often leaving behind traces of the file's data. This characteristic allows for the possibility of recovery, provided that the data hasn't been overwritten by new information.

In traditional file systems like FAT (File Allocation Table) or NTFS (New Technology File System), deleting a file only removes its reference in the file allocation table and frees up space for future data storage. The actual data remains on the disk until it is overwritten by new files. Therefore, if the space occupied by the deleted file has not been overwritten, the file can be recovered.

2. Techniques for Recovering Deleted Data

The process of recovering deleted data can be complex and depends on several factors, including the file system, the time since deletion, and whether the data has been overwritten. Below are some key techniques for recovering deleted data:

2.1 File Carving

File carving is a technique used to recover files from raw data on a disk image. When files are deleted, their entry in the file system directory is removed, but the actual file content may still remain on the storage device. File carving does not rely on the file system's metadata (such as filenames or directory structures); instead, it searches for specific file signatures (also called magic numbers) that indicate the beginning of a file. Carving tools use these signatures to identify and reconstruct files, even when their names and locations are no longer available.

For example, JPEG files often start with the hexadecimal sequence "FF D8" and end with "FF D9." Carving tools can search for these patterns and recover deleted images, even if they are fragmented across the disk.

2.2 Slack Space Analysis

Slack space refers to the unused space within a file's storage allocation unit (cluster). When a file is written to a disk, it is stored in clusters, and if the file doesn't completely fill the cluster, the remaining space is referred to as slack space. Even after the file is deleted, remnants of the data may remain in slack space.

Investigators use specialized tools to analyze slack space and recover fragments of deleted files. This process is often used to recover small pieces of data that could lead to important forensic evidence, such as portions of documents or images.

2.3 Using File System Metadata

In some cases, deleted files may still be recoverable through the file system's metadata, which can contain information such as the file's name, location, and other properties. Tools that analyze file system metadata can recover files that were deleted but have not yet been overwritten by new data. For example, in NTFS systems, a deleted file's MFT (Master File Table) entry may still exist for a period, allowing investigators to recover file information.

Forensic tools can examine this metadata to identify the location of the deleted file and recover it. However, the success of this method depends on the file system in use, the time that has passed since deletion, and whether the metadata has been overwritten.

2.4 Recovering from Unallocated Space

When files are deleted, their data is often relocated to unallocated space, which is marked as available for new data. Forensic investigators can scan unallocated space for traces of deleted files, as this space may still contain remnants of previously stored information.

By using specialized software, investigators can search unallocated space for file fragments or traces of deleted data. If no new data has overwritten this space, investigators may be able to recover the full or partial content of deleted files, including sensitive evidence that may have been intentionally erased.

2.5 Undeleting via Backup and Shadow Copies

Some operating systems, such as Windows, use backup systems and shadow copies to protect against data loss. Windows, for example, creates shadow copies of files and directories, which can be used to restore data if needed. Even if a file is deleted, the backup or shadow copy may still contain the original data.

Forensic investigators can access these backups or shadow copies to recover deleted files, provided that the backup or shadow copy exists and hasn't been purged. This is especially useful in cases where the file was deleted recently or the device was regularly backed up.

3. Tools for Recovering Deleted Data

A variety of forensic tools are available to help investigators recover deleted data. These tools are designed to support various file systems and can assist in analyzing disk images, recovering files, and presenting evidence in a legally admissible format.

3.1 EnCase

EnCase is one of the leading forensic software solutions used for digital evidence recovery. It allows investigators to analyze disk images, recover deleted files, and perform in-depth searches for hidden or deleted data. EnCase provides a comprehensive suite of tools for file carving, slack space analysis, and metadata recovery.

3.2 FTK (Forensic Toolkit)

FTK is another widely used forensic tool for recovering deleted data. FTK specializes in file carving and indexing, allowing investigators to quickly locate and recover deleted files, even if they have been fragmented. FTK also offers advanced filtering and reporting features, making it ideal for large-scale investigations.

3.3 PhotoRec

PhotoRec is an open-source data recovery tool that specializes in recovering deleted files, including images, videos, and documents. It supports a wide range of file types and file systems and is particularly useful for carving and recovering deleted data from unallocated space.

3.4 X1 Social Discovery

Forensic investigators can also use X1 Social Discovery, a tool designed for recovering social media data, emails, and web browsing history. This tool can extract and recover deleted files from web applications, social media platforms, and messaging services, which are often crucial in investigations involving cybercrime or personal disputes.

3.5 Disk Drill

Disk Drill is a user-friendly data recovery tool that can help recover deleted files from a variety of file systems. While it is more commonly used by individuals and businesses for general data recovery, it can also be useful in forensic investigations, particularly for recovering files from external storage devices or non-traditional file systems.

4. Challenges in Recovering Deleted Data

Recovering deleted data is not always straightforward, and several challenges may arise during the process:

Data Overwriting: The most significant challenge to data recovery is when the deleted file's space has been overwritten by new data. Once the space has been overwritten, the original file is irretrievable, making it essential to perform data recovery as soon as possible after deletion.

Encryption: Files that have been encrypted may be difficult to recover without the proper decryption keys. Encryption adds an additional layer of complexity to data recovery, as the original content may be unreadable without the key.

File Fragmentation: Files that have been fragmented across the disk are more difficult to recover, as they may be split into multiple pieces. Fragmented files may require more sophisticated carving techniques to fully reconstruct the file.

Advanced Deletion Techniques: Some individuals use secure deletion methods that overwrite deleted files multiple times, making recovery much more difficult. These techniques are designed to prevent forensic recovery of deleted data, and investigators may not be able to recover such data if these methods are employed.

5. Legal Considerations in Recovering Deleted Data

When recovering deleted data, forensic investigators must be mindful of legal considerations. The recovery process should be conducted with the utmost care to ensure the integrity of the evidence and prevent contamination. Additionally, investigators must ensure that the recovered data is admissible in court by maintaining the chain of custody and adhering to applicable legal standards.

Recovering deleted data is a fundamental aspect of digital forensics, as many critical pieces of evidence are often found in files that have been intentionally or unintentionally deleted. By leveraging a combination of techniques such as file carving, slack space analysis, and metadata recovery, investigators can often recover deleted files that provide crucial information for an investigation. However, this process requires a thorough understanding of file systems, careful use of forensic tools, and an awareness of the challenges that may arise. Effective recovery of deleted data can play a pivotal role in solving cases and uncovering vital evidence.

7.5 Verification of Forensic Images

Verification of forensic images is a critical process in digital forensics that ensures the integrity, authenticity, and accuracy of the images created from digital devices. A forensic image is a bit-by-bit copy of a storage device, such as a hard drive, USB stick, or SD card, which preserves the original data in its entirety, including all files, hidden or deleted data, and unallocated space. Given that forensic images are often used as evidence in legal proceedings, the verification process plays a vital role in ensuring that the evidence remains intact and can be trusted.

This chapter delves into the importance of verifying forensic images, the methods employed to verify their integrity, and best practices to ensure the image's validity for use in legal contexts.

1. The Importance of Verification

The verification of forensic images is necessary to ensure that the copied data is identical to the original device, with no alterations, errors, or corruption. Digital forensics relies heavily on the principle of preserving the original evidence. Any change made to the forensic image can compromise its admissibility in court, potentially leading to the exclusion of crucial evidence or even accusations of tampering.

Verification is a crucial part of the chain of custody, the process that tracks the handling of evidence from the moment it is collected to when it is presented in court. The chain of custody establishes the integrity of the evidence, and verifying the forensic image ensures that the data has not been altered, tampered with, or compromised during the investigation.

Key reasons for verifying forensic images include:

- **Ensuring Data Integrity**: Verification confirms that the forensic image is an exact replica of the original device and has not been changed in any way during the imaging process.
- **Maintaining Legal Admissibility**: Courts require strict adherence to the principles of evidence handling, and an unverified forensic image may be deemed inadmissible in legal proceedings.
- **Ensuring Accuracy of Analysis**: Investigators rely on forensic images to extract and analyze data. If the image is not verified, there is a risk that the analysis may be based on incomplete or inaccurate data.

2. Methods of Forensic Image Verification

The process of verification typically involves two key components: creating a hash value of both the original device and the forensic image and comparing these hash values to ensure they match. Hashing is a cryptographic technique that generates a unique value (a hash) for a set of data. Even the slightest change in the data will result in a completely different hash, which makes this method a reliable way to verify integrity.

2.1 Hashing the Original Device

When a digital device is first seized, a forensic investigator will create a hash value of the original device, typically using a cryptographic hash function like MD5, SHA-1, or SHA-256. This hash is a fixed-length string of characters that uniquely represents the entire contents of the device. Commonly used hash functions include:

- **MD5 (Message Digest Algorithm 5):** Produces a 128-bit hash value, often used for its speed and simplicity. While MD5 is widely used, it is not considered as secure as more modern hashing algorithms due to vulnerabilities that can lead to hash collisions.
- **SHA-1 (Secure Hash Algorithm 1):** Produces a 160-bit hash value and was once the standard for forensic hashing. However, SHA-1 is also susceptible to collision attacks and is no longer considered secure for high-security applications.
- **SHA-256 (part of the SHA-2 family):** Produces a 256-bit hash value and is widely regarded as more secure than MD5 and SHA-1. It is commonly used in modern digital forensics for verifying evidence.

Once the hash of the original device is computed, it serves as a baseline for comparison. This hash value will be recorded and stored securely in the forensic investigation documentation.

2.2 Hashing the Forensic Image

Next, the forensic investigator will create an image of the device, typically using forensic software tools like EnCase, FTK Imager, or X1. After the forensic image is created, the same cryptographic hash function (used for the original device) is applied to the image file. The resulting hash value of the forensic image must match the hash of the original device if the imaging process has been performed correctly and the data has remained unchanged.

If the hashes match, it verifies that the forensic image is an exact copy of the original device, including all files, unallocated space, and metadata. If there is a mismatch, the investigator must determine the cause, which could be due to errors during the imaging process or the introduction of external factors (such as malware or corrupt sectors).

2.3 Using Hash Databases

In some cases, investigators may also compare the hash values of forensic images against hash databases to detect known files or verify the integrity of the data. These databases contain hashes of known files, such as operating system files, commonly used software, or hash values from previous cases. By comparing the image's hash values with these databases, investigators can identify whether the image contains any known files or if the data appears to be tampered with.

For example, investigators might use the National Software Reference Library (NSRL) or other hash libraries to check the integrity of files in a forensic image. This can help detect altered, deleted, or overwritten files, and it can also aid in validating the authenticity of the forensic image.

3. Verifying the Chain of Custody

Verification also extends to the process of maintaining the chain of custody, which tracks every individual who handles the forensic image and the conditions under which it is stored. Proper documentation is essential for ensuring that the image is not tampered with at any point in the process. This includes:

- Recording the time and date the forensic image was created.
- Documenting the identity of the person who created the forensic image.
- Ensuring proper storage conditions, such as using secure storage devices and maintaining access logs.
- Using sealed containers or tamper-evident packaging to protect the image from unauthorized access or modification.

If the chain of custody is broken or the documentation is incomplete, it can cast doubt on the integrity of the forensic image and may jeopardize the admissibility of the evidence in court.

4. Best Practices for Verifying Forensic Images

To ensure the proper verification of forensic images, investigators should adhere to the following best practices:

4.1 Use Multiple Hash Functions

While MD5 and SHA-1 were traditionally used for verification, modern best practices recommend using more secure hash functions like SHA-256. Some investigators opt to hash forensic images with multiple algorithms to ensure that the integrity check is as robust as possible.

4.2 Document the Hash Values

Both the hash of the original device and the hash of the forensic image should be meticulously documented. This documentation should include details such as the time the hash was generated, the hash function used, and the investigator's identity. This ensures transparency and provides proof of the image's integrity.

4.3 Secure the Hash Values

Hash values must be securely stored to avoid tampering or alteration. Storing hash values in a secure, access-controlled environment ensures that any changes to the original data or the forensic image can be detected. This could involve secure digital storage or storing hash values in a physical logbook under lock and key.

4.4 Verify on a Separate System

To ensure that the forensic image has not been altered, verification should ideally be performed on a separate system or environment, isolated from the image's original creation. This ensures that the verification process does not inadvertently modify the forensic image.

5. Challenges in Image Verification

Although verification is a critical process, there are several challenges that forensic investigators may face:

- **Hash Collisions**: A hash collision occurs when two different sets of data produce the same hash value. While this is extremely rare, it can present a problem if a collision occurs with a commonly used hashing algorithm like MD5. Investigators should use more secure and collision-resistant hash algorithms like SHA-256 to mitigate this risk.
- **Data Corruption**: Data corruption during the imaging process or storage can cause mismatches in hash values. It is essential to use robust imaging software, conduct regular checks, and secure storage devices to minimize the risk of data corruption.

- **Secure Deletion**: In cases where a device has been subjected to secure deletion techniques (e.g., overwriting data multiple times), verification of forensic images may not be possible because the original data is no longer present to compare.

Verification of forensic images is an essential part of digital forensics, ensuring the integrity, accuracy, and authenticity of digital evidence. The process involves hashing both the original device and the forensic image, then comparing the hash values to ensure they match. Proper verification safeguards the evidence's legal admissibility, maintains the integrity of the investigation, and upholds the chain of custody. By following best practices and addressing common challenges, forensic investigators can verify the authenticity of digital evidence and ensure its reliability for use in legal proceedings.

8. Network Forensics: Tracking Digital Footprints

Network forensics involves monitoring, capturing, and analyzing network traffic to uncover the digital footprints left by criminals, attackers, or unauthorized users. In this chapter, you'll explore the tools and techniques used to capture network data, such as packet sniffing and traffic analysis with tools like Wireshark. You'll learn how to trace network activity, identify malicious behavior, and reconstruct communications to reveal critical evidence. This chapter also discusses the challenges of dealing with encrypted traffic, dynamic IP addresses, and the growing complexity of network environments, helping you develop the skills to track and interpret digital footprints across diverse networks.

8.1 Packet Capture and Analysis (Wireshark, TCPDump)

Packet capture and analysis are essential components of network forensics, enabling investigators to monitor, capture, and analyze network traffic for signs of suspicious activity or criminal behavior. The ability to examine the data packets flowing through a network can provide invaluable insights into unauthorized access, malware infections, data exfiltration, and other forms of cybercrime. Two of the most commonly used tools for packet capture and analysis are Wireshark and TCPDump. Both tools allow forensic investigators to observe the flow of data across a network and identify any anomalies or malicious activities that may be occurring in real-time or through historical traffic analysis.

This chapter explores the fundamentals of packet capture and analysis, with a focus on how Wireshark and TCPDump are used in digital forensic investigations. We'll discuss how packet capture works, the importance of analyzing network traffic, and how these tools can be used to identify potential evidence of network intrusions or cybercrimes.

1. Overview of Packet Capture

Packet capture refers to the process of intercepting data packets as they travel across a network. Data packets are small units of data transmitted over a network, each containing information like the sender and recipient's IP addresses, port numbers, protocol type, payload, and other metadata. By capturing these packets, investigators can examine the communication between systems on the network, identify potential security breaches, and recover evidence of illegal activity.

There are two main ways to capture network traffic:

- **Promiscuous Mode**: When a network interface is in promiscuous mode, it can capture all packets on the network, not just those addressed to it. This is typically used by forensic investigators to monitor all traffic on a network segment and gather data from devices that may not directly be communicating with the investigator's system.
- **Monitor Mode**: In wireless networks, monitor mode allows the capturing of all packets from a wireless network, even if they are not intended for the capturing device. This mode is useful in monitoring Wi-Fi networks for malicious activity or unauthorized devices.

The captured packets are typically stored in a file format such as PCAP (Packet Capture), which can later be analyzed using tools like Wireshark or TCPDump.

2. Tools for Packet Capture and Analysis

Two of the most widely used tools for packet capture and analysis in digital forensics are Wireshark and TCPDump. Both are powerful, open-source tools, but they serve different purposes and have unique strengths. Let's explore each tool in more detail.

2.1 Wireshark

Wireshark is a graphical, open-source network protocol analyzer that allows investigators to capture and interactively browse network traffic. It is one of the most popular tools used by network forensics experts due to its user-friendly interface, comprehensive feature set, and support for over 2,000 different network protocols. Wireshark captures packets in real time, and its powerful filtering and analysis tools enable forensic experts to examine specific traffic of interest.

Features of Wireshark:

- **Real-Time Packet Capture**: Wireshark can capture network traffic in real time, allowing investigators to monitor ongoing network communication.
- **Deep Packet Inspection**: Wireshark provides detailed analysis of packet contents, enabling investigators to inspect every layer of the network stack (including the application, transport, network, and data link layers).
- **Protocol Decoding**: Wireshark automatically decodes network protocols, presenting the data in human-readable formats, which simplifies the identification of unusual or malicious activity.
- **Advanced Filtering**: Wireshark provides an extensive set of filtering options, including the ability to filter by IP address, protocol type, TCP/UDP port, and other

criteria. This makes it easy to isolate specific traffic and investigate network events of interest.

- **Visualization**: Wireshark allows investigators to visualize network data, including packet flows and timing, which can help in understanding the context of network communications and identifying patterns indicative of malicious activity.

Wireshark in Action:

- **Packet Capture**: To begin capturing data in Wireshark, users select the network interface to monitor (e.g., Ethernet or Wi-Fi) and initiate the capture. The program records all packets transmitted over the selected interface and displays them in real time.
- **Analysis**: Once packets are captured, investigators can analyze them by examining each packet's details, such as source and destination IP addresses, packet size, sequence numbers, and payload data. Wireshark allows users to follow specific network streams (e.g., a TCP session) to trace the entire communication between two systems.
- **Exporting Data**: Captured packets can be saved in PCAP format, which can then be shared or analyzed later using other forensic tools.

2.2 TCPDump

TCPDump is a command-line packet capture tool that is primarily used on UNIX-like operating systems (e.g., Linux, macOS). While it lacks the graphical interface of Wireshark, TCPDump is highly efficient and suitable for use in command-line environments, particularly when analyzing network traffic on remote servers or devices where a GUI may not be available. TCPDump is widely used in professional network forensics due to its speed and simplicity.

Features of TCPDump:

- **Command-Line Interface**: TCPDump operates through a command-line interface, where users can specify parameters to control the capture process, making it suitable for automation and remote usage.
- **Filter-Based Capture**: TCPDump allows for powerful packet filtering using Berkeley Packet Filter (BPF) syntax. Investigators can filter traffic by source/destination IP, port, protocol, and more.
- **Capture and Export**: TCPDump captures packets in real time and allows them to be saved in PCAP format, which can later be analyzed using other tools like Wireshark.

- **Low Overhead**: Since TCPDump is a lightweight command-line tool, it can be used with minimal system resources, making it ideal for low-overhead captures in environments with limited resources.

TCPDump in Action:

- **Packet Capture**: To capture packets, investigators initiate TCPDump with a specific command and set filters based on their investigation needs (e.g., tcpdump host 192.168.1.1 to capture traffic from a particular host).
- **Analysis**: After packets are captured, TCPDump displays information in real time, such as packet type, IP addresses, and port numbers. Analysts can also capture detailed data for specific protocols like HTTP or DNS.
- **Exporting Data**: As with Wireshark, TCPDump can save packet captures to PCAP files, which can be exported for later analysis or used as evidence in legal proceedings.

3. Importance of Packet Capture in Digital Forensics

Packet capture plays a crucial role in digital forensics for several reasons:

- **Network Intrusion Detection**: Packet capture enables the detection of unusual network behavior, such as unauthorized access attempts, botnet communications, or abnormal traffic patterns indicative of a cyberattack.
- **Malware Analysis**: Capturing packets from infected devices can provide insights into the command and control (C2) servers communicating with malware on a compromised network, helping forensic investigators trace the origin and spread of malware.
- **Data Exfiltration**: Network analysis can identify data exfiltration attempts, where sensitive information is being transferred from a compromised system to an external location. This is particularly useful in cases of corporate espionage or hacking.
- **Incident Response**: During an ongoing security incident, packet capture allows investigators to monitor real-time network traffic, making it easier to identify active threats, mitigate damage, and take corrective actions.
- **Legal Evidence**: In cases involving cybercrime, data theft, or intellectual property violations, packet captures can provide legal evidence of the attack or breach. Forensic investigators can use packet capture files to reconstruct the timeline of an attack or validate claims made by the defense in court.

4. Best Practices for Packet Capture

To ensure that packet capture and analysis are effective and legally admissible, forensic investigators should follow several best practices:

- **Secure Capture Environment**: Ensure that the device used for packet capture is secure and isolated from the network to avoid tampering or interference.
- **Legal and Ethical Considerations**: Always obtain proper authorization to capture and analyze network traffic, ensuring compliance with local laws and regulations, especially in cases involving private or encrypted communications.
- **Filter Data**: Use filters to capture only relevant traffic to reduce the amount of data being collected. This makes it easier to find important evidence and prevents the analysis of irrelevant or excessive data.
- **Ensure Chain of Custody**: Maintain a clear and verifiable chain of custody for all captured packets. Document the time, date, and personnel involved in the capture process to ensure the integrity and admissibility of the evidence.
- **Storage and Backup**: Store captured data in secure locations and create backups to prevent loss or tampering of evidence.

Packet capture and analysis are vital techniques in network forensics, providing investigators with the ability to monitor, capture, and analyze data traffic for evidence of malicious activity, network intrusions, or criminal behavior. Wireshark and TCPDump are two powerful tools that forensic investigators commonly use for packet capture and analysis. By employing these tools effectively and adhering to best practices, investigators can uncover crucial evidence in cybercrime investigations, ensuring the integrity of the evidence and its admissibility in court.

8.2 Identifying Unauthorized Access

Unauthorized access to a network or system is a serious security concern and a common target for cybercriminals, hackers, and malicious insiders. Detecting unauthorized access is a crucial aspect of network forensics, helping investigators identify intrusions, track unauthorized users, and prevent data breaches. By analyzing network traffic, system logs, and security events, forensic investigators can uncover evidence of unauthorized access and determine the scope, method, and impact of the attack.

This section explores the techniques and methodologies involved in identifying unauthorized access within a network environment. We'll discuss how network forensics tools, security monitoring, and incident response strategies can help recognize suspicious activity and unauthorized users, providing insights into breach detection and response.

1. Understanding Unauthorized Access

Unauthorized access refers to situations where individuals, entities, or software programs gain access to a network, system, or data without proper authorization or permission. This could involve cybercriminals exploiting vulnerabilities, insiders abusing their privileges, or external actors gaining access through weak or stolen credentials.

Common types of unauthorized access include:

- **External Hackers**: Attackers who infiltrate a system from outside the organization, often using techniques like brute-force attacks, phishing, or exploiting security flaws.
- **Insider Threats**: Employees or contractors who misuse their access privileges to access or exfiltrate sensitive data, either maliciously or negligently.
- **Privilege Escalation**: Unauthorized users gaining higher privileges within a system by exploiting vulnerabilities, allowing them to access sensitive information or perform malicious actions.
- **Credential Theft**: Attackers obtaining valid login credentials, often through phishing, malware, or data breaches, and using them to access systems or data.

Detecting unauthorized access typically requires constant monitoring of network traffic, logs, and user behavior to spot unusual or abnormal activities indicative of a security breach.

2. Techniques for Detecting Unauthorized Access

Forensic investigators employ a variety of techniques to detect unauthorized access. These methods involve analyzing system logs, monitoring network traffic, and identifying patterns that suggest malicious activity or breaches.

2.1 Analyzing Network Traffic

Network traffic analysis is one of the most effective methods for detecting unauthorized access. By capturing and analyzing the data packets flowing through a network, investigators can identify signs of intrusion or attempts to exploit vulnerabilities. Common indicators of unauthorized access include:

- **Unusual Port Scanning**: Attackers often scan networks using various ports to identify open or vulnerable services that can be exploited. Excessive or unusual port scanning activity may indicate an attacker is probing the network.
- **Anomalous Traffic Patterns**: A sudden increase in traffic, especially on unusual ports or protocols, may suggest a breach. For example, large data transfers, especially to unknown or external IP addresses, could indicate data exfiltration by an unauthorized party.
- **Failed Login Attempts**: A large number of failed login attempts from a particular IP address or a series of attempts with different usernames can suggest brute-force attacks, where attackers are attempting to guess login credentials.
- **Login from Suspicious Locations**: If users are logging into the network from geographic locations that are unexpected or inconsistent with their normal behavior, it could signal unauthorized access.

2.2 Log File Analysis

Logs are a goldmine for investigators trying to detect unauthorized access, as they record system events and user activity. By analyzing system, security, and application logs, investigators can identify signs of intrusion or unauthorized actions. Key logs to examine include:

- **Authentication Logs**: These logs track login attempts, both successful and failed, and provide insight into when and from where an individual or system logged in. Repeated failed login attempts or successful logins from unrecognized IP addresses are clear indicators of unauthorized access.
- **Access Control Logs**: These logs record which users accessed specific files or resources within a system. Abnormal or unauthorized file access patterns can reveal attempts to steal or manipulate data.
- **Event Logs**: Many systems, including Windows, record events related to system health, user actions, and security events in event logs. Unusual event sequences, such as user privileges being changed or system settings being modified, can point to a compromise.
- **Firewall Logs**: Firewalls track inbound and outbound network traffic, allowing investigators to detect unusual traffic patterns or connections to suspicious IP addresses. These logs can also help identify unauthorized access attempts from external sources.

2.3 User Behavior Analysis

User behavior analysis (UBA) is an increasingly important technique in detecting unauthorized access. By establishing a baseline of normal user behavior and monitoring deviations from that pattern, investigators can identify activities that suggest unauthorized access or account compromise. Key behavioral indicators include:

- **Unusual Access Times**: If a user is accessing sensitive systems or files outside of their normal working hours, it may indicate an unauthorized attempt to exfiltrate data or access critical information without supervision.
- **Abnormal Data Access Patterns**: If a user is accessing files or systems that they don't typically interact with or have no legitimate need to access, it could be a sign that their account has been compromised.
- **High Volume of Access**: A user who suddenly begins to access large amounts of data or make numerous requests for resources may be involved in a data breach or unauthorized information retrieval.

Behavioral analytics tools and machine learning algorithms are increasingly being used to detect these anomalies in real time, offering more proactive ways to spot unauthorized access before significant damage occurs.

3. Tools and Techniques for Identifying Unauthorized Access

Several tools and techniques are available for forensic investigators to identify unauthorized access within a network environment. These tools range from packet capture and log analysis software to specialized security information and event management (SIEM) systems.

3.1 SIEM Systems

Security Information and Event Management (SIEM) systems are critical for detecting unauthorized access, as they collect, aggregate, and analyze log data from various sources, including network devices, firewalls, and servers. SIEM platforms provide real-time monitoring and can automatically detect suspicious behavior, such as multiple failed login attempts or unusual network traffic patterns. Popular SIEM tools include:

- **Splunk**: Splunk aggregates and analyzes machine data in real time, helping organizations detect unauthorized access through advanced searches, visualizations, and alerts.
- **IBM QRadar**: QRadar collects log data from a variety of sources, including network devices and security tools, and uses correlation rules to identify potential threats or breaches.

- **AlienVault USM**: A unified security management platform that combines SIEM with other threat detection and vulnerability management capabilities, helping identify unauthorized access quickly.

3.2 Intrusion Detection Systems (IDS) and Intrusion Prevention Systems (IPS)

Intrusion Detection Systems (IDS) and Intrusion Prevention Systems (IPS) are designed to monitor network traffic for signs of malicious activity. IDS tools analyze network traffic in real-time and alert investigators when unauthorized access is detected, while IPS tools go one step further and actively block suspicious activity. Key IDS/IPS tools include:

- **Snort**: Snort is an open-source IDS/IPS that monitors network traffic for signatures of known attacks, including unauthorized access attempts.
- **Suricata**: Suricata is an open-source IDS that can detect network intrusions and unauthorized access attempts by analyzing packet capture data.

3.3 Packet Capture Tools (Wireshark, TCPDump)

Packet capture tools like Wireshark and TCPDump can be used to examine network traffic in real time and look for signs of unauthorized access, such as strange packets, unauthorized IP addresses, or unusual port usage. These tools are invaluable for identifying potential breaches or malicious activity on a network.

4. Responding to Unauthorized Access

Once unauthorized access is detected, it is crucial to take immediate action to contain the breach, mitigate its impact, and begin an investigation. Key steps in responding to unauthorized access include:

- **Containment**: Isolate compromised systems or accounts to prevent further unauthorized access or damage. This may involve disconnecting a device from the network or disabling a compromised user account.
- **Eradication**: Once the breach is contained, eliminate any malware, backdoors, or other malicious artifacts left behind by the attacker.
- **Recovery**: Restore systems to a secure state and ensure that all vulnerabilities are patched before bringing them back online.
- **Investigation and Documentation**: Conduct a thorough investigation to determine the scope of the breach, including what data was accessed, how the attacker gained access, and what vulnerabilities were exploited. Document all findings for legal or regulatory purposes.

Identifying unauthorized access is a critical part of digital forensics and network security. Through the use of network traffic analysis, log file inspection, and advanced behavioral analysis, forensic investigators can uncover signs of unauthorized access and track down cybercriminals or malicious insiders. By utilizing tools like Wireshark, TCPDump, SIEM systems, and IDS/IPS solutions, investigators can quickly detect and respond to breaches, minimizing the damage and ensuring the integrity of the network environment.

8.3 Tracing Emails and Communication Logs

Email and communication logs are among the most valuable sources of evidence in digital forensics, offering key insights into the nature of cybercrimes, fraud, harassment, or even espionage. Tracing emails and communication logs can provide investigators with the information needed to track the sender's identity, understand the context of the communication, and establish timelines of events. This process is crucial not only in cybercrime investigations but also in cases such as data breaches, intellectual property theft, and corporate espionage.

This section will explore the various techniques and tools for tracing emails and communication logs, explaining how investigators can gather, analyze, and interpret digital traces to build a compelling case. By understanding how email systems and communication platforms store and transmit data, forensic experts can uncover key evidence that may otherwise remain hidden.

1. Email Forensics: The Basics

Emails are often used as a primary means of communication in criminal activity, and therefore, they are a critical component of any investigation. Email forensic analysis involves investigating the metadata and content of email messages to determine the identity of the sender, the legitimacy of the message, and the intent behind it. Key areas that investigators focus on include:

- **Email Headers**: Email headers contain a wealth of information, including the sender's IP address, the recipient's email address, time stamps, routing information, and the email servers involved. By analyzing email headers, forensic investigators can trace the path an email took from sender to recipient, helping to identify whether the message originated from a legitimate source or an attacker attempting to mask their identity.

- **IP Addresses**: Embedded within email headers is the originating IP address, which can be used to pinpoint the geographical location and the internet service provider (ISP) used by the sender. This can help investigators track down the identity of a malicious actor or determine if the email was sent from a compromised machine.
- **Content Analysis**: The content of emails can reveal important evidence, including threats, instructions for malicious activities, or evidence of illegal transactions. Analyzing the language, context, and attachments (such as malware or documents) can help investigators understand the nature of the communication.

2. Tools for Tracing Email Origins

Forensic investigators use a variety of tools and techniques to trace the origins of an email, reconstruct its path, and uncover the sender's identity. These tools provide invaluable assistance in analyzing email headers and content for malicious intent, as well as verifying the authenticity of the communication.

2.1 Header Analysis Tools

There are several tools available for parsing and analyzing email headers, making it easier for investigators to extract key metadata without manually interpreting complex header information. Some of the commonly used tools include:

- **MXToolbox**: A popular tool for analyzing email headers and looking up domain information, MXToolbox can help investigators trace the sender's IP address, identify the email's origin, and detect anomalies in the header that could indicate forgery or malicious activity.
- **Email Header Analyzer**: Provided by tools like Google's G Suite or MessageHeader (free online tools), these tools allow investigators to paste an email header and get an immediate breakdown of the sender's IP address, routing information, and timestamps.
- **Forensic Email Examiner**: This advanced tool assists investigators in analyzing the content, metadata, and attachments of emails. It can reconstruct email threads, check for authentication failures, and identify forged headers.

2.2 IP Geolocation Tools

Once an IP address is extracted from an email header, geolocation tools can help pinpoint the physical location of the sender. Investigators can use the following tools to trace the geographical origin of the IP address:

- **GeoIP**: Services like MaxMind's GeoIP or IP2Location offer powerful databases and APIs to geolocate IP addresses. They provide not only the country but also the city, ISP, and sometimes even the specific location (e.g., a company or a data center).
- **Whois Lookup**: Investigators can perform a Whois lookup to gather details about the organization that owns the IP address or domain, which can lead to additional clues regarding the identity of the sender or the infrastructure used in the crime.

2.3 Analyzing Email Attachments

Often, emails contain attachments that can be essential to the investigation. Malware, viruses, or encrypted files could be part of the evidence left behind by a cybercriminal. Email attachment analysis includes:

- **Hash Analysis**: By generating and comparing hash values for attachments, forensic investigators can determine if the file has been altered, helping to verify whether the file is authentic or has been tampered with.
- **Malware Detection**: Tools like VirusTotal can be used to scan attachments for known malware signatures, and sandboxing tools can run suspicious files in a safe environment to observe their behavior.
- **Document Analysis**: Investigators can also examine the metadata of documents attached to emails. This might include information such as the creation date, author, and editing history, which could help establish the authenticity of the document or reveal the involvement of a particular individual in the criminal activity.

3. Tracing Communication Logs Beyond Email

While email is one of the most common forms of communication, digital forensics also involves investigating other communication channels such as instant messaging, social media, and VoIP (Voice over IP) communications. Communication logs from platforms like WhatsApp, Slack, or Telegram can also provide valuable evidence for investigators.

3.1 Instant Messaging and Social Media Forensics

Forensic analysis of messaging platforms involves analyzing server logs and extracting data from backup systems. Investigators may trace usernames, IP addresses, timestamps, and other identifying metadata associated with messages.

- **Social Media Accounts**: Forensic investigators can analyze social media account activity logs and server data to track conversations, posts, or private messages that may contain critical evidence.
- **Encrypted Communications**: Many messaging services, including WhatsApp, Signal, and Telegram, use end-to-end encryption to secure messages. In these cases, investigators may need to rely on metadata, phone backups, or other circumstantial evidence to trace communications and link them to specific suspects.

3.2 VoIP Communications

VoIP communication logs, such as those from Skype or Zoom, contain vital metadata like timestamps, call logs, user IDs, and connection IPs. Investigators can examine these logs to trace communication patterns, identify call participants, and verify the authenticity of claims made during the investigation.

4. Challenges in Tracing Emails and Communication Logs

While email and communication log analysis can be incredibly useful in forensic investigations, several challenges make the process difficult:

- **Spoofing and Forged Headers**: Cybercriminals often spoof email addresses or modify email headers to obscure their identity. This can complicate the tracing process, requiring investigators to use advanced techniques to authenticate the message.
- **Encryption**: Many modern communication systems use end-to-end encryption, making it challenging to intercept or read messages without access to the encryption keys or without cooperation from service providers.
- **Anonymity Services**: Cybercriminals may use services such as VPNs, Tor, or proxy servers to mask their true location, making it harder to trace their activity back to a physical origin.

Tracing emails and communication logs is a vital aspect of digital forensic investigations. Through the analysis of email headers, IP addresses, content, and attachments, forensic investigators can piece together the timeline of events and potentially identify perpetrators of cybercrimes. By leveraging advanced tools and techniques, investigators can identify fraudulent activities, track down malicious actors, and uncover hidden patterns of communication in criminal investigations. As communication technology continues to evolve, so too must the methods and tools used in digital forensics to stay one step ahead of cybercriminals.

8.4 DNS Forensics and IP Mapping

Domain Name System (DNS) forensics and IP mapping play an essential role in tracing cybercrimes, identifying malicious activity, and uncovering digital footprints left behind by attackers. By examining DNS logs and mapping IP addresses, investigators can reveal crucial information about an attacker's identity, the systems they accessed, and their geographical location. DNS forensics helps forensic professionals track domain resolution paths, identify the domains involved in criminal activities, and pinpoint the connections between different digital infrastructure components.

This section will cover the significance of DNS forensics and IP mapping in digital investigations, how these tools are used to trace and track digital activity, and the techniques for extracting valuable evidence from DNS logs and IP addresses.

1. The Role of DNS in Cyber Investigations

The Domain Name System (DNS) is a fundamental component of the internet, acting as the "phonebook" that translates human-readable domain names into machine-readable IP addresses. Each time a user or attacker connects to a website or a server, DNS queries are made to resolve the domain name to an IP address, enabling the communication between the client and the server. DNS forensics involves analyzing these DNS queries and responses to uncover critical evidence related to cybercrime activities.

Key points of DNS forensic investigation include:

- **Domain Resolution**: When an attacker communicates with a malicious website or remote server, their activity is often recorded in DNS logs, including the domain name, IP address, and time stamps. Forensic investigators analyze these logs to trace the attacker's activity across multiple systems and domains.
- **DNS Lookup Patterns**: Analyzing patterns in DNS lookups can help identify suspicious behavior, such as frequent lookups for newly registered domains, rapid domain name changes (used in botnet activity), or connections to known malicious domains.
- **DNS Records**: DNS records contain valuable information, such as the associated IP addresses of domain names, TTL (time-to-live) values, mail server configurations (MX records), and authoritative DNS servers. This data can provide investigators with information about the infrastructure involved in the cybercrime.

2. Techniques for DNS Forensics

Forensic investigators rely on various tools and methods to perform DNS forensics, enabling them to track malicious activity, identify compromised systems, and map out the connections between attackers and their targets. Some of the primary methods for conducting DNS forensics include:

2.1 Analyzing DNS Logs

DNS logs contain a record of every DNS query that a user, service, or attacker has made to a DNS server. These logs provide key data points, such as:

- **Query Time**: The exact time an attacker queried a domain, which helps establish a timeline of events.
- **Requested Domain Name**: The domain being queried, which could lead investigators to websites or malicious services used in the attack.
- **IP Address**: The originating IP address that initiated the query, allowing investigators to map the source of the attack.
- **Response Data**: The resolved IP addresses for the queried domains, which help track the locations of the servers involved.

By examining DNS logs, investigators can pinpoint domain names associated with cybercrimes, such as phishing websites, C2 (Command and Control) servers, and malware distribution points.

2.2 DNS Query Analysis for Malicious Patterns

One of the key tasks in DNS forensics is identifying malicious patterns within DNS query logs. Malicious actors often exhibit certain behaviors that can be detected by analyzing DNS traffic. Common signs of malicious DNS activity include:

- **High Frequency of Lookups**: A sudden surge in DNS queries to a specific domain or a pattern of repeated lookups could indicate an attack or data exfiltration activity.
- **Obfuscation with Domain Generation Algorithms (DGAs)**: Some attackers use DGAs to generate large numbers of domain names to evade detection. By looking for domains with unusual or random strings in their names, investigators can identify possible DGA-driven attacks.
- **Query Anomalies**: Unusual or unexpected DNS queries, such as requests to rarely used top-level domains (TLDs), non-existent domains, or suspicious IP addresses, may indicate an attacker's attempt to hide their activity.

2.3 DNS Tunneling and Data Exfiltration Detection

DNS is a commonly exploited protocol for data exfiltration, as it is typically allowed to bypass firewalls and other security controls. Attackers may tunnel data through DNS queries, encoding data in the subdomain portions of DNS requests to exfiltrate sensitive information.

To detect DNS tunneling and data exfiltration, forensic investigators:

- **Look for Large DNS Payloads**: DNS requests that contain unusually large payloads (e.g., excessively long domain names) could indicate data being exfiltrated.
- **Examine Suspicious DNS Traffic**: Investigators analyze traffic patterns that deviate from normal DNS usage, such as a significant increase in query volume or requests to obscure domains.
- **Check for Hidden Subdomains**: Attackers sometimes encode information in the subdomain, which may appear as random strings of characters. Investigators can search for and decode these to uncover hidden data.

2.4 Historical DNS Data Retrieval

DNS records can also be used to track the historical movement of an IP address or domain, providing valuable context in criminal investigations. Services such as DNSHistory or SecurityTrails allow investigators to search for historical DNS data, offering insights into which domain names were previously associated with a given IP address.

Historical DNS data can help:

- **Identify Previous Connections**: Investigators can uncover past associations between malicious IP addresses and known bad domains.
- **Link Multiple Attacks**: Tracking a specific domain or IP address over time can reveal patterns in the attacker's behavior, allowing investigators to connect multiple attacks or identify potential co-conspirators.
- **Uncover Masked Activity**: If attackers have been using dynamic DNS services or frequently changing their domains, historical data can help to identify these patterns and track their infrastructure.

3. IP Mapping and Geolocation Analysis

IP mapping involves mapping an IP address to its geographical location or identifying the infrastructure behind the IP. When investigators identify an IP address associated with a suspicious activity or attack, they can use various tools to trace its geographical origin or ownership.

3.1 IP Geolocation

Geolocating an IP address can provide investigators with the approximate physical location of the attacker, which is especially useful for tracking down attackers or narrowing down a search area. By using geolocation services such as MaxMind or IP2Location, investigators can map the IP address to a specific city or country. However, this method has limitations, especially when attackers use VPNs or proxies to mask their location.

3.2 Whois Lookup

A Whois lookup is another important tool for mapping IP addresses. It provides information about the organization or entity that owns a particular IP address or domain name. For investigators, Whois data can help identify the domain registrar, ISP, or hosting provider associated with a malicious domain or IP address, providing critical information to track down perpetrators.

3.3 IP Reputation Services

IP reputation services, such as Threatminer or Cisco Umbrella, offer tools to assess the reputation of an IP address. These services analyze whether an IP has been associated with previous malicious activity, such as spamming, phishing, or botnet control. If an IP address is flagged by these services, it can provide investigators with important clues about its potential involvement in cybercriminal activity.

4. Challenges in DNS Forensics and IP Mapping

While DNS forensics and IP mapping are powerful techniques for tracking cybercriminals, they also come with certain challenges:

- **Use of VPNs and Proxies**: Attackers often use VPNs or proxies to mask their true location, which can make IP geolocation and IP mapping more difficult.
- **Dynamic DNS**: Cybercriminals may use dynamic DNS services to rapidly change the IP addresses associated with their domains, making it harder for investigators to track them over time.

- **Obfuscation and Encryption**: Attackers may use encrypted DNS traffic or implement DNS tunneling to bypass security measures and hide their activities from detection.

DNS forensics and IP mapping are essential techniques for tracing cybercrimes and uncovering digital footprints in network-based investigations. By analyzing DNS logs, IP addresses, and geolocation data, forensic investigators can uncover valuable insights into the identity and activities of attackers. These methods allow investigators to track malicious domains, detect data exfiltration, and map out an attacker's infrastructure, providing critical evidence in the fight against cybercrime. As cybercriminals continue to evolve their methods, DNS forensics and IP mapping will remain crucial tools for digital forensic professionals working to solve complex digital crimes.

8.5 Detecting and Investigating Network Intrusions

Network intrusions represent one of the most significant threats in the modern digital landscape. They can lead to data breaches, intellectual property theft, financial loss, and, in some cases, even national security threats. Detecting and investigating network intrusions is a complex process that requires a combination of advanced technology, expert knowledge, and sound investigative techniques. It involves identifying unauthorized access to a network, understanding the methods used by the intruder, and gathering evidence that can be used in legal proceedings or to mitigate future risks.

This section will explore the methods used for detecting network intrusions, how forensic investigators investigate network-based attacks, and the tools and techniques that assist in identifying malicious activities and tracing their sources.

1. The Importance of Network Intrusion Detection

Network intrusion detection is crucial for maintaining the security and integrity of digital infrastructures. A network intrusion can range from a simple unauthorized login attempt to a sophisticated attack involving malware, data exfiltration, or a full-blown Distributed Denial of Service (DDoS) attack. Detecting these intrusions in real-time is essential to minimizing the damage they cause and responding effectively.

Key reasons why network intrusion detection is critical include:

- **Early Detection of Attacks**: Intruders often attempt to gain unauthorized access to a network before launching a full attack. Early detection can allow network administrators to block the intruder and prevent data breaches.
- **Maintaining Data Integrity**: Once an intruder gains access to a network, they can tamper with, delete, or steal sensitive data. Detecting the intrusion as soon as possible helps ensure that data remains intact.
- **Compliance and Reporting**: For businesses in highly regulated industries (such as healthcare or finance), detecting and reporting network intrusions promptly is necessary to comply with laws and regulations.

2. Types of Network Intrusions

Network intrusions can take many forms, each with its own signature and method of operation. Understanding the different types of intrusions helps investigators design effective detection and response strategies.

2.1 Unauthorized Access Attempts

Unauthorized access attempts occur when an attacker tries to gain access to a system, network, or application without permission. These attempts may involve various tactics, such as brute-force attacks (guessing passwords), exploiting vulnerabilities in software, or social engineering tactics to trick users into providing access credentials.

- **Brute Force Attacks**: Attackers use automated tools to guess passwords by trying multiple combinations at high speed. These attacks are often easy to detect due to the high volume of failed login attempts.
- **Credential Stuffing**: Attackers use previously stolen credentials from other breaches to try and gain access to accounts on other platforms, typically by automating the login process.
- **Phishing and Social Engineering**: Attackers may impersonate a trusted entity to deceive users into revealing sensitive login credentials or other security information.

2.2 Malware Infections

Malware, including viruses, worms, Trojans, and ransomware, is often used as a means of gaining unauthorized access to a network. Once installed, malware can facilitate further exploitation of the network by giving the attacker remote control, stealing sensitive data, or even causing operational disruptions.

- **Trojans**: These are often disguised as legitimate software to trick users into installing them, allowing attackers to control infected systems remotely.
- **Ransomware**: Ransomware encrypts data and demands payment for decryption. This type of malware is especially dangerous for organizations, causing both operational disruption and financial damage.
- **Worms**: Self-replicating malware that spreads across networks without user intervention, often exploiting unpatched vulnerabilities in software.

2.3 Denial of Service (DoS) Attacks

Denial of Service (DoS) and Distributed Denial of Service (DDoS) attacks are designed to overwhelm a network, server, or website with traffic, making it unavailable to legitimate users. DDoS attacks are particularly difficult to detect and mitigate because they involve a large number of attacking systems (often botnets).

- **DoS Attacks**: The attacker uses a single computer to flood the target network with traffic, rendering it inaccessible.
- **DDoS Attacks**: These attacks are launched from multiple systems, usually from a network of compromised computers known as a botnet, making the attack far more potent and harder to stop.

2.4 Insider Threats

Insider threats are malicious actions taken by someone within the organization, such as an employee or contractor. These threats can be challenging to detect because the attacker already has access to the internal network and may have legitimate credentials. Insider threats include data theft, sabotage, and espionage.

3. Methods for Detecting Network Intrusions

Detecting network intrusions requires a combination of real-time monitoring, alert systems, and forensic analysis tools. These methods help identify anomalous behavior on a network and enable quick response to potential threats.

3.1 Intrusion Detection Systems (IDS) and Intrusion Prevention Systems (IPS)

Intrusion Detection Systems (IDS) and Intrusion Prevention Systems (IPS) are critical tools for detecting and responding to network intrusions.

- **IDS**: An IDS monitors network traffic for signs of suspicious activity. It can alert administrators to potential intrusions by detecting known attack patterns (signature-based detection) or identifying unusual traffic patterns (anomaly-based detection).
- **IPS**: An IPS goes a step further by not only detecting intrusions but also blocking malicious traffic in real-time. IPS solutions are often integrated with firewalls and network management systems for automated defense.

IDS/IPS systems use a variety of detection techniques, including:

- **Signature-based Detection**: This method involves looking for known attack patterns, such as specific byte sequences or malicious payloads.
- **Anomaly-based Detection**: This method establishes a baseline of normal network behavior and flags any activity that deviates significantly from that baseline.
- **Heuristic-based Detection**: This approach uses algorithms to identify new or unknown attacks by looking for suspicious patterns of behavior.

3.2 Network Traffic Analysis and Packet Inspection

Forensic investigators often rely on network traffic analysis and packet inspection to detect intrusions. By capturing and analyzing network packets, investigators can identify unauthorized communication attempts, suspicious activity, or data exfiltration.

- **Wireshark**: A popular packet analysis tool, Wireshark allows forensic investigators to capture network traffic and analyze it for signs of malicious activity. Suspicious or unusual packets can be flagged, and the full conversation between attacker and victim can be reconstructed.
- **NetFlow**: NetFlow analysis provides insight into the flow of data across a network. By examining NetFlow data, investigators can spot unusual traffic patterns, such as spikes in data transfers or unexpected connections to external servers.

3.3 Log Analysis

Network devices, such as firewalls, routers, and servers, generate logs that record network activities. Log analysis is an important part of the investigative process, as it can reveal information about network traffic, failed login attempts, or unauthorized access to sensitive resources. Investigators examine these logs for unusual activity, such as repeated login attempts, strange IP addresses, or unfamiliar devices.

- **SIEM Systems (Security Information and Event Management):** SIEM systems aggregate logs from multiple sources, making it easier for investigators to identify patterns of suspicious behavior. They use correlation rules and alerting mechanisms to notify administrators of potential intrusions.

3.4 Honeypots and Deception Technologies

Honeypots are decoy systems set up to attract attackers, diverting them from real systems and allowing investigators to observe their methods. By monitoring the activity in a honeypot, investigators can gather valuable information about the tools, techniques, and targets of an attacker, helping to strengthen overall security defenses.

4. Investigating Network Intrusions

Once a network intrusion is detected, investigators must thoroughly examine the affected systems to understand the scope and impact of the attack. Key steps in investigating network intrusions include:

4.1 Evidence Collection

The first step in investigating an intrusion is to collect and preserve evidence. This may include capturing volatile data from running systems, preserving network logs, and making forensic images of compromised systems. Chain of custody must be maintained to ensure the evidence is admissible in court if needed.

4.2 Analyzing Attack Techniques

Investigators use techniques such as packet analysis, log analysis, and malware reverse engineering to understand how the attacker gained access, what tools they used, and what systems were affected. This analysis helps build a timeline of the attack and provides insights into potential vulnerabilities that need to be addressed.

4.3 Identifying the Attacker

By correlating evidence from various sources (DNS logs, IP geolocation, malware signatures, etc.), investigators attempt to trace the attacker's identity or the infrastructure used in the attack. In some cases, this may involve collaboration with law enforcement or service providers to identify the source of the attack.

5. Challenges in Detecting and Investigating Network Intrusions

Network intrusion detection and investigation are fraught with challenges. Attackers constantly evolve their tactics, using methods such as encryption, obfuscation, and the use of proxies to evade detection. Other challenges include:

- **Data Overload**: The sheer volume of network traffic generated by modern systems can make it difficult for investigators to detect intrusions without robust filtering and analysis tools.
- **Sophisticated Attacks**: Some intrusions, such as advanced persistent threats (APTs), are carefully planned and executed over long periods, making them difficult to detect.

Detecting and investigating network intrusions is a crucial aspect of maintaining cybersecurity and preventing criminal activities in digital networks. By employing a combination of intrusion detection systems, traffic analysis tools, and log analysis, investigators can identify and respond to threats in real-time. The process of investigation involves collecting evidence, understanding attack methods, and tracing the attacker's identity. However, the evolving nature of cyber threats presents ongoing challenges that require constant innovation in detection and investigative techniques.

9. Mobile Forensics: Unlocking Evidence on the Go

Mobile devices have become central to our daily lives, containing a wealth of personal and investigative data. This chapter dives into the world of mobile forensics, focusing on the techniques and tools used to extract valuable evidence from smartphones, tablets, and other portable devices. You'll learn how to handle different operating systems like Android and iOS, recover deleted messages, call logs, and app data, and uncover location history and other sensitive information. The chapter also addresses the challenges of dealing with device encryption, password protection, and remote wiping, equipping you with the skills to unlock critical evidence on the go.

9.1 Tools for Mobile Data Extraction

Mobile devices have become integral to our daily lives, containing vast amounts of personal, professional, and even criminal evidence. As a result, mobile data extraction plays a pivotal role in digital forensics investigations. Extracting data from mobile devices can provide investigators with crucial insights into communications, activities, and behaviors that may be tied to criminal activities, civil disputes, or corporate investigations. However, mobile data extraction is not a straightforward process—devices come in various operating systems, models, and configurations, each with its own unique data structures, encryption methods, and security features.

This section focuses on the tools available for mobile data extraction, including their capabilities, limitations, and how they are used in forensic investigations.

1. Types of Mobile Data Extraction

There are three primary types of mobile data extraction:

Physical Extraction: Involves acquiring an exact copy of the entire memory of a mobile device, including deleted files, hidden data, and system files that may not be visible through normal usage. This method provides the most complete data recovery and is typically used in cases where full evidence is needed. However, physical extraction may be more difficult to perform on modern devices due to encryption and security measures.

Logical Extraction: This method involves extracting data from the file system, including contacts, messages, call logs, photos, and application data. Logical extraction is often easier and faster than physical extraction, but it may not recover deleted data or hidden files.

File System Extraction: A more advanced technique that extracts data directly from the file system of a device without accessing the full physical memory. This method typically recovers data that is stored on the device in a specific format (such as for apps or system logs) and is effective for targeting specific data types without accessing the entire memory.

Each method is employed based on the type of device, the situation, and the type of evidence needed for the investigation.

2. Mobile Data Extraction Tools

The market for mobile forensic tools is robust, offering both commercial and open-source solutions. These tools range from hardware-based solutions to software platforms and may offer a variety of features, such as bypassing lock screens, recovering deleted data, or extracting data from encrypted devices.

2.1 Cellebrite UFED (Universal Forensic Extraction Device)

Cellebrite UFED is one of the most widely used and trusted tools in mobile forensics. It offers a wide range of capabilities for extracting and analyzing data from mobile devices. UFED is known for its comprehensive support for various mobile operating systems (iOS, Android, BlackBerry, etc.) and its ability to bypass password protections, access encrypted data, and recover deleted information.

Key Features:

- Supports extraction from a wide range of devices, including smartphones, tablets, GPS devices, and SIM cards.
- Provides logical, physical, and file system extraction methods.
- Includes decryption capabilities for protected devices and apps.
- Recover deleted or hidden data, such as text messages, emails, photos, and app data.
- Offers advanced data analysis and reporting tools.

2.2 XRY by Micro Systemation (MSAB)

XRY is another leading mobile forensic solution, often favored by law enforcement agencies for its reliability and ability to extract data from a wide range of devices, including smartphones, feature phones, and tablets. XRY offers support for a variety of extraction methods, and its mobile data extraction capabilities are regularly updated to support new devices and operating system versions.

Key Features:

- Provides logical, physical, and file system extraction methods.
- Supports a wide array of mobile devices, including those from mainstream manufacturers such as Apple, Samsung, Huawei, and LG.
- Can bypass security features such as PIN codes, passwords, and biometric locks.
- Capable of extracting data from encrypted devices and apps, including app data and encrypted communication logs.
- Offers cloud data extraction from services like Google and Apple accounts.

2.3 Oxygen Forensics Detective

Oxygen Forensics Detective is a powerful mobile data extraction and analysis tool known for its versatility and ability to extract data from a wide range of mobile devices, including smartphones, tablets, and other smart devices. Oxygen Forensics is equipped with tools for data acquisition, analysis, and reporting, making it a favorite among forensic investigators.

Key Features:

- Extracts data from mobile devices running iOS, Android, and other operating systems.
- Capable of retrieving deleted data, including text messages, call logs, photos, and videos.
- Supports extraction of cloud data from mobile devices.
- Provides advanced analysis features, such as timeline creation, app analysis, and keyword search.
- Offers remote data extraction from mobile devices using cloud backup and storage solutions.

2.4 Autopsy and Mobile Forensics Module

Autopsy, an open-source digital forensics platform, provides mobile forensics capabilities through its integration with the Mobile Forensics Module. Autopsy is widely used in forensic investigations and supports a variety of evidence extraction processes, including mobile device data.

Key Features:

- Free and open-source, making it accessible for organizations with limited budgets.
- Supports extraction from Android devices through USB debugging and root access.
- Integrates with other forensic tools to offer advanced mobile data analysis.
- Useful for analyzing data extracted from mobile devices, including deleted and hidden files.
- Supports evidence tracking, reporting, and management features.

2.5 Belkasoft Evidence Center

Belkasoft Evidence Center is a comprehensive digital forensic tool that can extract and analyze data from mobile devices, computers, and online services. It offers a range of mobile data extraction capabilities, including logical, physical, and file system extraction, with strong support for both iOS and Android platforms.

Key Features:

- Supports extraction from a wide range of mobile devices, including iOS and Android.
- Offers the ability to extract and analyze app data, messages, call logs, contacts, and more.
- Features a built-in password cracking tool that can help unlock devices with complex passcodes or patterns.
- Capable of analyzing cloud data from mobile devices, including iCloud and Google accounts.
- Allows investigators to build timelines and track events based on data extracted from mobile devices.

3. Extraction Challenges and Limitations

While mobile data extraction tools are powerful, investigators may encounter several challenges in the extraction process, including:

3.1 Encryption and Lock Screen Protection

Modern mobile devices are equipped with various security features, including encryption and lock screens (PINs, passwords, fingerprints, facial recognition). These features can significantly hinder data extraction efforts. Many mobile forensics tools are designed to bypass or defeat these protections, but some devices may require advanced techniques, such as brute force attacks or the use of specialized hardware.

3.2 Device Variability and Compatibility

Mobile devices come in many forms and run on different operating systems (iOS, Android, etc.). While forensic tools are designed to support a broad range of devices, new devices and OS updates may present compatibility issues. Forensic investigators must continually update their tools to ensure they support the latest devices and operating system versions.

3.3 Data Corruption or Damage

In cases where the mobile device is damaged (e.g., water damage, broken screens, or malfunctioning hardware), data extraction becomes more complicated. Specialized tools and techniques may be required to recover data from damaged devices, including the use of forensic data recovery hardware and the expertise of data recovery professionals.

3.4 Legal and Ethical Considerations

As mobile data often contains highly personal information, investigators must be mindful of legal and ethical considerations when performing data extractions. Legal requirements such as obtaining proper search warrants, maintaining chain of custody, and ensuring data privacy and protection must always be followed.

Mobile data extraction is a critical component of modern digital forensics investigations. Tools such as Cellebrite UFED, XRY, Oxygen Forensics Detective, and Autopsy have revolutionized how investigators extract and analyze data from mobile devices. However, extracting data from mobile devices is not without its challenges, including encryption, device variability, and legal concerns. With the growing complexity of mobile devices and the constant evolution of mobile operating systems, forensic investigators must remain adaptable, continually updating their tools and skills to keep pace with emerging threats and technologies.

9.2 Investigating Android vs. iOS Devices

In the field of mobile forensics, one of the most significant distinctions investigators must consider is the difference between Android and iOS devices. These two operating systems dominate the smartphone market, but they have distinct architectures, security measures, and data storage structures. This section explores the key differences between investigating Android and iOS devices, focusing on the unique challenges, methods, and tools involved in forensic investigations on each platform.

1. Operating System Differences

Android and iOS differ fundamentally in their operating systems. Android is an open-source platform based on the Linux kernel, while iOS is a closed-source system developed by Apple. These distinctions lead to variations in how data is stored, encrypted, and accessed.

Android: Android devices run on a version of the Linux kernel, and the platform allows for more customization and third-party software. The open nature of Android makes it more accessible for forensic investigators to extract data, although it also means that Android devices vary widely in terms of hardware, software versions, and vendor customizations (e.g., Samsung's One UI, Google Pixel's stock Android).

iOS: iOS, on the other hand, is a closed ecosystem tightly controlled by Apple. iPhones and iPads are designed with a consistent user experience and often use proprietary hardware, making data extraction slightly more standardized. However, the closed nature of the system and Apple's strong emphasis on security make data extraction from iOS devices more challenging than from Android devices.

2. Data Storage and File Systems

The way Android and iOS devices store data also differs significantly. Understanding these differences is key to conducting a successful forensic investigation.

Android Devices: Android smartphones typically use the EXT4 file system, which is similar to the Linux file system. Android also has two primary storage areas: internal storage (which houses system files and user data) and external storage (such as microSD cards). These storage areas may contain valuable data, but accessing them depends on the device's rooting status (for non-rooted devices, only the accessible file system can be retrieved). Rooting an Android device can provide full access to the file system, but it may also complicate the extraction process and invalidate the warranty.

iOS Devices: iOS devices use a proprietary HFS+ or APFS (Apple File System) depending on the iOS version. APFS, introduced in iOS 10.3, provides enhanced encryption and more advanced data management. iOS devices do not typically support external storage like Android devices, relying instead on internal storage, which is tightly integrated with the system. The file system on iOS is encrypted by default, and access to certain data can be restricted based on the device's security settings, especially if the device is locked with a passcode, fingerprint, or face recognition.

3. Data Extraction Methods

Extracting data from Android and iOS devices involves different methods, tools, and techniques. Understanding these differences is crucial to choosing the appropriate forensic approach.

Android Data Extraction:

Android devices are typically more accessible than iPhones because they have fewer built-in restrictions on data access. Forensic investigators can use several methods to extract data from Android devices:

ADB (Android Debug Bridge): ADB allows investigators to interact with Android devices via a command-line interface. It enables the extraction of data from unlocked Android devices, including contacts, SMS, call logs, application data, and more.

Physical Extraction: This is a process of copying the entire memory of the device, which can be done on many Android devices, especially those with older versions of the operating system. This method allows investigators to recover deleted data and hidden files, but it is not always possible on newer models with strong encryption and advanced security features.

Rooting: Rooting an Android device grants full access to the file system, but it is a controversial method that can potentially alter the evidence and compromise the integrity of the device. Rooting is often required for extracting data from locked or encrypted devices, though it can be time-consuming and carry risks of data loss.

Logical Extraction: If the device is unlocked, logical extraction methods can be used to access data, including contacts, messages, app data, and media files. This process is faster than physical extraction and is often the first approach in Android investigations.

iOS Data Extraction:

Extracting data from iOS devices is more challenging due to the higher level of security and encryption Apple employs. However, several methods and tools are commonly used by forensic investigators:

iTunes Backup: If an iPhone or iPad is backed up to iTunes or iCloud, investigators can access the backup to recover user data, such as contacts, text messages, app data, and more. iTunes backups are encrypted, which means investigators may need the device's passcode or the backup password to decrypt the data.

Physical Extraction: Physical extraction of data from iOS devices was once possible without the passcode by using forensic tools, but Apple has introduced more robust security measures (e.g., Secure Enclave and iOS encryption). Physical extraction is now limited to older models or devices without strong passcode protection.

Logical Extraction: This method is used when the device is unlocked and can provide access to a range of data, including call logs, contacts, messages, and app data. It is less invasive than physical extraction and is typically the preferred method for iOS investigations.

Bypassing Lock Screen: Tools such as Cellebrite's UFED and GrayKey are used to bypass the lock screen and gain access to the device. However, this often requires the investigator to have physical access to the device and may take time, especially on newer devices with advanced encryption.

4. Security and Encryption Considerations

Both Android and iOS devices implement strong encryption to protect user data, but the methods of encryption and the level of security vary between the two platforms.

Android Encryption: Android devices use encryption as part of their default security features (especially with devices running Android 5.0 or later). The encryption keys are often tied to the device's lock screen security, meaning investigators will require the PIN, pattern, or password to decrypt the device. Additionally, Android's open-source nature makes it easier for security researchers and forensic investigators to develop custom tools to bypass or decrypt Android devices.

iOS Encryption: iOS devices are encrypted by default with a hardware-based encryption system (via the Secure Enclave), and the encryption key is tied to the device's passcode.

Unlike Android, Apple uses strong measures to prevent unauthorized access, and even forensic tools have limited success in bypassing the lock screen. Recent versions of iOS have made it even harder to access the device without the correct passcode, and in some cases, devices with newer iOS versions are virtually impenetrable.

5. Data Types and What Can Be Extracted

The types of data that can be extracted from Android and iOS devices differ, largely due to the operating systems and available apps. Below are the primary data types commonly recovered from each platform:

Android:

- SMS, MMS, and instant messaging data (e.g., WhatsApp, Facebook Messenger)
- Call logs and contacts
- Photos, videos, and media files
- App data (including third-party apps)
- Browser history and cookies
- Email (Gmail, Outlook, etc.)
- GPS location history and Wi-Fi connections

iOS:

- SMS, iMessages, and instant messaging data (including WhatsApp, Telegram, etc.)
- Call logs and contacts
- Photos, videos, and media files
- App data (including third-party apps)
- Safari browsing history, bookmarks, and cookies
- iCloud and iTunes backups
- GPS location history

While both Android and iOS devices store and handle data in different ways, forensic investigators have developed specialized tools and techniques to extract evidence from each platform. Android devices generally offer greater flexibility in terms of data extraction methods due to the open nature of the operating system, though security measures like encryption and lock screens can still pose challenges. iOS devices, with their advanced encryption and security protocols, often present more obstacles, requiring specialized tools and techniques for effective data extraction. Understanding the differences between these two operating systems is essential for any mobile forensic investigator in order to select the appropriate tools and methods for each case.

9.3 Recovering Deleted SMS and Call Logs

In digital forensics, one of the most critical types of evidence that can be recovered from mobile devices are SMS messages (Short Message Service) and call logs. These data types often contain critical information in criminal investigations, civil disputes, and corporate compliance matters. However, recovering deleted SMS messages and call logs from mobile devices can present significant challenges due to the way these data are stored, deleted, and potentially overwritten.

This section will explore how SMS and call logs are stored on mobile devices, the process for recovering deleted messages and call logs, the forensic tools available for this purpose, and the challenges investigators face in this area.

1. SMS and Call Log Storage

SMS Storage: On both Android and iOS devices, SMS messages are stored in a database file format, which allows the messages to be indexed for quick retrieval by the user. Typically, the data resides in internal storage, either in an SQLite database on Android or as part of the local backup system on iOS. The message content, along with associated metadata (such as the sender's number, timestamp, and status), is stored in these files.

Call Log Storage: Call logs are similarly stored in a database format and contain essential information, such as the phone numbers dialed, the incoming or outgoing status, the timestamp, and the duration of each call. Call logs are often stored in separate files or databases depending on the operating system.

Deleted Data: When SMS messages or call logs are deleted by a user, the data is typically not immediately erased from the storage medium. Instead, the operating system marks the storage space as available for new data. This means that, in many cases, deleted SMS messages and call logs can be recovered, provided they have not been overwritten by new data.

2. How Deleted SMS and Call Logs Are Stored

- **Android Devices**: On Android devices, SMS and call log data are stored in a database called the SQLite database. The deletion of SMS or call logs may only mark the data as deleted, and the records may still reside in the database for some time until the data is overwritten by new content.
- **SQLite Database**: SQLite databases store text-based information, and this is typically where deleted messages or call logs remain until the system reuses that space. For example, even when an SMS message is deleted, the message remains stored on the device until another piece of data is written in its place, allowing forensic investigators to recover it.
- **iOS Devices**: On iOS devices, SMS and call logs are stored within SQLite databases or as part of the backup process, either in iTunes or iCloud. Even when SMS or call logs are deleted, the data often remains within the device's storage or backup until the space is overwritten by new data, which makes it recoverable through forensic methods.
- **iCloud and iTunes Backup**: Both iCloud and iTunes backup files can contain copies of SMS and call logs. When devices are backed up regularly, deleted messages or logs can sometimes be recovered from these backups, even if the data was removed from the device itself.

3. Recovering Deleted SMS and Call Logs

Forensic investigators use a combination of physical, logical, and file system data extraction methods to recover deleted SMS messages and call logs from mobile devices.

3.1 Logical Extraction:

In logical extraction, the device is connected to a forensic tool, and data that is not overwritten is extracted. The tool interacts with the device's file system to retrieve accessible SMS and call log data. However, deleted messages or call logs are often not available through this method unless the device's memory has not been overwritten.

Android: Logical extraction typically recovers messages and call logs that are still intact on the device. However, deleted items might not be included unless they are still marked as present within the storage and have not been overwritten by new data.

iOS: Logical extraction allows investigators to retrieve information stored on the device, including data from installed apps and system files. Deleted SMS and call logs can sometimes be found within this method if the data hasn't been overwritten or removed during a backup synchronization process.

3.2 Physical Extraction:

Physical extraction provides a complete copy of the entire memory of the mobile device, including both visible and deleted data. This method is particularly effective for recovering deleted data, including SMS and call logs that have not yet been overwritten.

Android: Physical extraction on Android devices often involves rooting the device to bypass certain restrictions and gain full access to the file system. Tools like Cellebrite UFED or XRY can perform physical extraction, recovering deleted SMS messages and call logs from the device's memory, even if the data is no longer visible to the user.

iOS: For iOS devices, physical extraction requires bypassing the device's encryption or security measures. Tools like GrayKey and Cellebrite UFED can help retrieve deleted SMS and call logs from iPhones, including bypassing PINs, passwords, and biometric locks. Physical extraction on iOS is often more challenging due to Apple's more stringent security mechanisms.

3.3 File System Extraction:

File system extraction gives investigators access to the file system of the mobile device, allowing for the examination of files directly and the recovery of deleted data that hasn't been overwritten.

Android: In Android devices, file system extraction allows forensic tools to access and analyze the internal storage, which may include deleted SMS or call logs. This process can be more effective for accessing and recovering data from older devices or those that haven't been updated with the latest encryption and security features.

iOS: For iOS devices, file system extraction is more challenging due to Apple's use of strong encryption methods, such as the Secure Enclave and APFS (Apple File System). However, forensic investigators may still recover deleted data from an iOS device using tools that can bypass encryption or utilize iTunes and iCloud backups.

4. Forensic Tools for Recovering Deleted SMS and Call Logs

Various forensic tools are used to recover deleted SMS messages and call logs from mobile devices. These tools provide different extraction methods and have varying capabilities for handling different operating systems and security features.

4.1 Cellebrite UFED:

Cellebrite UFED is one of the most widely used tools in mobile forensics and is capable of performing logical, physical, and file system extraction. It supports a wide variety of devices, including Android and iOS, and can recover deleted SMS messages and call logs from many devices, even if they have been erased from the user's interface. UFED also includes capabilities for bypassing device security features, such as PINs and passwords, enabling the recovery of data from locked devices.

4.2 XRY:

XRY is another widely used mobile forensic tool that supports logical, physical, and file system extraction methods. Like UFED, XRY is capable of recovering deleted SMS and call logs from both Android and iOS devices. It can also bypass security features and recover data from encrypted devices, making it valuable for investigators attempting to recover deleted data.

4.3 Oxygen Forensics Detective:

Oxygen Forensics Detective is another powerful forensic tool that supports a broad range of mobile devices, including both Android and iOS. It can perform logical, physical, and cloud data extractions and is particularly useful for recovering deleted SMS messages and call logs. Oxygen Forensics Detective also includes cloud backup analysis, which can be helpful for recovering deleted data from services like iCloud or Google Drive.

4.4 Autopsy:

Autopsy, while more commonly used for computer forensics, includes modules that support the extraction and analysis of data from mobile devices. It can be used in combination with other tools to analyze data from Android and iOS devices, including deleted SMS and call logs, particularly when examining SQLite databases and other file structures.

5. Challenges in Recovering Deleted SMS and Call Logs

Encryption and Security: Modern mobile devices, particularly iPhones, are heavily encrypted, making data recovery more difficult. Encryption can prevent forensic tools from accessing deleted data unless the investigator has the necessary passcode or uses advanced techniques to bypass security.

Data Overwriting: Once SMS messages or call logs are deleted, the storage space they occupied is marked as available. If new data is written to that space, it can overwrite the deleted data, making recovery impossible. The more the device is used after the deletion, the greater the chance that the data will be overwritten.

Device Model Variability: The method of data storage and deletion can vary significantly between different devices and operating system versions. Investigators need to be familiar with specific models and versions to select the correct recovery method and tool.

Recovering deleted SMS messages and call logs from mobile devices is a vital part of many forensic investigations. With the right tools and techniques, investigators can often recover deleted data, even from encrypted or locked devices. However, challenges like encryption, data overwriting, and device variability make this process complex and require expertise in both the technology and the legal considerations surrounding mobile forensics. By using physical, logical, and file system extraction methods, forensic investigators can often piece together crucial evidence from deleted SMS and call logs, contributing to the resolution of criminal cases, civil disputes, and corporate investigations.

9.4 Analyzing App Data and Location History

In modern digital forensics, mobile devices are an invaluable source of evidence, with app data and location history providing critical insights into a user's activities and behavior. As the use of mobile apps continues to proliferate, investigators increasingly rely on extracting and analyzing app data and location history to solve cases ranging from criminal investigations to civil litigation. Both app data and location data are deeply integrated into mobile devices and provide a rich source of evidence that can be analyzed to understand a person's movements, interactions, and behaviors.

This section will explore the process of analyzing app data and location history from mobile devices, the challenges associated with these data types, and the tools used to extract and interpret this information.

1. App Data on Mobile Devices

Mobile apps generate a wide range of data that is stored locally on the device or synced with cloud services. This data includes user-generated content, logs, preferences, interactions, and metadata associated with each app. The forensic significance of app data lies in the insights it can provide into a person's digital life and activities.

1.1 Types of App Data

- **User Data**: This includes photos, messages, notes, documents, and other content directly created or modified by the user within an app. For example, a messaging app might store text messages, images, and video files exchanged with others.
- **Metadata**: Metadata associated with app data includes timestamps, file sizes, and other details that provide context about when and how the data was created, accessed, or modified. For example, an email app stores not only the content of emails but also details such as the time of receipt, sender, and recipient.
- **Logs and Cache**: Many apps generate log files that track the app's behavior, including errors, warnings, and performance data. Cached data, which apps store locally for faster access, can also contain valuable information such as previously viewed pages or search histories.
- **App-Specific Databases**: Some apps, such as social media apps or e-commerce apps, store data in SQLite databases, which contain structured records of user activities. This could include friend lists, transaction history, or even the locations where the user has interacted with the app.

1.2 Locating and Extracting App Data

- **Android Devices**: On Android devices, app data is typically stored in the /data/data directory, which contains app-specific databases, preferences, and configuration files. To access this data, forensic investigators often need to root the device or use specialized extraction tools like Cellebrite UFED or XRY. Once access is granted, tools can pull the app data, including files and database records.
- **iOS Devices**: On iOS devices, app data is stored in the App Sandbox folder and is protected by Apple's security features. To extract app data, investigators can use forensic tools like Cellebrite UFED or XRY, or rely on backups made via iTunes or iCloud. Some apps may encrypt their data, making it necessary for investigators to bypass encryption mechanisms or use decryption keys.

1.3 App Data Analysis and Relevance

- **Messaging Apps**: Investigators often focus on recovering and analyzing data from messaging apps, such as WhatsApp, Facebook Messenger, or SMS apps. These apps store not only conversations but also metadata such as the timestamp of each message, sender, recipient, and location if location services were enabled.
- **Social Media Apps**: Social media apps (like Facebook, Instagram, or Twitter) can provide a wealth of information, including user posts, friend lists, interactions, and

geotags. For example, posts on Facebook may include a user's status updates, comments, and location data, offering valuable clues to the user's activities.

- **Banking or E-commerce Apps**: These apps provide transaction logs, purchase histories, and shipping addresses, which can be important for financial investigations or cases involving fraud.

2. Location History: Tracking Movement and Behavior

Location data is another crucial form of evidence on mobile devices. Mobile phones continuously collect and store location information via GPS, Wi-Fi, Bluetooth, and cellular network triangulation. This data can provide investigators with a detailed record of the user's movements, visits to specific locations, and real-time behavior patterns.

2.1 Sources of Location Data

- **GPS**: The GPS system allows mobile devices to pinpoint the user's location within a few meters by triangulating signals from satellites. Many apps, particularly navigation apps like Google Maps, use GPS data to track and store a user's location history.
- **Wi-Fi**: Wi-Fi networks can also provide location data when devices are connected to a known network. The device can determine its approximate location by identifying the Wi-Fi router's signal strength and its known position.
- **Cellular Network Triangulation**: Even when GPS is disabled, mobile devices can use cell towers to approximate location by triangulating signals from nearby towers.
- **Bluetooth**: Bluetooth beacons can provide location data when devices are in close proximity to Bluetooth-enabled devices. For example, Bluetooth data can be used to track a user's movement within a building.

2.2 Collecting Location History

- **Google Location History**: Android devices that are linked to a Google account often store detailed location history via Google Maps. This location history can be accessed through the user's Google account and provides a timeline of their movements, often with timestamps and place names. Investigators can request this data from Google using proper legal channels, such as a subpoena.
- **Apple's Location Services**: iPhones also store location data as part of the device's Location Services, which includes the GPS data, Wi-Fi networks, and nearby Bluetooth devices. This data is often included in iTunes backups or can be

extracted directly from the device. Additionally, Apple Maps tracks location history in the form of places the user has visited or frequently visits.

- **Third-Party Apps**: Many third-party apps, such as fitness trackers, weather apps, and social media platforms, also collect location data, sometimes even more extensively than the device's native apps. For example, apps like Strava, Snapchat, or Facebook often store geotagged content that reveals when and where a user has taken specific actions.

2.3 Analyzing Location Data

- **Mapping and Visualization**: Once collected, location data can be analyzed and mapped to create a timeline of the user's movements. By plotting the coordinates from the GPS, Wi-Fi, or cell tower data, investigators can pinpoint locations that are crucial to a case. Investigators often use specialized tools like Gephi, ArcGIS, or Google Earth to visualize the location history and track movements over time.
- **Geofencing**: Geofencing involves creating virtual boundaries around specific locations. If a user enters or exits this area, an alert is triggered. Investigators can use geofencing to track when and where a suspect or person of interest was located during a specific time frame. This is particularly useful in cases such as criminal investigations where a suspect's movements need to be verified.
- **Location Correlation**: Investigators may cross-reference location data with other forms of evidence, such as call logs, messages, or surveillance footage. For example, if a suspect's mobile device was detected at a crime scene based on GPS or Wi-Fi data, investigators can correlate this with timestamped messages or calls made from the device during that time.

3. Challenges in Analyzing App Data and Location History

- **Data Deletion**: Many mobile apps allow users to delete data, including app content, messages, and location history. However, deletion doesn't always mean the data is completely gone; it may still be recoverable unless overwritten. The challenge is determining which data has been permanently deleted and which can still be retrieved using forensic tools.
- **Encryption**: Both app data and location history can be encrypted by the operating system or the app itself. For example, some apps encrypt user data to prevent unauthorized access, requiring forensic experts to bypass encryption mechanisms or utilize decryption methods. Forensic investigators may need decryption keys or the user's password to extract and analyze this data.
- **User Privacy and Permissions**: Many mobile apps ask for location and personal data permissions, but these permissions can be revoked by users, complicating

investigations. Also, apps may limit access to historical location data or require specific access rights. Investigators must be mindful of legal requirements and privacy concerns when accessing and analyzing this sensitive data.

4. Forensic Tools for Analyzing App Data and Location History

- **Cellebrite UFED**: A leading tool for extracting data from mobile devices, Cellebrite UFED supports app data extraction, including from popular apps like WhatsApp, Facebook, and Instagram, and can pull GPS and location history from Android and iOS devices.
- **XRY**: XRY by MSAB is another powerful tool that allows forensic investigators to recover app data and location history from mobile devices. It can extract and analyze data from both Android and iOS devices, including deleted app content, geolocation data, and cloud backups.
- **Oxygen Forensics Detective**: Oxygen Forensics Detective is capable of extracting and analyzing app data and location history from both Android and iOS devices. It supports geolocation analysis and allows investigators to visualize location data over time.

The analysis of app data and location history from mobile devices plays a crucial role in modern digital forensics. By recovering app data and tracking location history, forensic investigators can uncover valuable evidence about a suspect's activities, movements, and interactions. However, the process comes with challenges, such as data deletion, encryption, and privacy concerns. By leveraging advanced forensic tools and techniques, investigators can successfully navigate these challenges and extract critical data that can aid in solving crimes, disputes, and other investigative matters.

9.5 Mobile Device Encryption Challenges

Mobile device encryption is one of the most significant challenges in modern digital forensics. As the use of smartphones and tablets becomes ubiquitous, the need for encryption to protect user data has intensified. However, this rise in encryption presents significant obstacles for digital forensic investigators who need to access critical evidence stored on mobile devices. In this section, we will explore the challenges posed by encryption on mobile devices, the impact on digital forensics investigations, and the methods used to overcome these challenges.

1. The Importance of Encryption on Mobile Devices

Mobile device encryption is designed to protect sensitive data, including personal information, communications, and media, from unauthorized access. Both Android and iOS devices incorporate encryption as a core security feature to ensure user privacy and data protection. For instance:

- **Full Disk Encryption (FDE):** On devices such as iPhones (with iOS 8 and later) and Android devices (running Lollipop or later), full disk encryption encrypts the entire device storage. This means that data is unreadable without the proper decryption key, which is typically tied to a user password or PIN.
- **File-Based Encryption (FBE):** Introduced in Android 7.0 (Nougat), file-based encryption allows different files or directories to be encrypted with different keys. This provides more flexibility for accessing certain parts of the device when needed while keeping other files securely encrypted.
- **End-to-End Encryption (E2EE):** Many apps, such as WhatsApp, Telegram, and Signal, offer end-to-end encryption for messages. This means that the app's server cannot decrypt the content of the messages, ensuring that only the sender and receiver have access to the data.

While encryption is crucial for protecting user privacy and security, it complicates the process of obtaining evidence during a forensic investigation.

2. Challenges of Mobile Device Encryption for Investigators

The key challenge for digital forensic investigators lies in the fact that encryption effectively locks them out of critical evidence unless they can bypass or unlock it. Some of the key challenges include:

2.1 Locked Devices and Passwords

- **Strong Passwords/PINs**: Many users set strong, complex passwords or PINs to secure their mobile devices. The encryption keys used to encrypt the device's data are linked to these passwords or PINs, making the devices effectively unreadable without the correct password. Investigators must either have the password or find a way to bypass it. Some devices also use multi-factor authentication, adding additional layers of security.
- **Brute Force Attacks**: If investigators do not have access to the password or PIN, they may resort to brute force attacks—systematically trying different combinations until the correct one is found. However, modern devices are designed to limit the number of attempts (e.g., Android may wipe the device after a certain number of

incorrect attempts), making brute force attacks time-consuming and ineffective on devices with strong passwords.

2.2 Biometric Authentication

- **Fingerprint and Face Recognition**: Many modern smartphones (especially iPhones and Android devices) incorporate biometric authentication features such as fingerprint scanners and facial recognition. While convenient for users, these features present significant challenges for investigators who lack access to the biometric data. Unless investigators can access the device using the user's fingerprint or face (or bypass the biometric security with specialized tools), the encrypted data remains locked.
- **Advanced Biometric Features**: Some devices use more sophisticated biometric features (such as iris scans or voice recognition) that further complicate decryption. The challenge is that these methods cannot always be bypassed or replicated for forensic access, especially without cooperation from the device owner.

2.3 Encryption of Cloud and Backups

- **Cloud Encryption**: Many users store a significant portion of their mobile data in the cloud (e.g., iCloud, Google Drive, Dropbox). This cloud data is typically encrypted by the service provider. Without the appropriate credentials (username and password), forensic investigators cannot access the cloud data. Even if investigators access the cloud data via legal means (e.g., search warrants), the data may still be encrypted or protected by additional layers of authentication.
- **Backup Encryption**: In addition to cloud storage, users often back up their mobile devices to cloud services or local computers. For example, iPhones use iCloud backups, while Android devices can back up data to Google Drive or to a local computer via USB. These backups are often encrypted, and accessing them without the proper password or key can be extremely difficult. Furthermore, some backup services also encrypt individual files, further complicating forensic analysis.

2.4 Encryption and App Data

- **End-to-End Encrypted Apps**: Many messaging and communication apps, such as WhatsApp, Signal, and Telegram, use end-to-end encryption (E2EE) to ensure that only the sender and recipient can read messages. While E2EE is a valuable privacy feature for users, it poses a significant challenge to investigators. Even if an investigator can gain access to the device, decrypting the communication stored within these apps is often not possible without access to the app's encryption keys. Without those keys, all that may remain is metadata such as timestamps and phone numbers, leaving the actual message content out of reach.

- **App-Specific Encryption**: Some apps, such as banking apps, social media apps, and photo storage apps, may also apply their own encryption mechanisms. These apps could store sensitive information such as transaction logs, personal communications, or images behind encryption barriers that are difficult or impossible to bypass without the user's credentials.

3. Methods to Overcome Encryption Challenges

While mobile encryption poses significant challenges, there are tools and techniques that forensic investigators can use to attempt to bypass or unlock encrypted mobile devices and access evidence. These methods include:

3.1 Legal and Ethical Considerations

- **Warrants and Subpoenas**: In some jurisdictions, investigators can obtain a legal warrant or subpoena compelling the user or the device owner to provide access to the device, including passwords or biometric data. These legal orders are often the only means by which investigators can bypass encryption ethically and legally.
- **Cooperation with the Device Owner**: In some cases, investigators may be able to work with the device owner to gain access to encrypted data. However, this option is not always feasible, especially in cases where the device owner is uncooperative, or the user has refused to provide passwords under legal rights such as the Fifth Amendment in the United States.

3.2 Forensic Tools and Techniques

- **Cellebrite UFED**: Cellebrite UFED is one of the most commonly used forensic tools for extracting data from mobile devices. It is capable of bypassing certain types of encryption, particularly on older devices, and can also extract data from locked or damaged devices. UFED uses a variety of methods, including software exploits and hardware-based extraction, to bypass encryption and unlock mobile devices.
- **GrayKey**: GrayKey is a device used to bypass the encryption on both iOS and Android devices. It has been used by law enforcement agencies to unlock devices, especially those with complex passwords or biometric authentication. GrayKey uses physical access to the device and often exploits software vulnerabilities to attempt to extract the encryption key.

- **Brute-Force Tools**: Some forensic investigators use brute-force tools designed to work with mobile devices. These tools attempt to unlock the device by trying different PIN or password combinations until the correct one is found. This process, however, can take considerable time depending on the complexity of the password and the security settings of the device.
- **Physical Access and Chip-Off Techniques**: In more extreme cases, forensic investigators can resort to physical access techniques, such as chip-off forensics. This involves removing the storage chip from a mobile device, then reading the chip directly to recover data. However, this method is complex, time-consuming, and requires a high level of technical expertise. Additionally, newer devices may have more advanced encryption that is difficult to bypass even with chip-off techniques.

3.3 Cloud Access and Backup Analysis

- **Cloud Data Recovery**: If investigators cannot access the device itself, they can attempt to recover data stored in the cloud using legal means. For instance, through subpoenas or search warrants, investigators can compel cloud providers like Apple, Google, or Dropbox to release user data. However, this data may still be encrypted, and investigators may need the user's credentials to gain access.
- **Backup Forensics**: Investigators may also focus on obtaining device backups, either from cloud storage services or from local backups stored on a computer. These backups may contain valuable data, such as app data, photos, messages, and contacts, that could serve as evidence.

Mobile device encryption presents significant challenges to forensic investigators who need to access critical evidence. While encryption is vital for protecting user privacy and data security, it complicates forensic investigations by preventing unauthorized access to encrypted data. Investigators must navigate technical, legal, and ethical challenges when attempting to bypass encryption, using tools such as Cellebrite UFED, GrayKey, and brute-force techniques, as well as leveraging cloud data and backups. As encryption methods continue to evolve, digital forensic professionals must stay abreast of the latest developments to overcome encryption challenges and ensure they can access relevant evidence while adhering to legal and ethical standards.

10. Cloud Forensics and Virtual Environments

As more data moves to the cloud and into virtualized environments, digital forensic investigators must adapt to new challenges in evidence collection and analysis. This chapter explores the complexities of cloud forensics, including how to access and preserve data stored across distributed cloud platforms. You'll learn how to track digital evidence within multi-tenant cloud systems, investigate virtual machines, and examine virtual storage solutions. The chapter also covers the legal and technical hurdles of working with cloud providers, data ownership, and jurisdictional issues, providing you with the knowledge needed to investigate virtualized and cloud-based environments effectively.

10.1 The Architecture of Cloud Systems

The architecture of cloud systems is the foundational framework that supports the storage, processing, and management of data across distributed networks. As digital forensics increasingly intersects with cloud computing, understanding the architecture of cloud systems is essential for investigators aiming to access and analyze digital evidence stored in the cloud. Cloud environments differ from traditional on-premises data storage solutions, and their distributed, multi-tenant nature presents unique challenges and opportunities for digital forensics professionals. This section explores the core components and characteristics of cloud architecture, focusing on its structure, data management, security, and the implications for forensic investigations.

1. Cloud Computing Models

Cloud computing operates under several service models, each with its own architectural components and implications for digital forensics. These models define how cloud services are delivered and how users interact with the cloud infrastructure.

1.1 Infrastructure as a Service (IaaS)

- **Definition**: IaaS provides virtualized computing resources over the internet, allowing users to rent virtual machines, storage, and networking hardware. Common IaaS providers include Amazon Web Services (AWS), Microsoft Azure, and Google Cloud Platform (GCP).
- **Forensics Implications**: In IaaS, users are responsible for managing their virtual machines and operating systems, while the cloud provider manages the underlying

physical infrastructure. Forensic investigators may face challenges when accessing data stored in virtual machines or retrieving logs that are distributed across different nodes in the cloud infrastructure.

1.2 Platform as a Service (PaaS)

- **Definition**: PaaS provides a platform and environment for developers to build, deploy, and manage applications without managing the underlying infrastructure. Examples include Google App Engine, Microsoft Azure App Service, and Heroku.
- **Forensics Implications**: PaaS environments abstract away much of the hardware and operating system details. Investigating cloud-based applications built on PaaS can be more complex, as data may be stored in a variety of locations, and investigators may need to understand the application layer to extract useful evidence.

1.3 Software as a Service (SaaS)

- **Definition**: SaaS delivers software applications over the internet on a subscription basis. Examples include Google Workspace, Microsoft 365, Dropbox, and Salesforce.
- **Forensics Implications**: SaaS applications store data primarily in the cloud, managed entirely by the provider. Investigating SaaS applications typically involves accessing cloud storage and interacting with the application's web interface or API. Forensic experts must navigate the provider's data structures and potentially request data from the provider via legal means, such as subpoenas or court orders.

2. Cloud Deployment Models

Cloud deployment models determine how cloud services are implemented and made available to users. The deployment model impacts the architecture and security of the cloud, with significant implications for forensic investigations.

2.1 Public Cloud

- **Definition**: A public cloud is a cloud infrastructure where services are offered to the general public or a large industry group and are owned by third-party cloud providers. Examples include AWS, Microsoft Azure, and Google Cloud.
- **Forensics Implications**: In a public cloud, the cloud provider owns and operates the hardware, and multiple tenants share the same physical infrastructure.

Investigating digital evidence in a public cloud can be challenging due to the multi-tenancy model, where data from multiple clients may be co-located. Forensic investigators must be careful to separate and preserve evidence from the relevant tenant's data while respecting legal boundaries and privacy concerns.

2.2 Private Cloud

- **Definition**: A private cloud is a cloud infrastructure used exclusively by a single organization. It can be hosted on-premises or by a third-party provider.
- **Forensics Implications**: A private cloud offers greater control over the infrastructure and security. Investigators can have more direct access to data stored in a private cloud, especially if they are working within an organization's own infrastructure. However, the forensic process may still involve complex access controls, encryption, and virtualization techniques that need to be navigated carefully.

2.3 Hybrid Cloud

- **Definition**: A hybrid cloud combines private and public cloud infrastructure, allowing for data and applications to be shared between them. This model offers flexibility in terms of data storage and processing power.
- **Forensics Implications**: Hybrid clouds create challenges for investigators, as data may exist in both public and private cloud environments. Data transfers between the two can complicate the investigation, requiring forensic professionals to track where the data resides at any given time, how it is transferred, and the security measures in place for both private and public environments.

2.4 Community Cloud

- **Definition**: A community cloud is a shared infrastructure that is used by a specific group of organizations with shared interests, such as compliance requirements or security needs.
- **Forensics Implications**: Community clouds involve a shared infrastructure, similar to public clouds, but with stricter controls and often tailored to meet the needs of the community. Investigators must coordinate with cloud providers and member organizations to access data and preserve evidence, ensuring that privacy and data protection regulations are followed.

3. Cloud Architecture Components

The core components of cloud architecture form the backbone of cloud-based services and dictate how data is processed, stored, and transmitted. Understanding these components is crucial for forensic professionals who need to navigate the cloud environment and access digital evidence.

3.1 Virtualization Layer

- **Definition**: The virtualization layer abstracts the physical hardware and enables the creation of virtual machines (VMs) and other virtualized resources. This layer is managed by hypervisors like VMware, KVM, or Hyper-V.
- **Forensics Implications**: Virtualization allows for the rapid provisioning and deployment of virtual machines, but it also makes it more difficult to pinpoint where specific data is stored, as data can be distributed across physical servers. Forensic investigators must have the necessary tools and permissions to access virtual machine images and logs, which may be scattered across the cloud infrastructure.

3.2 Storage Layer

- **Definition**: The storage layer provides data storage and management services, typically using a distributed approach. Common cloud storage solutions include object storage (e.g., Amazon S3), block storage (e.g., Amazon EBS), and file storage (e.g., Google Drive, Dropbox).
- **Forensics Implications**: Investigating cloud storage can be complex, as cloud providers use distributed architectures, which means data is often stored across multiple physical locations. Forensic investigators must access storage logs and metadata to track where and when data was stored, modified, or accessed. Encryption is commonly used in cloud storage, adding another layer of complexity to forensic efforts.

3.3 Network Layer

- **Definition**: The network layer provides the communication channels between users and the cloud infrastructure. This includes routing, load balancing, and network security controls such as firewalls and intrusion detection systems.
- **Forensics Implications**: The network layer is crucial for tracking network traffic, including data transfers and access attempts. Forensic investigators can analyze network traffic to uncover communication patterns, unauthorized access, or malicious activities. Cloud providers often use complex security configurations to monitor and protect network activity, making it essential for investigators to have access to the appropriate logs and traffic data.

3.4 Management and Orchestration Layer

- **Definition**: This layer manages and automates cloud services, including provisioning resources, scaling infrastructure, and ensuring proper load distribution. It includes tools like Kubernetes and cloud management platforms provided by cloud providers.
- **Forensics Implications**: The management layer is critical in understanding how resources are allocated and how cloud services are orchestrated. Forensics professionals may need to examine configuration logs and orchestration tools to understand how data is handled across multiple cloud environments. The management layer can also provide access to logs detailing cloud service operations, which can be critical in tracing unauthorized activities or breaches.

The architecture of cloud systems is a complex, multi-layered framework that underpins cloud computing services. Forensic investigators must understand the various models of cloud computing (IaaS, PaaS, SaaS), deployment types (public, private, hybrid), and the components that make up the cloud infrastructure. Challenges arise due to the distributed nature of cloud storage, multi-tenancy, and encryption, which can make accessing and preserving digital evidence more difficult than with traditional on-premises systems. By understanding how cloud environments are structured and operated, forensic investigators can better navigate these systems, locate relevant evidence, and adhere to legal and ethical standards while conducting cloud-based investigations. As cloud computing continues to evolve, digital forensics professionals must stay informed and adapt to new technologies and challenges to ensure effective and accurate investigations in the cloud.

10.2 Evidence Collection in Cloud Environments

Evidence collection in cloud environments presents unique challenges for digital forensics professionals due to the distributed, multi-tenant nature of cloud architectures. Unlike traditional systems where data is stored on a single physical device or server, cloud environments spread data across multiple data centers and geographic locations. Forensic investigators must adapt their approaches to account for the intricacies of cloud systems, which often involve complex layers of virtualization, encryption, and network protocols. This section explores the key principles and techniques involved in collecting digital evidence from cloud environments, the challenges forensic professionals face, and the best practices to ensure proper evidence acquisition and preservation.

1. Understanding Cloud Data Ownership and Access

Before collecting evidence from cloud environments, forensic investigators must first understand the legal and ownership aspects of the data they are examining. Unlike traditional on-premises systems, where the user or organization typically owns the hardware and data, cloud data is often stored and managed by third-party cloud service providers (CSPs). These providers own the physical infrastructure, while customers rent virtual resources.

- **Tenant vs. Provider Responsibilities**: In a multi-tenant cloud model, data from multiple organizations is stored on shared infrastructure. Investigators must clearly identify the data they are interested in and ensure they have the necessary permissions to access it. Often, cloud service agreements (CSAs) and terms of service define access controls and procedures for handling data in case of a forensic investigation.
- **Service Level Agreements (SLAs):** Forensic investigators should consult the cloud service provider's SLA to understand the scope of data retention policies, legal obligations, and available tools for data retrieval. SLAs can provide insight into what data is accessible and for how long it is retained, which can be essential for planning a forensic investigation.

2. Challenges in Cloud Evidence Collection

Cloud-based evidence collection involves several unique challenges that digital forensics professionals must navigate:

2.1 Data Volatility and Dynamic Nature

Cloud environments are highly dynamic, with virtual machines (VMs), storage volumes, and other resources being created, deleted, or modified frequently. This volatility can make it challenging to capture a consistent snapshot of the environment when evidence needs to be preserved.

- **Dynamic Provisioning**: Cloud systems are designed to scale resources on-demand, and VMs or storage volumes can be moved or replicated across multiple physical servers. Evidence collection may require forensic experts to coordinate with cloud providers to ensure they access the correct instance or storage location.
- **Temporary and Ephemeral Data**: Some data in the cloud is temporary or ephemeral, such as session data or cached information that may disappear after

a short period. Investigators must be aware of the fleeting nature of certain data types and act quickly to preserve evidence before it is overwritten or deleted.

2.2 Multi-Tenancy and Data Separation

In public cloud environments, multiple customers (tenants) share the same physical hardware. Cloud service providers implement virtual boundaries to ensure that tenants' data is kept separate. However, the shared infrastructure raises concerns about data leakage, cross-contamination, and access control issues.

- **Tenant Isolation**: Investigators must ensure that evidence from one tenant is not mistakenly mixed with that of another. This requires careful planning and validation to ensure that evidence is preserved from the correct sources.
- **Access to Multi-Tenant Data**: In cases where an investigator must access logs or data that span multiple tenants, gaining proper authorization from the cloud provider is critical to avoid violating privacy or legal requirements.

2.3 Encryption and Privacy Concerns

Many cloud service providers use encryption to protect data both in transit and at rest. While encryption is essential for data security, it complicates the process of evidence collection by making it harder for forensic investigators to access usable data without the proper decryption keys.

- **Data Encryption**: Investigators need to understand how encryption is applied within the cloud environment. Encrypted data stored in cloud systems may not be immediately accessible without the proper keys or credentials. This could require legal processes to obtain decryption keys or access to encryption systems through court orders or subpoenas.
- **End-to-End Encryption**: Cloud providers may also implement end-to-end encryption, where even the provider cannot decrypt the data. In such cases, obtaining the necessary encryption keys or user credentials is essential to decrypt the evidence.

2.4 Jurisdiction and Legal Considerations

Cloud data can be stored in multiple physical locations across different countries and regions. This geographical distribution can present jurisdictional challenges, as laws governing the collection of digital evidence may vary depending on where the data is physically located.

- **Cross-Border Investigations**: Investigators must navigate the complex web of international laws and agreements that govern cross-border data transfers and access. For example, data stored in one country may be subject to that country's laws, while data stored in another jurisdiction may be governed by different legal standards.
- **Data Sovereignty**: Some countries have laws that govern the storage and access of data within their borders. In some cases, cloud service providers may restrict access to data or require specific legal processes before releasing evidence from certain regions, which can delay investigations.

3. Cloud Evidence Collection Techniques

The process of collecting evidence in a cloud environment follows similar principles to traditional digital forensics, but it requires cloud-specific tools and techniques to ensure that data is properly acquired and preserved.

3.1 Cloud Provider APIs and Interfaces

Cloud service providers offer APIs (Application Programming Interfaces) and management interfaces that can be used to interact with cloud resources and retrieve evidence. These tools allow forensic investigators to access storage systems, virtual machines, network logs, and other cloud-based resources in a structured and consistent manner.

- **Accessing Logs and Metadata**: Cloud providers often generate logs of system activities, including access requests, configuration changes, and network traffic. These logs and metadata are crucial in an investigation, as they can reveal how data was accessed, modified, or deleted.
- **Cloud API Access**: Most cloud providers offer programmatic access to data through APIs. Investigators can use these APIs to automate evidence collection processes, ensuring that they capture all relevant data within the cloud environment.

3.2 Cloud Snapshots and Disk Images

Cloud providers often offer the ability to take "snapshots" of virtual machines or storage volumes. These snapshots capture the exact state of a cloud resource at a specific point in time, allowing forensic investigators to preserve a copy of the environment for further analysis.

- **Creating Snapshots**: Snapshots allow forensic investigators to create an exact replica of a cloud resource, including its file system, configuration, and state at the time of collection. This is crucial for preserving evidence in a cloud environment where resources can be dynamically altered or moved.
- **Verifying Snapshots**: Just like traditional disk images, cloud snapshots must be verified to ensure that they have not been tampered with and that they accurately represent the state of the original resource at the time of collection.

3.3 Collaboration with Cloud Providers

Cloud service providers can play a crucial role in evidence collection, especially in cases where investigators are unable to access certain data directly due to encryption, multi-tenancy, or other limitations.

- **Data Request Procedures**: Forensic professionals must work closely with cloud providers to follow the proper channels for requesting data. This may involve issuing subpoenas, search warrants, or court orders to compel the provider to hand over specific data or provide access to forensic tools that can be used for evidence collection.
- **Cloud Provider Forensic Tools**: Some cloud providers offer dedicated forensic tools designed to help investigators access and analyze data from their platforms. These tools may include forensic reporting capabilities, logging interfaces, or dedicated support for legal requests.

4. Best Practices for Cloud Evidence Collection

To ensure the integrity of the evidence and to comply with legal and ethical standards, forensic investigators should follow best practices when collecting evidence from cloud environments.

- **Document Everything**: Keep detailed records of all actions taken during the evidence collection process. This includes noting the time, method of collection, and any communications with cloud providers. Documentation is crucial for ensuring the chain of custody and for defending the integrity of the evidence in court.
- **Ensure Data Integrity**: Use tools like cryptographic hash functions to verify the integrity of the evidence before and after collection. Any tampering with data during the collection process can undermine its admissibility in court.

- **Coordinate with Legal Teams**: Always work with legal teams to ensure that the collection process adheres to applicable laws and privacy regulations, especially when dealing with sensitive or personal data stored in the cloud.

Evidence collection in cloud environments presents unique challenges due to the dynamic, distributed nature of cloud computing systems. Forensic professionals must adapt their traditional methods and use specialized tools to collect evidence in a way that preserves its integrity and complies with legal and ethical standards. Understanding the architecture of cloud systems, working with cloud service providers, and leveraging cloud-specific tools like snapshots and APIs are key to successful evidence collection. As cloud technologies evolve, forensic professionals must stay informed and adapt their practices to ensure they can effectively navigate these complex environments.

10.3 Tracking Data in Multi-Tenant Environments

Tracking data in multi-tenant cloud environments is one of the most challenging aspects of cloud forensics. In a multi-tenant architecture, multiple customers (tenants) share the same physical hardware resources, including storage, processing power, and network infrastructure. This creates complexities for forensic investigators who must distinguish between data belonging to different tenants and accurately track and collect digital evidence while maintaining legal and technical compliance. This section explores the challenges of tracking data in multi-tenant environments, the tools and techniques used to overcome these challenges, and best practices to ensure data integrity and admissibility.

1. Understanding Multi-Tenant Cloud Architecture

In a multi-tenant cloud, multiple organizations or individuals share the same physical infrastructure (such as servers, storage, or networking), but each tenant's data is logically separated using software-defined boundaries. This logical separation is achieved through virtualization technologies, containerization, and access control mechanisms, which are designed to isolate the data and resources of one tenant from another.

- **Shared Infrastructure**: The physical resources, including compute nodes and storage devices, are shared among multiple tenants, with each tenant's data residing in isolated virtual environments. However, since they share the same physical infrastructure, it becomes essential for forensic professionals to understand the environment thoroughly to ensure the correct identification and tracking of relevant data.

- **Virtualization and Containers**: Cloud environments often use virtualization technologies (e.g., hypervisors) and containerization (e.g., Docker) to create isolated environments for tenants. These technologies allow multiple virtual machines (VMs) or containers to run on a single physical machine, each hosting its own applications, data, and operating system. Investigators must be able to track the virtualized resources used by the target tenant while avoiding interference from other tenants.

2. Data Attribution and Isolation in Multi-Tenant Systems

One of the primary challenges in multi-tenant environments is ensuring proper attribution and isolation of data. Since multiple tenants use shared resources, forensic investigators need to accurately trace and identify data belonging to a specific tenant without breaching the privacy or security of other tenants' data.

2.1 Attribution of Data to Specific Tenants

Data attribution refers to the process of linking data or actions within the cloud to a specific tenant. In a multi-tenant cloud, the same physical hardware may be used by many different tenants, making it difficult to identify which tenant's data resides on which virtual machine, storage volume, or network log.

- **Metadata and Log Files**: Cloud service providers generate metadata and logs for all actions within the cloud environment, including data creation, access, modification, and deletion. This metadata can help investigators attribute actions to specific tenants. For example, access logs can show which virtual machine or container accessed specific data or performed a certain action, providing clues as to which tenant is responsible.
- **Unique Identifiers**: Each tenant within a cloud environment is often assigned a unique identifier (tenant ID or account number). This can be crucial when tracking data through the system, particularly when performing forensic analysis of logs, network traffic, or storage systems. Investigators can use these unique identifiers to track down tenant-specific data and ensure that they are examining the correct data set.

2.2 Maintaining Data Isolation

Data isolation is a critical component of multi-tenant cloud environments, as it prevents one tenant's data from being accessible or tampered with by others. However, this isolation is implemented through software mechanisms, which are susceptible to misconfigurations, vulnerabilities, or flaws in access control that can allow unauthorized access to a tenant's data.

- **Access Control**: Properly configured access control mechanisms, including role-based access control (RBAC), identity and access management (IAM), and multi-factor authentication (MFA), help ensure that only authorized users can access a tenant's data. When tracking data in multi-tenant environments, forensic investigators must verify that they have the correct access permissions to gather evidence without violating any other tenant's rights or breaching privacy laws.
- **Data Leakage Risks**: If there are issues with data isolation—such as security breaches, misconfigured settings, or vulnerabilities—data belonging to one tenant could be exposed to others. Forensic investigators must be aware of these risks and take steps to verify that the data they are collecting belongs to the correct tenant, and is not the result of data leakage.

3. Evidence Collection Techniques in Multi-Tenant Environments

Collecting evidence from multi-tenant cloud environments requires special techniques that account for the challenges of data attribution and isolation. Some of the most common techniques include using cloud provider APIs, logging data, and snapshot collection.

3.1 Using Cloud Provider APIs

Cloud providers offer APIs (Application Programming Interfaces) that allow forensic investigators to interact programmatically with the cloud resources. These APIs provide access to storage volumes, virtual machines, logs, and other data that can be crucial for tracking digital evidence.

- **Accessing Tenant-Specific Data**: By utilizing cloud provider APIs, forensic investigators can pull logs, configurations, and metadata related to specific tenants. These APIs can also help collect virtual machine images, file system snapshots, and other critical evidence.
- **Tenant-Specific Access Controls**: Investigators must authenticate through the API using appropriate credentials and ensure that the API calls are scoped to only the specific tenant's resources, preventing access to data belonging to other tenants. This ensures compliance with privacy regulations and prevents unintentional data leakage.

3.2 Snapshot Collection and Analysis

Cloud providers offer snapshot functionalities, which capture the exact state of a virtual machine or storage volume at a given point in time. These snapshots can be critical when collecting evidence from multi-tenant environments, as they preserve the data and configuration of a tenant's environment.

- **Tenant-Specific Snapshots**: Forensic investigators can request snapshots of specific virtual machines or storage volumes associated with the target tenant. These snapshots provide a comprehensive view of the tenant's environment, preserving files, configurations, and other data that may be crucial for the investigation.
- **Ensuring Accuracy**: Investigators should ensure that the snapshots they collect are accurate and reflect the state of the tenant's data at the relevant time. Snapshot verification can help ensure that the evidence is not tampered with or altered during the collection process.

3.3 Network Traffic Analysis

In multi-tenant environments, network traffic may pass through shared infrastructure, making it challenging to identify traffic associated with a specific tenant. However, network logs and packet captures can provide valuable information about how data is transferred or accessed, which can be useful for tracing evidence.

- **Using Network Monitoring Tools**: Tools like Wireshark, tcpdump, and cloud-native network monitoring tools can capture and analyze traffic passing through the cloud's virtual network. By filtering traffic based on tenant-specific identifiers (e.g., IP addresses, user accounts), investigators can track communications and data flow associated with a specific tenant.
- **Identifying Unauthorized Access**: Network traffic analysis can also help identify instances where one tenant's data is accessed or tampered with by another tenant. Monitoring unauthorized access is essential for ensuring data integrity and investigating potential security incidents or breaches.

4. Legal and Ethical Considerations in Multi-Tenant Cloud Forensics

When conducting forensic investigations in multi-tenant environments, investigators must be mindful of the legal and ethical issues related to data privacy, security, and access control.

4.1 Chain of Custody and Documentation

Maintaining a strict chain of custody is essential when collecting evidence in multi-tenant cloud environments. All actions taken during the investigation must be thoroughly documented, including any interactions with cloud service providers, access to specific data, and the tools and methods used to collect the evidence.

- **Ensuring Integrity**: Any breach in the chain of custody can render evidence inadmissible in court. Proper documentation helps ensure that the evidence remains intact and that it can be defended in legal proceedings.
- **Data Privacy Compliance**: Investigators must ensure that they follow the applicable data privacy laws and comply with data protection regulations, such as GDPR or HIPAA, when handling tenant-specific data. The improper handling of private or sensitive data could lead to legal consequences or claims of malpractice.

4.2 Cross-Tenant Privacy Concerns

Since multiple tenants share the same physical resources in a cloud environment, there is always a risk that data from one tenant could be accessed by another due to misconfigurations, security vulnerabilities, or human error. Forensic investigators must take steps to ensure that evidence collection does not inadvertently violate the privacy of other tenants.

- **Segregation of Evidence**: To avoid cross-contamination of data, investigators must isolate the evidence related to a specific tenant and ensure that no data from other tenants is included in the collected evidence.

Tracking data in multi-tenant cloud environments requires careful attention to detail and a deep understanding of the unique challenges posed by shared infrastructure. Forensic investigators must leverage cloud provider tools, ensure proper data isolation, and use techniques like snapshot collection and network traffic analysis to collect evidence without breaching privacy or legal boundaries. By following best practices for attribution, access control, and chain of custody, investigators can successfully track and collect evidence in multi-tenant cloud environments while ensuring that the evidence is valid and admissible in legal proceedings.

10.4 Investigating Virtual Machines and Hypervisors

In cloud forensics, virtual machines (VMs) and hypervisors are pivotal components that require specialized knowledge and techniques for proper investigation. Virtualization technology, including hypervisors, allows multiple virtual environments to operate on a single physical host, enabling efficient resource allocation and flexibility in cloud environments. Forensic investigators face unique challenges when dealing with virtualized infrastructure, as traditional physical forensic techniques may not be sufficient. This section delves into the importance of virtual machines and hypervisors in cloud forensics, the specific challenges they pose, and the tools and methods used to conduct forensic investigations in virtualized environments.

1. Virtual Machines and Hypervisors: Overview

A virtual machine is a software-based emulation of a physical computer system that runs an operating system (OS) and applications. A hypervisor, on the other hand, is the virtualization layer that enables multiple virtual machines to run on a single physical host machine. It manages the resources of the physical machine and allocates them to each VM based on their requirements.

Hypervisor Types: There are two primary types of hypervisors:

- **Type 1 Hypervisors (Bare-metal):** These run directly on the host hardware, such as VMware ESXi or Microsoft Hyper-V. They are typically more secure and efficient but are harder to analyze from a forensic standpoint, as they operate directly on the hardware.
- **Type 2 Hypervisors (Hosted):** These run on top of an operating system, like Oracle VirtualBox or VMware Workstation. Type 2 hypervisors are often more accessible to forensic investigators, as they operate within a host OS, which may provide easier access to logs and other critical data.

In cloud environments, virtualization is critical for resource management and scalability. Cloud service providers utilize hypervisors to create and manage large pools of VMs that serve multiple customers, each with isolated virtual environments.

2. Challenges in Investigating Virtualized Environments

Forensic investigators face unique challenges when dealing with virtual machines and hypervisors. These challenges arise from the complexity of virtual environments, the difficulty of distinguishing between virtual and physical evidence, and the possible lack of visibility into the hypervisor layer itself.

2.1 Physical vs. Virtual Evidence

One of the primary challenges in investigating VMs is differentiating between virtual and physical evidence. Since VMs operate in software on virtualized hardware, investigators must understand how data is stored and processed in virtual environments, which differs significantly from physical systems.

- **Data Storage**: Virtual machines store data in virtual disk files, which are often stored as image files on physical storage devices. For example, VMware uses .vmdk files, while VirtualBox uses .vdi. These virtual disk files contain the entire operating system, applications, and data of the VM, making them essential forensic artifacts. Investigators must extract and analyze these files, keeping in mind that they may also be linked to specific snapshots, clones, or other configurations that can affect their analysis.
- **VM Snapshots and Clones**: Virtual machines can be easily snapshot or cloned, creating a point-in-time copy of a VM's entire state. Forensic investigators must carefully handle these snapshots and understand the relationships between the original VM, its snapshots, and any clones, as these can provide different versions of data and system configurations.

2.2 Visibility of the Hypervisor Layer

Hypervisors control the virtual machines running on a physical host and maintain the system's virtualized hardware. However, direct access to the hypervisor layer can be restricted, especially in cloud environments, which makes gathering forensic evidence from this layer more challenging.

- **Hypervisor Logs**: Hypervisors generate logs that track the state of the virtual machines, such as when they were started, suspended, or shut down, as well as when snapshots were created. These logs are critical for identifying the timeline of VM activity and potential tampering or data exfiltration attempts.
- **Limited Access**: In cloud environments, the cloud service provider (CSP) typically controls access to the hypervisor and may not grant investigators direct access to these logs, making forensic analysis more difficult. Investigators must rely on indirect sources of evidence, such as system logs from VMs, or work with the CSP to obtain hypervisor-level data.

2.3 Isolation Between Virtual Machines

Virtual machines are designed to be isolated from each other, meaning that one VM should not be able to access the data or processes of another VM. However, vulnerabilities in the hypervisor or misconfigurations can lead to "VM escape" attacks, where one VM gains unauthorized access to the host or other VMs.

Isolation Breaches: Investigators must consider the possibility of VM escape incidents, where malicious actors may have exploited vulnerabilities in the hypervisor to move laterally between VMs or even access the host system. This introduces the potential for cross-VM contamination of evidence, making it harder to pinpoint the source of a security breach.

3. Investigative Techniques for Virtual Machines and Hypervisors

While investigating virtualized environments presents certain obstacles, there are several tools and techniques that forensic investigators can use to gather evidence, maintain data integrity, and reconstruct timelines of events.

3.1 Extracting Virtual Disk Images

To analyze the data stored in a virtual machine, investigators must first extract the VM's virtual disk image, which contains the OS, files, and data from the VM. Depending on the hypervisor in use, these disk images are stored in different file formats, such as .vmdk (VMware), .vdi (VirtualBox), or .vhd (Hyper-V).

- **Disk Image Extraction**: Specialized tools like FTK Imager, EnCase, or the built-in tools provided by hypervisor vendors can be used to extract virtual disk images. Investigators should ensure that they are extracting the correct version of the VM, taking into account any snapshots or clones.
- **File System Analysis**: After extracting the virtual disk image, investigators can mount it as a separate volume and analyze the file system for evidence. The tools used for traditional disk forensic analysis (e.g., EnCase, FTK) can also be applied to virtual disk images, allowing investigators to examine file structures, recover deleted data, and search for specific evidence.

3.2 Analyzing Hypervisor Logs

While direct access to hypervisor logs may be limited in cloud environments, on-premise or hybrid environments may allow investigators to obtain these logs. Hypervisor logs provide valuable information about VM creation, destruction, migration, and other administrative actions.

Log Extraction: Tools like VMware vSphere and Microsoft Hyper-V Manager allow investigators to extract and review logs from the hypervisor. These logs can provide insight into when specific VMs were powered on or off, when snapshots were created, and any administrative actions performed on the virtual machines.

3.3 Investigating Suspicious Hypervisor Activity

In the event of a security incident, investigators should look for unusual activity in the hypervisor layer that might indicate a breach, such as unauthorized VM migrations, cloning, or changes in the VM's configuration.

Configuration Files: Hypervisor configuration files contain metadata about the VMs, such as their memory usage, network configurations, and associated virtual disks. Analyzing these files can help track the state of the virtual machines, detect anomalies, and confirm that a virtual machine has been tampered with or manipulated.

3.4 Snapshot Analysis

VM snapshots capture the entire state of a virtual machine, including its memory, disk, and processor state. Snapshots can be critical for identifying when certain actions took place or when data was modified or deleted.

Snapshot Timestamps: Investigators should pay attention to the timestamps of snapshots to establish timelines and understand the sequence of events. For example, if a snapshot was taken shortly before a system crash or a suspected breach, it may provide critical insights into what the system looked like at that time.

4. Legal and Ethical Considerations

When conducting forensics in virtualized environments, investigators must be aware of the legal and ethical implications associated with accessing and analyzing virtual machine data. Issues such as data privacy, chain of custody, and the preservation of evidence must be handled with care.

- **Chain of Custody**: Maintaining a clear chain of custody for virtual evidence is critical for ensuring its admissibility in court. Each step taken to extract, preserve, and analyze virtual machine data should be meticulously documented.
- **Data Privacy**: As with all digital forensics investigations, investigators must ensure that they respect the privacy of individuals and organizations. This includes

ensuring that data from other tenants or VMs not related to the investigation is not accessed or inadvertently included in the evidence.

Investigating virtual machines and hypervisors in cloud forensics requires a specialized set of tools and techniques. While virtualization provides scalability and flexibility, it also introduces challenges in distinguishing between physical and virtual evidence, gaining access to hypervisor-level data, and maintaining proper isolation between virtualized environments. By understanding the underlying architecture of VMs and hypervisors, forensic investigators can effectively collect and analyze evidence, identify suspicious activity, and ensure that their findings are legally sound and admissible in court. As cloud technology continues to evolve, so too will the methods and tools used to investigate virtualized environments.

10.5 Legal and Technical Issues in Cloud Forensics

Cloud forensics presents a complex blend of technical and legal challenges that investigators must navigate carefully to ensure that digital evidence is properly collected, preserved, and analyzed. These challenges arise from the inherent nature of cloud computing, where data is stored in virtualized, distributed, and often geographically dispersed environments. This section explores the key legal and technical issues that forensic investigators must address when conducting cloud-based investigations, highlighting both the opportunities and pitfalls associated with cloud forensics.

1. Legal Issues in Cloud Forensics

The legal landscape surrounding cloud forensics is complex and varies across jurisdictions, making it critical for investigators to understand the legal frameworks governing cloud-based evidence collection and handling. These legal challenges revolve around data privacy, jurisdictional issues, and chain of custody, among others.

1.1 Data Privacy and Protection Laws

One of the primary legal concerns in cloud forensics is the adherence to data privacy and protection laws. Since cloud providers often store data across multiple locations, sensitive data may be subject to different regulations depending on where the data resides. For example, the European Union's General Data Protection Regulation (GDPR) imposes strict rules on how personal data should be handled, including requirements for data minimization, consent, and the right to be forgotten.

- **Cross-Border Data Transfers**: Cloud service providers typically distribute data across multiple regions and countries. As a result, investigators must be mindful of the legal implications of accessing data stored in different jurisdictions, especially when it involves cross-border investigations. For example, a cloud provider might store data in the United States while serving a client based in the EU, raising questions of compliance with data protection laws like GDPR.
- **Third-Party Data Access**: Investigators must also consider the legal implications of accessing third-party data stored in the cloud. Cloud providers often have terms of service agreements that limit or restrict access to the data stored on their platforms. Investigators may need permission from the service provider or even a court order to access this data, which could delay or complicate the investigation.

1.2 Jurisdiction and Venue

In cloud forensics, determining the appropriate jurisdiction can be a major challenge. Cloud data may be stored across various geographical locations and can move between regions dynamically. When data is dispersed across different countries, the laws of the country where the data resides may apply, creating complications for investigators who are working within a specific jurisdiction.

- **Multi-Tenant Environments**: Cloud environments are often shared by multiple clients, each using their own virtual resources. As a result, investigators must avoid inadvertently accessing data belonging to other tenants when conducting a forensic investigation. This can raise ethical and legal concerns about privacy and data protection.
- **Data Ownership and Control**: Determining who owns the data in the cloud can be another legal hurdle. Cloud providers typically assert ownership over the infrastructure, while the customer retains ownership of the data. However, terms of service agreements often give providers the right to access, modify, or even delete data in certain circumstances. These nuances must be considered when obtaining and analyzing cloud-based evidence.

1.3 Chain of Custody and Evidence Handling

Maintaining a clear and documented chain of custody is a fundamental aspect of any forensic investigation. In cloud forensics, preserving the integrity of evidence is more challenging due to the virtual and often ephemeral nature of cloud resources.

- **Virtual Evidence**: Unlike traditional physical evidence, cloud-based evidence may not be static or tangible. For example, investigators might deal with virtual machines or cloud storage that can be dynamically modified, moved, or even deleted by the provider. This makes it harder to track the original state of evidence, requiring investigators to adopt specialized methods for capturing and preserving cloud-based data.

- **Data Duplication**: Cloud service providers often replicate data across multiple locations for redundancy and availability. Forensic investigators must ensure that they are obtaining the correct version of the data and that it has not been altered or duplicated inappropriately during the collection process. This requires tools capable of capturing consistent, verifiable snapshots of cloud resources.

2. Technical Issues in Cloud Forensics

The technical challenges in cloud forensics stem from the unique architecture of cloud environments, where data can be fragmented, encrypted, and stored across a distributed network of servers. Investigators must employ specialized tools and techniques to properly analyze cloud data while adhering to the legal and ethical considerations discussed above.

2.1 Data Fragmentation and Distribution

In cloud environments, data is often fragmented and distributed across multiple servers to optimize storage and access speeds. This presents a challenge for forensic investigators who need to piece together evidence from disparate sources.

- **Distributed Systems**: Cloud providers use distributed storage systems such as Hadoop, Amazon S3, and Google Cloud Storage, where data is spread across multiple physical locations. Investigators must be able to reconstruct the data from these distributed systems, often requiring knowledge of the provider's internal storage architecture.
- **File Metadata and Access Logs**: Investigators need to be able to access and analyze metadata associated with cloud-based files, which might include creation times, modification timestamps, and access logs. These metadata records can provide essential context and help piece together a timeline of events. However, access to this metadata may be restricted depending on the cloud provider's policies.

2.2 Cloud Data Volatility

Cloud data is often more volatile than traditional physical data. Data stored in the cloud can be rapidly modified or deleted, and cloud resources can be spun up and destroyed on-demand. This makes it crucial for forensic investigators to act quickly and employ techniques that can capture the evidence before it is lost.

- **Ephemeral Resources**: Cloud providers frequently offer ephemeral computing resources, such as temporary virtual machines or containers, which are allocated and deallocated as needed. These resources may not retain data after they are terminated, making it essential for investigators to act fast to capture relevant data from such resources before they are destroyed.
- **Dynamic Data**: Cloud service providers often offer features like auto-scaling and load balancing, which can lead to changes in the data's storage location. Investigators must account for these dynamic changes and ensure that they are capturing the right data in the correct context.

2.3 Encryption in the Cloud

Encryption is a critical tool for securing data in cloud environments, but it also complicates forensic investigations. Data in the cloud is often encrypted both in transit and at rest, which can make it difficult for investigators to access and analyze the data without the proper decryption keys.

- **End-to-End Encryption**: Many cloud providers offer end-to-end encryption, where the provider encrypts data before it is uploaded and ensures that it remains encrypted while stored in the cloud. Forensic investigators may face challenges if they do not have access to the encryption keys, especially if the encryption is managed entirely by the provider.
- **Key Management**: If the encryption keys are stored within the cloud environment, investigators may need to work with the cloud service provider to gain access to these keys. Alternatively, if the keys are held by the customer, investigators may need to obtain them via legal means, such as a subpoena or court order.

2.4 Lack of Standardized Tools

Unlike traditional digital forensics, where standardized tools are commonly used, cloud forensics lacks universal tools that can be applied to all cloud platforms. Investigators must adapt to the cloud service provider's unique architecture, APIs, and data storage mechanisms.

- **Cloud-Specific Forensic Tools**: Each cloud provider has its own set of tools, APIs, and interfaces for managing and analyzing data. For example, Amazon Web Services (AWS) has AWS CloudTrail for logging, and Microsoft Azure has Azure

Security Center. Investigators must be familiar with these tools and how to extract and analyze cloud data from each specific platform.

- **Challenges in Data Extraction**: Many cloud providers limit the types of data that can be exported or accessed by external users, making it difficult for investigators to extract evidence without direct cooperation from the provider.

Cloud forensics presents a unique set of legal and technical challenges that require investigators to be familiar with both the technical architecture of cloud environments and the legal regulations governing data privacy and cross-border access. The rapid evolution of cloud technology, combined with the distributed, ephemeral, and encrypted nature of cloud resources, requires investigators to employ specialized tools and techniques to gather, preserve, and analyze evidence. As cloud computing continues to grow, so too will the complexities of cloud forensics, making it essential for investigators to stay informed about evolving laws, emerging technologies, and best practices in the field.

11. Cryptography and Decryption Techniques

Cryptography plays a crucial role in securing digital data, but it can also pose significant challenges for forensic investigators. This chapter delves into the different types of encryption used to protect sensitive information, including symmetric and asymmetric encryption methods. You'll learn about common encryption algorithms and how they are applied to secure files, communications, and storage. The chapter also covers decryption techniques, exploring tools and methods used to break or bypass encryption, from brute-force attacks to cryptographic weaknesses. With an understanding of these concepts, you'll be equipped to navigate the complexities of encrypted data and uncover critical evidence hidden behind encryption walls.

11.1 Types of Encryption and Their Applications

Encryption is the backbone of digital security, ensuring that sensitive information remains confidential and protected from unauthorized access. In the field of digital forensics, understanding the different types of encryption and their applications is essential for investigators seeking to recover and analyze evidence in a secure manner. This section delves into the various encryption types commonly used in digital systems and their specific applications, particularly in relation to digital forensics and the challenges they pose to investigators.

1. Symmetric Encryption

Symmetric encryption is one of the most commonly used encryption methods, where the same key is used for both encryption and decryption. This method is fast and efficient, making it suitable for encrypting large volumes of data.

1.1 Characteristics

- **Single Key Usage**: In symmetric encryption, both the sender and receiver use the same secret key to encrypt and decrypt data. The main challenge with symmetric encryption is securely sharing the key.
- **Efficient for Large Data**: Symmetric encryption algorithms are generally faster than asymmetric ones, making them well-suited for scenarios where large datasets need to be encrypted or decrypted quickly.

1.2 Common Algorithms

- **Advanced Encryption Standard (AES):** AES is one of the most widely used symmetric encryption algorithms today, particularly favored for its speed and security. It is commonly used to encrypt data at rest in storage devices, including external drives, cloud storage, and mobile devices.
- **Data Encryption Standard (DES):** Although largely obsolete today due to vulnerabilities, DES was one of the first symmetric encryption algorithms used for encrypting data. Its use has been largely replaced by more secure algorithms like AES.
- **Triple DES (3DES):** This is an enhancement of DES that applies the DES algorithm three times to each data block, providing improved security. However, it is slower and has largely been superseded by AES.

1.3 Applications in Forensics

- **Full Disk Encryption (FDE):** Symmetric encryption is frequently used for full disk encryption, protecting the contents of a device from unauthorized access. Investigators may need to bypass this encryption during forensic investigations, often requiring access to the encryption key or using brute-force or cryptographic analysis techniques.
- **Encrypted Data in Transit:** Symmetric encryption is often used for securing data in transit, such as email communications, VPNs, and secure file transfers. Forensic investigators may need to intercept or decrypt these transmissions when investigating cybercrimes or data breaches.

2. Asymmetric Encryption

Asymmetric encryption, also known as public-key cryptography, uses a pair of keys: one for encryption (the public key) and one for decryption (the private key). This method is widely used in securing online communications and digital signatures.

2.1 Characteristics

- **Key Pair:** Asymmetric encryption relies on a key pair—one public and one private key. The public key is used to encrypt data, while the corresponding private key is used to decrypt it. This ensures that only the intended recipient, who possesses the private key, can decrypt the information.
- **Slower than Symmetric Encryption:** While more secure in many cases, asymmetric encryption is slower than symmetric encryption due to the complexity of the cryptographic operations involved.

2.2 Common Algorithms

- **RSA (Rivest-Shamir-Adleman):** RSA is one of the most widely used asymmetric encryption algorithms, especially for securing communications on the internet, such as SSL/TLS for HTTPS websites. RSA is commonly employed in digital signatures, secure key exchanges, and email encryption (e.g., PGP).
- **Elliptic Curve Cryptography (ECC):** ECC is a more modern and efficient form of asymmetric encryption, using elliptic curves for key generation. It provides similar security to RSA with much smaller key sizes, making it faster and less resource-intensive.

2.3 Applications in Forensics

- **Public Key Infrastructure (PKI):** PKI systems, which rely on asymmetric encryption, are used to secure communications and authenticate digital identities. Investigators may encounter PKI-based encryption when analyzing email communications or digitally signed documents.
- **Digital Signatures**: Asymmetric encryption is commonly used for creating digital signatures that verify the authenticity and integrity of data. Forensic investigators may analyze digital signatures in documents or files as part of fraud investigations or to verify the authenticity of evidence.

3. Hashing and Hash Functions

While not technically encryption in the strict sense, hashing is an essential cryptographic operation that is widely used in digital forensics for ensuring data integrity and authenticity.

3.1 Characteristics

- **One-Way Function**: Hashing involves using a mathematical function (called a hash function) to convert an input (such as a file or password) into a fixed-size string of characters. Hash functions are one-way, meaning they cannot be reversed to retrieve the original input.
- **Data Integrity**: Hashes are used to verify that data has not been altered. A small change in the input results in a drastically different hash output, making it an effective tool for detecting tampering with evidence.

3.2 Common Algorithms

- **MD5 (Message Digest Algorithm 5):** MD5 was once widely used for generating hashes, but it is now considered insecure due to vulnerabilities that allow for collision attacks (i.e., different inputs producing the same hash).
- **SHA-1 and SHA-2 (Secure Hash Algorithm):** SHA-1 was once popular but is now considered insecure due to collision vulnerabilities. SHA-2, which includes SHA-256 and SHA-512, is considered more secure and is widely used in modern cryptographic applications, including digital signatures and certificates.

3.3 Applications in Forensics

- **Data Integrity and Verification**: Hashes are extensively used in forensics to verify the integrity of digital evidence. Investigators often generate hash values for evidence (such as disk images) and compare them at different stages of the investigation to ensure that the evidence has not been altered or tampered with.
- **Password Cracking**: Hashing is often used for storing passwords in a secure manner. In forensic investigations, investigators may encounter password hashes in database dumps or other storage systems. They may attempt to crack these hashes through methods such as brute force or rainbow tables to recover the original passwords.

4. Full Disk Encryption (FDE)

Full disk encryption (FDE) is a method of encrypting the entire content of a disk, including the operating system and all files, so that data is unreadable without the correct decryption key.

4.1 Characteristics

- **Encrypts Entire Disk**: FDE ensures that all data on a disk is encrypted by default, making it secure from unauthorized access. This includes both operating system files and user data.
- **Requires Decryption Key**: To access the data, investigators must have the decryption key or be able to bypass the encryption using techniques such as password recovery or brute-force attacks.

4.2 Common Software

- **BitLocker**: A Microsoft encryption tool for Windows operating systems, BitLocker encrypts the entire system drive. It is often used by organizations to secure sensitive data stored on laptops and desktops.
- **FileVault**: FileVault is Apple's encryption solution for macOS devices, which encrypts the entire hard drive and is often used in both consumer and enterprise environments to protect sensitive data.

4.3 Applications in Forensics

- **Protecting Sensitive Data**: Full disk encryption is commonly used to protect sensitive or classified data on a device. Investigators often encounter encrypted devices during criminal investigations, and breaking or bypassing full disk encryption can be one of the most significant challenges in forensic analysis.

5. Disk and File Encryption Tools

Many tools are available to encrypt individual files or entire disks, allowing users to control access to specific data.

5.1 Common Tools

- **VeraCrypt**: VeraCrypt is an open-source encryption tool that allows users to create encrypted volumes and disks. It provides strong encryption and is frequently used for securing files and partitions on Windows, macOS, and Linux.
- **TrueCrypt**: TrueCrypt, though no longer actively maintained, was one of the most popular open-source tools for creating encrypted volumes. Forensic investigators may still encounter TrueCrypt-encrypted volumes in some cases.

5.2 Applications in Forensics

- **Encrypted File Storage**: Forensic investigators may need to recover encrypted files stored on a device, which can involve bypassing or cracking encryption to access the content. Disk and file encryption tools are commonly encountered in corporate and criminal investigations where data privacy is a concern.

Encryption plays a pivotal role in securing digital data, but it also presents significant challenges for digital forensics. Whether through symmetric encryption, asymmetric encryption, hashing, or full disk encryption, each encryption method has its own set of applications and challenges. Forensic investigators need to understand how each type works, how it is used in real-world systems, and how to overcome the hurdles it presents when attempting to recover and analyze digital evidence. As encryption technologies evolve, digital forensic investigators must stay abreast of new developments and continuously adapt their methodologies to keep up with the increasing complexity of encrypted data.

11.2 Password Recovery and Brute-Force Methods

In the world of digital forensics, password recovery plays a crucial role in unlocking data that may be encrypted or locked behind a password. Whether it's for accessing a device, a specific file, or an encrypted disk, forensic investigators often encounter situations where the target data is protected by passwords. In such cases, password recovery methods and brute-force techniques are employed to regain access to the data. This section will delve into these methods, their applications, challenges, and the tools used to perform them.

1. Understanding Password Protection

Passwords are commonly used to protect digital data from unauthorized access, securing everything from operating systems and software applications to encrypted files and communication services. However, passwords also act as barriers to forensic investigators, who need to access data for legal or investigative purposes. There are two types of password protection that are often encountered:

- **Plaintext Passwords**: These are stored in a readable form, often in a file or a database. While they are easier to recover if the storage method is unprotected or weak, they are less commonly used today due to security concerns.
- **Hashed Passwords**: More commonly, passwords are hashed before being stored. Hashing converts the password into a fixed-size string of characters. The process is one-way, meaning that investigators cannot reverse the hash to recover the original password directly. However, they can attempt to break the hash through various password recovery techniques.

2. Password Recovery Methods

There are several password recovery methods, ranging from simple to highly complex techniques. These methods are deployed based on the encryption used, the complexity of the password, and the tools available.

2.1 Dictionary Attacks

A dictionary attack is a password-cracking method that uses a pre-compiled list of likely passwords—often based on common words, phrases, or patterns. In this method, the attacker attempts to match the hash of the password to each word in the list.

- **Strengths**: It is faster than brute-force methods because it uses a curated list of common passwords. Many people use easily guessable passwords like "password123," "qwerty," or their names, which are often found in a dictionary file.
- **Limitations**: This method only works if the password is relatively simple or based on common words. It is ineffective against complex passwords that do not appear in the dictionary file.

2.2 Brute-Force Attacks

A brute-force attack is one of the most exhaustive methods for cracking passwords. In this approach, every possible combination of characters is tried until the correct password is found.

- **Strengths**: Brute-force attacks are guaranteed to find the correct password eventually, as long as the attacker has enough time and computational power.
- **Limitations**: Brute-force attacks can be incredibly slow, especially when the password is long or contains a mix of upper and lower case letters, numbers, and symbols. The more complex the password, the longer it will take to crack.

2.3 Hybrid Attacks

Hybrid attacks combine elements of both dictionary and brute-force attacks. The attacker will start with a dictionary file but will also modify the entries by adding numbers, symbols, or other characters at the beginning or end, or even replace letters with similar-looking characters (e.g., "password" becomes "p@ssw0rd").

- **Strengths**: Hybrid attacks increase the likelihood of cracking passwords that are not strictly common words but are based on easily guessable patterns.
- **Limitations**: While hybrid attacks are faster than brute-force, they are still limited by the strength of the original password and the complexity of the variations used in the dictionary.

2.4 Rainbow Table Attacks

Rainbow table attacks are a more advanced technique used to crack hashed passwords. Rainbow tables are precomputed tables containing the hash values for a wide range of possible plaintext passwords. They allow for much faster password recovery since the attacker can simply look up the hash in the table instead of computing the hash for each password guess.

- **Strengths**: Rainbow table attacks can be significantly faster than brute-force or dictionary attacks since the attacker only needs to compare hashes instead of generating them.
- **Limitations**: Rainbow tables are only effective for cracking unsalted hashes. Many modern password hashing techniques (such as bcrypt) use "salting," which adds a random string to the password before hashing, rendering rainbow tables ineffective. Additionally, rainbow tables are large and require significant storage.

2.5 Keylogging and Social Engineering

While not strictly a technical method, keylogging and social engineering are additional ways that passwords can be obtained. Keylogging involves recording the keystrokes of a user, either through software or hardware devices, to capture the password. Social engineering involves manipulating individuals to gain access to their passwords, such as through phishing attacks, where an attacker pretends to be a trusted entity to trick the target into revealing their credentials.

- **Strengths**: These methods do not rely on computational power and can be effective if the user is not cautious.
- **Limitations**: These are not digital forensics techniques per se and are often illegal or unethical. They also rely on human error or trust and are outside the scope of typical forensic investigations.

3. Tools for Password Recovery

Forensic investigators use a range of specialized tools to facilitate password recovery and decryption. These tools utilize various techniques, such as brute-force and dictionary attacks, and they often feature sophisticated algorithms to speed up the process.

3.1 John the Ripper

John the Ripper is one of the most widely used password cracking tools in the digital forensics field. It supports a variety of encryption algorithms and offers multiple attack modes, including brute-force and dictionary attacks. It also includes an option for performing "hybrid" attacks.

- **Strengths**: It supports many hashing algorithms and has a user-friendly interface. It is also highly customizable and can be optimized for high-performance hardware.
- **Applications**: John the Ripper is often used in forensic investigations to crack password-protected files, operating systems, and encrypted archives.

3.2 Hashcat

Hashcat is a powerful password recovery tool designed for high-speed cracking. It supports a wide range of hashing algorithms and is optimized to run on GPUs, significantly improving its speed.

- **Strengths**: Hashcat is one of the fastest tools available for cracking passwords, particularly when using GPU-based hardware acceleration.
- **Applications**: It is used in situations where a fast, exhaustive brute-force attack is required to recover passwords for encrypted files, archives, or network services.

3.3 Ophcrack

Ophcrack is an open-source tool that focuses on cracking Windows password hashes using rainbow tables. It is primarily used to recover lost or forgotten Windows login passwords.

- **Strengths**: Ophcrack is fast and effective for cracking older Windows password hashes (NTLM) that are not salted.
- **Applications**: Investigators use Ophcrack when working with Windows-based systems to recover login credentials or access encrypted data.

3.4 Passware

Passware is a commercial password recovery tool that supports a wide range of file types, including encrypted Office documents, PDF files, and Windows system passwords. It integrates both dictionary and brute-force methods for password cracking.

- **Strengths**: Passware supports a wide variety of encrypted file formats and can work with hardware acceleration to speed up cracking times.
- **Applications**: It is often used in enterprise-level forensic investigations to recover passwords from high-security systems or encrypted files.

4. Challenges in Password Recovery

While password recovery techniques are often effective, they come with significant challenges, particularly in complex, high-security environments.

4.1 Stronger Passwords and Encryption

As organizations and individuals adopt stronger password policies (longer, more complex passwords, often with multi-factor authentication), brute-force and dictionary attacks become increasingly time-consuming and less effective. Encrypted volumes, files, and communications that use advanced algorithms (such as AES-256) further complicate the recovery process, requiring more powerful computing resources.

4.2 Legal and Ethical Considerations

Password recovery is fraught with legal and ethical concerns. Forensic investigators must ensure that any password-cracking efforts are within the bounds of the law and are conducted with proper authorization. In many cases, cracking passwords without consent may violate privacy laws, especially if it involves personal or confidential information. Investigators must also ensure that the methods used do not alter the integrity of the evidence.

Password recovery and brute-force methods are essential tools in the arsenal of digital forensic investigators. While password protection is designed to safeguard sensitive data, forensic experts employ a combination of dictionary attacks, brute-force techniques, and specialized software tools to regain access to encrypted or password-protected information. However, with increasing password complexity and stronger encryption algorithms, password recovery has become more challenging. Forensic investigators must continually refine their skills and adapt to evolving security measures in order to successfully recover and analyze digital evidence in a secure and legally compliant manner.

11.3 Identifying Encrypted Data Containers

In the field of digital forensics, identifying encrypted data containers is a crucial aspect of an investigation. An encrypted data container is a file or storage device that has been intentionally protected by encryption to secure its contents. These containers can take various forms, ranging from file archives (like encrypted ZIP files) to entire disk volumes or partitions (such as those encrypted using BitLocker, VeraCrypt, or other disk encryption software). Recognizing these encrypted containers and understanding how to handle them appropriately is essential for forensic investigators, as it directly impacts the ability to access, analyze, and present digital evidence in an investigation.

This section explores the different types of encrypted data containers, the tools and techniques used to identify them, and the challenges forensic investigators face when dealing with encrypted files.

1. Types of Encrypted Data Containers

Encrypted data containers come in several forms, each requiring a different approach to identification and decryption. These containers are typically designed to hide and protect sensitive information from unauthorized access, and they can appear in multiple formats.

1.1 File-Based Containers

File-based containers are individual files or archives that are encrypted. These containers could be standard file types, such as compressed files or proprietary encrypted formats, that conceal data behind encryption algorithms.

Common Examples:

- **Encrypted Archive Files**: Files such as encrypted ZIP, RAR, or 7z archives are often used to store multiple files or folders. These archives are password-protected, and without the correct password or decryption key, accessing the contents is impossible.
- **Proprietary Formats**: Tools like TrueCrypt, VeraCrypt, and DiskCryptor can create encrypted file containers that act as secure "vaults" where users store sensitive files. These containers are files on a computer but behave like virtual disks that can be mounted and accessed when decrypted.
- **Identification Challenges**: These containers may appear as standard files (e.g., ZIP or EXE files) or as obscure formats that do not immediately reveal their encrypted nature. In some cases, files may have an ambiguous extension or an altered format that complicates detection.

1.2 Volume-Based Containers

Volume-based containers are larger and more complex than file-based containers. These are entire disk partitions or volumes that are encrypted to protect all the data within that specific space. Encryption is applied to the entire partition, making it difficult to differentiate between encrypted and unencrypted sections of the disk.

Common Examples:

- **Full-Disk Encryption (FDE):** Software like BitLocker (Windows), FileVault (macOS), or LUKS (Linux) can encrypt an entire disk partition, making it unreadable without the appropriate decryption key or password. These types of containers are often used to protect all data on a system.
- **Virtual Machine Disks**: Virtual machines (VMs) may use encrypted virtual disk files (e.g., VMDK files for VMware or VDI files for VirtualBox) to safeguard the contents of the virtual machine environment.
- **Identification Challenges**: These containers can be more difficult to identify since the encryption may apply to an entire volume or disk rather than just a single file. Investigators need to locate the specific volume, determine if it is encrypted, and assess how to access it.

1.3 Encrypted Cloud Containers

Cloud storage services, such as Google Drive, Dropbox, or OneDrive, often provide users with the option to encrypt their files before uploading them to the cloud. In some cases, these services use their own encryption (client-side encryption), while others may allow users to apply their own encryption before uploading.

Common Examples:

- **Encrypted Files in Cloud Services**: Many users may choose to encrypt sensitive files before storing them in cloud environments to protect against unauthorized access. This is common in corporate or personal security practices.
- **Encrypted Cloud Storage Platforms**: Specialized cloud services like Tresorit or Sync.com offer end-to-end encryption, meaning that only the user has access to the encryption key.
- **Identification Challenges**: The challenge lies in determining whether cloud-stored data is encrypted, especially when it's stored using third-party cloud providers. Investigators may have access to the files, but decryption could be impossible without the necessary encryption keys or passwords, which may be stored offsite.

2. Tools and Techniques for Identifying Encrypted Data Containers

Forensic investigators rely on a variety of tools and techniques to identify and analyze encrypted data containers. These tools help detect encrypted files or volumes, analyze their structure, and aid in the decryption process when possible.

2.1 File Signatures and Heuristics

File signatures (also called magic numbers) are unique identifiers that are embedded at the beginning of files and serve to indicate the type of file format. For example, a ZIP file typically starts with the hexadecimal signature 50 4B 03 04. Forensic tools can scan files and compare their signatures to known file formats, helping investigators identify potential encrypted archives or other protected containers.

Forensic Tools: Tools like X1 Search, FTK Imager, and EnCase use file signature matching and heuristics to scan and detect encrypted file containers, even when the encryption is not immediately apparent.

2.2 Disk Imaging and Volume Analysis

In the case of encrypted disk partitions or volumes, forensic investigators typically use disk imaging tools to create a bit-for-bit copy of the suspected disk or partition. Once the disk image is created, tools like FTK Imager, EnCase, or The Sleuth Kit are used to analyze the partition structure and detect encrypted volumes.

Detecting Hidden Volumes: Some encryption software (like VeraCrypt) allows users to create hidden volumes within a larger encrypted container. These volumes are invisible unless the correct decryption password is provided. Forensic tools use various techniques, such as searching for suspicious or unusual partition structures, to uncover hidden volumes.

2.3 File Carving and Data Recovery Tools

When dealing with encrypted files or volumes, investigators may use file carving techniques to recover fragments of files that may provide clues to the encryption method or reveal metadata about the container. Tools like Scalpel, PhotoRec, and Autopsy can perform file carving on disk images, which may help identify encrypted file types or recover partially deleted encrypted containers.

2.4 Cloud Forensics Tools

To handle encrypted data in cloud environments, specialized cloud forensics tools are used to examine cloud storage accounts and retrieve information about files stored in the cloud. Some of these tools include Cellebrite Cloud Analyzer, Oxygen Forensics Cloud Extractor, and Magnet AXIOM. These tools can examine user activity in cloud services and determine if the files stored in the cloud are encrypted.

3. Challenges in Identifying Encrypted Data Containers

Identifying encrypted containers poses several challenges, many of which stem from the nature of encryption itself. Some of the most significant challenges include:

3.1 Lack of Encryption Key or Password

The most obvious challenge in working with encrypted data containers is the lack of access to the encryption key or password. Without this key, forensic investigators can only attempt to recover the password through methods such as brute force, dictionary attacks, or exploiting weaknesses in the encryption algorithm (if any exist).

3.2 Obfuscation Techniques

Some individuals or organizations use obfuscation techniques to hide the existence of encrypted containers. For instance, encrypted files may be disguised with misleading file extensions, or hidden volumes may be created within larger containers to evade detection. These obfuscation techniques increase the difficulty of identifying encrypted data containers and require investigators to be familiar with the specific tools and methods used for obfuscation.

3.3 Legal and Ethical Concerns

Handling encrypted data containers often involves complex legal and ethical considerations. In some jurisdictions, investigators may need to obtain a warrant or have explicit consent to attempt decryption. Additionally, certain encryption methods (like those used in national security or by criminal organizations) may pose challenges in terms of jurisdiction and the applicability of laws around decryption.

The identification of encrypted data containers is an essential skill in digital forensics, as encrypted files and volumes often contain crucial evidence. Forensic investigators must use a combination of tools and techniques to detect encrypted containers, whether they are file-based, volume-based, or cloud-based. While identifying encrypted containers can be challenging, modern forensic tools, advanced analytical methods, and a solid understanding of encryption principles enable investigators to address these challenges effectively. Despite the hurdles presented by encryption, investigators play a key role in recovering and securing digital evidence, adhering to legal protocols, and ensuring that encrypted data containers are appropriately handled during investigations.

11.4 Tools for Decrypting Files

Decryption is one of the most complex and critical tasks in digital forensics, especially when investigators are confronted with encrypted files or data containers. Whether the encryption is password-based, based on a cryptographic key, or involves more sophisticated methods such as full-disk encryption, forensic investigators often need specialized tools to access the contents of encrypted files. This section delves into the various tools that are commonly used in the process of decrypting files, the mechanisms behind them, and the potential challenges that investigators may face.

1. Overview of Decryption in Digital Forensics

Decryption is the process of converting encrypted data back into its original, readable form using a cryptographic key or password. This task is essential for uncovering evidence hidden behind encryption in both physical and cloud environments. However, the effectiveness of decryption depends on several factors, including the strength of the encryption algorithm, the availability of the encryption key or password, and the expertise of the forensic examiner.

Decryption tools come in two primary categories:

- Password-based decryption tools, which attempt to crack or bypass encryption by guessing or recovering the password or key.
- Cryptanalysis tools, which analyze the encryption algorithm itself to find weaknesses that can be exploited to decrypt the data without needing the password.
- The ability to decrypt files relies heavily on the specific type of encryption being used, as well as the tools available to the investigator.

2. Password-Based Decryption Tools

Password-based decryption tools are widely used to crack the password protecting an encrypted file or disk volume. These tools rely on several decryption methods, such as brute force, dictionary attacks, or rainbow tables. Below are some of the most popular tools used in password-based decryption:

2.1. Passware Kit Forensic

Passware Kit Forensic is one of the most comprehensive decryption tools available for digital forensics professionals. This tool can decrypt a variety of file types, including documents (PDF, Word, Excel), archives (ZIP, RAR, 7z), and disk images (BitLocker, TrueCrypt, VeraCrypt). Passware Kit Forensic supports several password-cracking methods, such as:

- Brute force attacks (trying all possible password combinations)
- Dictionary attacks (using a list of potential passwords)
- Key recovery (when partial keys or information about the key is available)

Additionally, Passware Kit Forensic integrates with other forensic tools and provides full reporting capabilities, making it a valuable asset for law enforcement and private investigators.

2.2. ElcomSoft Password Recovery Tools

ElcomSoft offers a variety of password recovery tools that can handle various types of encrypted files, including archives, documents, and disk volumes. Their products, such as ElcomSoft Distributed Password Recovery (EDPR), allow users to recover passwords for a wide range of file types and encryption schemes. This tool is particularly effective for:

- ZIP and RAR archives
- Microsoft Office documents (Word, Excel, etc.)
- PDF files

The tool uses sophisticated methods such as:

- Dictionary attacks (based on predefined word lists)
- Brute force attacks (testing every possible password combination)
- Pattern-based attacks (for identifying commonly used password structures)

For more complex encryption schemes like BitLocker or encrypted iOS backups, ElcomSoft also provides specific solutions to recover passwords or encryption keys.

2.3. John the Ripper

John the Ripper is one of the most popular open-source password-cracking tools used by forensic professionals. Although originally designed to crack UNIX passwords, it has evolved to support a wide range of encryption algorithms, including those used in encrypted archives, disk images, and password-protected files. It supports:

- Brute force attacks
- Dictionary attacks
- Cryptanalysis attacks (exploiting weaknesses in encryption algorithms)

John the Ripper's flexibility and speed make it an excellent choice for testing multiple decryption methods, especially for commonly used encryption algorithms.

2.4. Hashcat

Hashcat is a high-performance password recovery tool that supports numerous hashing and encryption algorithms. It is particularly suited for decryption tasks involving cryptographic hashes, which are often used in password-based encryption schemes. Hashcat is capable of performing:

- Brute force attacks
- Dictionary attacks
- Hybrid attacks (using both brute force and dictionary methods)

Its advanced capabilities include the ability to use GPU acceleration for significantly faster processing, making it one of the most powerful tools in a forensic investigator's toolkit. Hashcat can crack passwords for file formats such as ZIP, RAR, and PDF, and even supports the decryption of disk encryption formats like TrueCrypt and VeraCrypt.

3. Cryptanalysis and Key Recovery Tools

While password-based decryption tools rely on recovering or guessing passwords, cryptanalysis tools focus on finding weaknesses within the encryption algorithm itself. These tools are especially useful when password recovery is not feasible, such as in cases of strong encryption without known password hints. Below are some commonly used cryptanalysis tools in digital forensics:

3.1. VeraCrypt and TrueCrypt Decryption Tools

For disk encryption solutions like TrueCrypt (no longer actively developed) and VeraCrypt, forensic investigators can use specific decryption tools to bypass or crack the encryption. These tools can be used to recover the encryption key from a disk image or mounted container, if the password or key is lost.

VeraCrypt's hidden volume feature (a hidden encrypted volume within a larger one) can make decryption more complicated, as investigators must first mount the correct outer volume before accessing the hidden volume. Tools like VeraCrypt Password Recovery or TrueCrypt Volume Recovery can help attempt to recover the password through brute-force or dictionary attacks.

3.2. Forensic Toolkit (FTK)

FTK Imager, while primarily an imaging and analysis tool, also provides functionality to decrypt files under certain conditions. For instance, FTK can decrypt certain file systems, such as those used by BitLocker or Full Disk Encryption (FDE). FTK is commonly used by investigators to both examine and recover encrypted data, provided they have access to the proper encryption keys.

3.3. Decryption of Encrypted Disk Images

For disk-based encryption, forensic tools like FTK Imager and X1 Social Discovery can be used to decrypt encrypted disk images if the password or encryption key is known. In cases where this is not possible, tools such as L0phtCrack or Oxygen Forensics are sometimes employed to attempt to recover or bypass encryption passwords through cryptographic weaknesses or brute-force techniques.

3.4. Cryptographic Libraries

Some forensic professionals also use cryptographic libraries, such as OpenSSL, to manually analyze and decrypt data. These libraries provide the low-level access needed to work with encryption algorithms like AES, RSA, and SHA-256. By understanding the encryption method and obtaining any necessary keys, investigators can decrypt data manually or via custom scripts.

4. Challenges in Decrypting Files

While numerous tools are available to aid in decryption, forensic investigators face several challenges during the process:

Strong Encryption: Modern encryption algorithms, such as AES (Advanced Encryption Standard) with long key lengths (e.g., AES-256), are virtually impossible to crack using brute-force methods within a reasonable time frame.

Password Complexity: Users often choose long, complex passwords, making brute-force or dictionary attacks far more difficult to execute effectively.

Hidden Containers: In some cases, encrypted files or volumes may contain hidden containers (e.g., hidden TrueCrypt volumes), which require additional steps for detection and decryption.

Legal and Ethical Issues: In some jurisdictions, attempting to decrypt encrypted data without proper authorization can violate laws or ethical standards, especially if the data is related to privacy rights or protected under specific legal frameworks.

Decrypting encrypted files is an essential yet challenging aspect of digital forensics. A variety of tools, ranging from password recovery solutions like Passware Kit and ElcomSoft, to cryptanalysis tools and forensic suites like FTK, provide investigators with the necessary means to access encrypted evidence. However, successful decryption often hinges on the encryption method used, the strength of passwords, and the availability of relevant keys. As encryption technology advances, forensic professionals must stay updated on the latest tools and techniques to ensure that they can effectively handle encrypted evidence in their investigations.

11.5 Forensic Challenges in Blockchain Systems

Blockchain technology, initially introduced as the underlying structure for cryptocurrencies like Bitcoin, has gained widespread attention for its potential to transform a variety of industries, including finance, supply chain, and even healthcare. Its primary appeal lies in its ability to provide transparent, decentralized, and immutable records of transactions. However, while blockchain systems offer many advantages, they also introduce unique forensic challenges that investigators must contend with. This section will explore the key forensic challenges in blockchain systems, focusing on their implications for investigators handling digital evidence.

1. Immutable Nature of Blockchain

One of the core features of blockchain technology is its immutability—once data is written to a blockchain, it cannot be altered or deleted without altering all subsequent blocks, which is practically infeasible due to the computational effort required. While this makes blockchain a robust system for secure and transparent record-keeping, it creates forensic challenges in several ways:

- **Evidence Retrieval**: In traditional digital forensics, investigators often rely on the ability to alter or delete data to preserve evidence or remove traces of malicious activity. With blockchain, however, the records are permanent and unchangeable, meaning any illicit activity recorded on the blockchain is often publicly visible and cannot be reversed.
- **Data Tampering**: Although tampering with blockchain data is difficult due to its decentralized nature, attackers may attempt to corrupt or manipulate blockchain transactions by exploiting vulnerabilities at the application or network level (e.g., 51% attacks in proof-of-work blockchains). Identifying such tampering requires analyzing external factors like network activity and software bugs.

2. Anonymity and Pseudonymity

Blockchain transactions are designed to be pseudonymous, meaning users can transact without revealing their real-world identities. This offers privacy and security but complicates forensic investigations:

- **Tracing User Identity**: While blockchain records are transparent, they are not tied to identifiable individuals. Wallet addresses, which represent users in a blockchain network, are not directly linked to personal information unless additional data points are obtained from other sources (e.g., exchanges or Know Your Customer (KYC) protocols). Identifying the real-world person behind a wallet address is a significant challenge for forensic investigators.
- **Mixing and Tumbling Services**: Criminals often use cryptocurrency mixers or tumblers to obscure the trail of funds between multiple wallets. These services shuffle transactions, making it exceedingly difficult to trace the origin and destination of funds. Investigators must look beyond the blockchain itself, incorporating analysis of off-chain data and transactions across multiple networks.

3. Cross-Chain Transactions and Multi-Asset Forensics

With the rise of cross-chain transactions (i.e., transactions that occur between different blockchain systems), forensic investigators face additional challenges. Users can transfer assets between blockchains through atomic swaps or intermediary services, which makes it harder to trace transactions to a single chain. This means that investigators must piece together data from multiple blockchains and external exchanges to track assets or investigate suspicious activity:

- **Interoperability**: The increasing use of multiple blockchain platforms, such as Ethereum, Bitcoin, and newer layer-2 solutions like Polygon or Solana, adds a layer of complexity for investigators who must learn the technical details of each chain and its respective transaction structures.
- **Tracking Cross-Chain Activities**: Investigators need to be familiar with tools that can track cross-chain activities and multi-asset transactions. This often involves the use of specialized blockchain explorers and analytic tools like Chainalysis or Elliptic, which aggregate transaction data from various sources to provide a cohesive view of a user's activities across different chains.

4. Lack of Standardization in Blockchain Forensics

Currently, blockchain forensics lacks uniform standards, and the tools used to analyze blockchain data are often proprietary or developed by private companies. This absence of standardization poses several challenges:

- **Tool Limitations**: Different blockchain networks may require specialized forensic tools to analyze their transactions and structures. For example, a tool like Blockchair may be useful for Bitcoin analysis but would be ineffective for Ethereum due to the differences in how data is stored and processed on each network.
- **Data Interpretation**: The lack of standardized protocols for analyzing blockchain data often leads to discrepancies in how evidence is interpreted. Without agreed-upon methods and tools, blockchain forensic results could vary depending on the software or expertise of the investigator, which may cause issues when the findings are presented in court.

5. Smart Contracts and Decentralized Applications (dApps)

Blockchain systems like Ethereum use smart contracts—self-executing contracts with the terms of the agreement written directly into code. These contracts run on decentralized applications (dApps) that can facilitate a wide range of transactions, including financial agreements, token transfers, and even decentralized governance. While smart contracts offer great utility, they also present a host of forensic challenges:

- **Automated Transactions**: Smart contracts can automatically execute transactions based on pre-determined conditions, which means that, if an illicit activity occurs, it may be difficult for investigators to pinpoint the responsible party since actions are carried out programmatically. Additionally, complex contract code could obscure the intent behind a transaction, requiring deeper code analysis.

- **Auditability Issues**: While the code underlying smart contracts is stored on the blockchain and can be publicly audited, many smart contracts are written by developers who may not follow best practices for security and transparency. Investigators may need to reverse-engineer or analyze poorly written contracts to understand how they work, and this process can be time-consuming and technically challenging.
- **Decentralized Finance (DeFi)**: The growth of DeFi platforms—decentralized exchanges, lending protocols, and derivatives markets—has created new avenues for illicit activity. Tracking and understanding financial transactions on these platforms requires knowledge of specific protocols and how they interface with blockchain networks.

6. Legal and Jurisdictional Issues

As blockchain transactions are decentralized and often cross borders, forensic investigators face legal and jurisdictional challenges when trying to access information related to blockchain activities. Since blockchain networks are globally distributed, with no central authority, investigating illegal activity on a blockchain can involve several legal issues:

- **International Cooperation**: Tracking down the individuals behind illicit blockchain activity often requires international cooperation between law enforcement agencies across multiple jurisdictions. However, the decentralized nature of blockchain means that evidence could be stored in multiple countries, complicating the process of obtaining search warrants or subpoenas.
- **Data Privacy and Sovereignty**: Data stored on blockchains may be subject to different privacy laws and regulations depending on the jurisdiction. In cases where blockchain evidence intersects with data protection laws (e.g., GDPR in Europe), investigators must navigate a complex legal landscape to ensure they are complying with privacy requirements while still collecting critical evidence.

7. Lack of Blockchain Forensic Expertise

Blockchain forensic investigations require a specialized skill set, and there is a shortage of trained professionals who can analyze blockchain data effectively. Investigators need to be proficient not only in traditional digital forensics but also in the technical aspects of blockchain technology, cryptography, and the tools used to analyze decentralized networks. As blockchain adoption grows, the demand for trained forensic professionals will increase.

While blockchain technology offers exciting opportunities in areas such as cryptocurrency, supply chain management, and digital identity verification, it also presents significant challenges for forensic investigators. The immutable nature of blockchain records, the pseudonymous nature of transactions, cross-chain activities, smart contracts, and legal issues all create unique hurdles when gathering and analyzing digital evidence. Forensic experts must adapt their methods, use specialized tools, and collaborate across jurisdictions to effectively investigate blockchain-related crimes. As blockchain technology continues to evolve, staying abreast of new developments and tools will be essential to overcome these challenges and ensure that blockchain evidence is properly handled in legal investigations.

12. Malware Analysis and Incident Response

Malware is one of the most pervasive threats in the digital world, and understanding how to analyze and respond to it is a critical skill for any forensic investigator. This chapter introduces you to the world of malware, from viruses and ransomware to Trojans and spyware. You'll learn how to identify, isolate, and analyze malicious software, using both static and dynamic analysis techniques to uncover its behavior and impact. The chapter also covers best practices for incident response, detailing how to handle an active cyberattack, contain the threat, and recover compromised systems while preserving crucial evidence for further investigation. With these tools and strategies, you'll be prepared to tackle the challenges posed by modern malware threats.

12.1 Reverse Engineering Malware

Reverse engineering malware is a critical process in digital forensics and cybersecurity. It involves deconstructing and analyzing malicious software (malware) to understand its functionality, behavior, and potential impact on an affected system. This process is essential for uncovering how malware operates, identifying its origin, and finding effective countermeasures. By dissecting malware, investigators can create strategies to mitigate future attacks and build more secure systems.

Reverse engineering is often used to analyze various types of malware, including viruses, worms, Trojans, ransomware, and spyware, to gain insights into their mechanisms. It also helps investigators determine whether an attack was part of a larger campaign, trace its source, and discover any vulnerabilities the malware may have exploited. This section explores the methodology of reverse engineering malware, the tools used in the process, and the challenges forensic investigators face when dealing with malware.

1. Understanding Malware Behavior and Its Purpose

The first step in reverse engineering malware is understanding the type of attack it represents and its intended effects. Malware can be designed for a variety of malicious purposes, including:

- **Data theft**: Malware can steal personal, financial, or corporate data and send it back to an attacker.
- **System damage**: Some malware may corrupt or delete critical files, disrupt system operations, or damage the integrity of data.

- **Backdoor access**: Malware may create backdoors that allow attackers to maintain persistent access to the infected system or network.
- **Ransomware**: Malware that encrypts files and demands payment for the decryption key.
- **Botnets**: Some malware is designed to turn infected systems into part of a botnet, which can then be used to launch large-scale attacks, such as distributed denial-of-service (DDoS) attacks.

Each of these types of malware has different goals, and understanding these goals is key to reverse engineering. For example, ransomware typically encrypts files and demands payment, while spyware focuses on collecting and sending sensitive data.

2. Key Phases of Reverse Engineering Malware

Reverse engineering malware involves a systematic approach, which can be broken down into several key phases:

2.1. Collection and Preservation of Evidence

Before analyzing the malware itself, investigators must ensure that they properly collect and preserve the infected system or file. This includes:

- **Isolating the malware**: Ensure the infected device or files are isolated from the network to prevent further damage or infection.
- **Forensic imaging**: Create a forensic image of the compromised system or storage device to preserve the integrity of the evidence before analysis begins.
- **Chain of custody**: Document the handling of the evidence to ensure it is admissible in court and traceable throughout the investigation.

2.2. Static Analysis

Static analysis involves studying the malware without executing it. This step can provide valuable insights into the structure and behavior of the malware, including:

- **File inspection**: Investigators examine the malware's file properties (e.g., size, date modified, file type) and check for any suspicious or malicious indicators.
- **Hexadecimal examination**: By opening the malware in a hexadecimal editor, investigators can inspect the raw binary code for strings, headers, and other recognizable patterns.

- **Disassembly**: Using disassemblers like IDA Pro or Ghidra, investigators convert the binary code into assembly language, making it easier to understand. This helps identify the functions and instructions used by the malware.
- **String analysis**: Searching for strings within the malware (e.g., domain names, IP addresses, hardcoded passwords) can provide valuable clues about its functionality or communication with external servers.

2.3. Dynamic Analysis

Dynamic analysis involves running the malware in a controlled, isolated environment (also known as a sandbox) to observe its behavior in real-time. The goal is to understand how the malware interacts with the system, what files it modifies, what processes it initiates, and what network activity it generates.

- **Behavioral monitoring**: Using tools like Process Monitor (ProcMon), Wireshark, and Sysinternals Suite, investigators can track the malware's system calls, file and registry modifications, and network activity.
- **Network traffic analysis**: Monitoring network traffic with tools like Wireshark allows investigators to capture outgoing and incoming communication from the malware. This can reveal how the malware communicates with its command and control (C&C) server, exfiltrates data, or spreads to other systems.
- **Sandboxing**: Tools such as Cuckoo Sandbox allow investigators to safely run malware in an isolated environment, providing a controlled setting to observe its behavior without risking infection of the live network.

2.4. Code Analysis and Debugging

In more advanced cases, malware reverse engineers may dive into deeper code analysis using debugging tools. Debuggers like OllyDbg, x64dbg, or WinDbg allow investigators to step through the code execution process and trace how the malware behaves at runtime. This process can reveal hidden functionality, such as encryption routines, self-replication methods, or anti-debugging techniques.

- **Disrupting Anti-Analysis Techniques**: Many malware authors incorporate anti-debugging and anti-virtual machine techniques to prevent analysis. These can include checks to detect virtual environments or debugger software. Reverse engineers must work around these defenses to fully understand the malware's capabilities.

- **Function tracing**: By tracing specific functions of the malware, such as decryption routines, command processing, or network communication, investigators can map out its internal workings and identify critical points in its execution flow.

2.5. Reporting and Documentation

After completing the reverse engineering process, the investigator needs to document their findings thoroughly. This documentation will include:

- **Malware description**: A detailed breakdown of the malware's purpose, features, and functionality.
- **Indicators of Compromise (IOCs)**: A list of file hashes, IP addresses, domain names, or other artifacts associated with the malware that can be used to detect or block it.
- **Impact analysis**: A summary of the potential or actual damage caused by the malware, including data theft, system downtime, or financial loss.
- **Recommendations**: Suggestions for remediation, such as removing the malware, patching vulnerabilities, or implementing preventative measures.

Reports should be clear, concise, and structured to facilitate both technical and non-technical audiences, such as legal teams or executives.

3. Tools Used in Malware Reverse Engineering

Various tools play a crucial role in the reverse engineering of malware, from static and dynamic analysis to debugging and forensic imaging. Some of the most commonly used tools include:

- **IDA Pro**: One of the most popular disassemblers and debuggers, IDA Pro allows reverse engineers to analyze the binary code of malware and translate it into assembly language for better understanding.
- **Ghidra**: A free, open-source reverse engineering tool developed by the NSA, Ghidra provides powerful disassembly, decompilation, and debugging features.
- **OllyDbg**: A 32-bit debugger for Windows that allows for dynamic analysis of malware, enabling investigators to step through code and identify key behavior.
- **Wireshark**: A packet analyzer used for monitoring network traffic and detecting any malicious communication initiated by the malware.
- **Process Monitor (ProcMon):** A tool that allows investigators to observe real-time system activity, including file, registry, and process operations.

- **Cuckoo Sandbox**: A popular open-source automated malware analysis system that runs malware in a controlled environment and generates comprehensive reports on its behavior.

4. Challenges in Reverse Engineering Malware

Reverse engineering malware presents several challenges, including:

- **Obfuscation and Encryption**: Malware authors often use obfuscation techniques to disguise their code and prevent easy analysis. This can include packing the malware into encrypted forms or using polymorphic code that changes with each execution.
- **Anti-analysis Techniques**: Many malware samples are designed to detect and thwart reverse engineering efforts, employing tricks such as delaying execution, detecting debugging tools, or checking if the malware is running in a virtual machine.
- **Time-Consuming Process**: Reverse engineering can be time-consuming and requires a high level of expertise. Some malware may be highly complex, involving hundreds or thousands of lines of code, which can make analysis a slow and iterative process.

Reverse engineering malware is a sophisticated and indispensable process in digital forensics. It allows investigators to understand the inner workings of malicious software, uncover hidden functionalities, and assess its potential damage. By using a combination of static and dynamic analysis, disassembly, and debugging tools, forensic experts can gain valuable insights that not only help with immediate incident response but also contribute to the development of better cybersecurity defenses. However, the process is complex, and investigators must overcome technical challenges such as obfuscation, anti-analysis techniques, and the increasing sophistication of modern malware. Despite these obstacles, effective reverse engineering plays a crucial role in defending against and mitigating the risks associated with digital threats.

12.2 Behavioral Analysis: Monitoring Malware in Action

Behavioral analysis of malware is an essential technique used by digital forensics experts to understand how malware operates and behaves when it is executed on a system. Unlike static analysis, which focuses on examining the code itself without running it, behavioral analysis involves running the malware in a controlled environment and monitoring its actions in real-time. This approach allows investigators to observe the full scope of the malware's activities, such as system modifications, network communications, and other interactions with the environment.

Malware is often designed to evade detection through various methods, such as encryption, obfuscation, and anti-analysis techniques. Behavioral analysis helps mitigate these challenges by allowing investigators to observe how the malware behaves once it bypasses static analysis techniques. This section discusses the key concepts, methodologies, and tools used in behavioral analysis, as well as the significance of monitoring malware in action for effective detection, analysis, and mitigation.

1. Importance of Behavioral Analysis in Malware Investigation

Behavioral analysis is particularly valuable in cases where malware has been obfuscated or is using advanced techniques to disguise its true functionality. By observing the actions of malware in a sandbox or controlled environment, investigators can:

- **Understand malware's objectives**: Behavioral analysis helps determine the purpose of the malware (e.g., data exfiltration, system corruption, denial-of-service attacks) by observing its actions.
- **Identify Indicators of Compromise (IOCs):** Observing the malware's actions can reveal critical IOCs, such as files created or modified, registry keys altered, or network traffic generated, which are vital for detecting and remediating the malware in other systems.
- **Detect evasive techniques**: Many advanced malware variants use sophisticated techniques to evade detection. Behavioral analysis can identify these methods, such as process injection, fileless execution, or rootkit behaviors.
- **Learn persistence mechanisms**: Malware often creates backdoors or other persistence mechanisms to maintain control over the system. Through behavioral analysis, investigators can uncover these mechanisms, which are essential for complete eradication.

Behavioral analysis is also beneficial for understanding how malware spreads within a network, how it communicates with external servers, and how it interacts with system processes. This enables investigators to track its origin and how it moves through the environment.

2. Key Stages of Behavioral Analysis

Behavioral analysis of malware can be broken down into several stages, which guide investigators in uncovering the full impact of the infection. These stages include:

2.1. Setting Up a Controlled Environment

The first step in behavioral analysis is to prepare a safe and isolated environment where the malware can be executed without posing a risk to live systems. This is typically done using a sandbox—a virtual machine or isolated system that mimics a real-world environment. Key considerations during setup include:

- **Virtualized environment**: Using a virtual machine (VM) allows the malware to run in isolation from the host system, preventing it from causing harm. Virtualization tools like VMware or VirtualBox are often used.
- **Snapshotting**: Before executing the malware, investigators create a snapshot of the environment. This allows them to roll back the system to its original state after the analysis, ensuring that any changes made by the malware do not persist beyond the test.
- **Network isolation**: The sandbox should be isolated from the broader network to prevent the malware from spreading. A controlled network environment may also be set up to monitor network traffic.

By ensuring that the environment is isolated and can be restored to its original state, investigators can safely observe the malware without fear of widespread damage.

2.2. Executing the Malware

Once the sandbox is prepared, the malware is executed within the controlled environment. At this stage, the primary objective is to monitor the actions of the malware as it runs. Investigators focus on key indicators such as:

- **File system activity**: Malware often creates, deletes, or modifies files during execution. Monitoring these actions helps identify the presence of malicious files and provides insight into the malware's objectives.
- **Registry changes**: Many types of malware modify system registries to ensure persistence or to disable security measures. Registry keys related to autostart, scheduled tasks, or security settings are often targeted.
- **Process activity**: Malware frequently spawns new processes, manipulates existing processes, or injects itself into other running programs. Monitoring the creation of suspicious processes is a key part of behavioral analysis.
- **Network traffic**: Malware often communicates with external command-and-control (C&C) servers or exfiltrates data. Investigators track any outgoing network

connections to identify malicious communication and the IP addresses of C&C servers.

Behavioral analysis tools that monitor these activities can help investigators capture and document the full range of actions taken by the malware.

2.3. Monitoring and Logging System Activities

During malware execution, real-time monitoring and logging are essential for capturing system activities. Tools like Process Monitor (ProcMon), Wireshark, and Regshot allow investigators to observe detailed information on the malware's actions:

- **File system activity**: File and folder creation, modification, and deletion events are logged, allowing investigators to identify files that may have been injected by the malware.
- **Registry analysis**: Changes to system registries are recorded, enabling investigators to detect alterations that could suggest malicious intent, such as the creation of new registry keys for persistence or disabling antivirus software.
- **API calls and system calls**: Malware often uses specific API calls or system calls to execute malicious activities, such as file manipulation, network connections, or process creation. Tools that track these calls provide valuable insights into the inner workings of the malware.

Logging and monitoring help create a comprehensive timeline of events, which can be critical for tracing the malware's behavior and understanding how it spreads or interacts with other systems.

2.4. Analyzing Network Traffic

Malware frequently communicates over the network, either to retrieve commands or send stolen data to an external server. Capturing network traffic using packet sniffers like Wireshark or TCPDump can reveal important information about the malware's communication patterns, such as:

- **Outbound connections**: Network traffic can reveal the IP addresses or domain names of C&C servers that the malware contacts.
- **Data exfiltration**: Malware that steals sensitive data (e.g., login credentials, financial information) often sends this data back to its controller. By analyzing network traffic, investigators can track this exfiltration.

- **Command-and-Control (C&C) communication**: Monitoring the malware's communication with a C&C server helps investigators understand how the attacker controls the malware and issues commands. C&C traffic may use common protocols such as HTTP, HTTPS, or custom protocols.

By observing these communications, investigators can identify network-based IOCs and even trace the source of the malware.

2.5. Documenting Findings and Generating Reports

Once the behavioral analysis is complete, investigators document their findings and compile detailed reports. This documentation typically includes:

- **Malware behavior overview**: A summary of the malware's activities, including how it interacts with the system, what files or processes it affects, and whether it communicates with external servers.
- **Indicators of Compromise (IOCs)**: A list of file hashes, IP addresses, domain names, registry keys, and other artifacts that can help in identifying the malware on other systems.
- **Impact analysis**: An evaluation of the malware's potential damage, including data theft, system disruption, or any other malicious activities.
- **Remediation steps**: Recommendations for eliminating the malware and securing the affected system, such as removing persistent registry keys, restoring files, and patching vulnerabilities.

Reports should be comprehensive enough to provide both technical and non-technical audiences with a clear understanding of the malware's behavior, its impact, and the necessary response actions.

3. Tools for Behavioral Analysis

Several tools are indispensable for behavioral malware analysis. These tools assist investigators in monitoring system activities, network traffic, and file system changes:

- **Process Monitor (ProcMon):** A tool that provides real-time monitoring of file system, registry, and process activities.
- **Wireshark**: A network protocol analyzer that captures and inspects network traffic generated by the malware.
- **Regshot**: A tool used to take snapshots of system registries before and after malware execution to identify changes.

- **Sandboxing tools**: Tools like Cuckoo Sandbox or Any.Run allow investigators to execute malware in a controlled, isolated environment and track its behavior.

Behavioral analysis is a powerful technique in malware forensics, enabling investigators to observe how malware interacts with a system and identifies critical IOCs. Through monitoring system activities, network traffic, and file changes, forensic experts can uncover the full scope of a malware attack, including its communication with external servers, persistence mechanisms, and data exfiltration methods. Despite the challenges of evasion and obfuscation techniques, behavioral analysis remains an essential tool for understanding, mitigating, and preventing malware threats. By carefully documenting findings and generating detailed reports, investigators ensure that the evidence is actionable and can inform both technical defenses and legal proceedings.

12.3 Memory Forensics for Malware Detection

Memory forensics is a crucial aspect of digital forensics, especially when it comes to detecting and analyzing malware. Unlike traditional disk-based forensic methods, which focus on static data stored in files and directories, memory forensics targets the volatile memory (RAM) of a system, where malware can hide, execute, or remain undetected by other forensic methods. Memory forensics involves analyzing the contents of a system's memory to uncover malicious activity, even when it has evaded detection on the file system. This chapter focuses on the importance of memory forensics in malware detection, the tools and techniques used, and its role in modern digital investigations.

1. The Importance of Memory Forensics in Malware Detection

Memory forensics is becoming increasingly vital in the detection and analysis of advanced persistent threats (APTs), rootkits, and fileless malware, which are designed to evade traditional file-based detection methods. These types of malware often execute or reside entirely in memory without leaving significant traces on disk, making them invisible to conventional antivirus software or disk-based forensic tools.

Key reasons why memory forensics is crucial for malware detection include:

Fileless Malware: Some modern malware, known as fileless malware, executes entirely in memory without writing any files to disk. This makes it particularly difficult to detect using traditional disk forensics or signature-based antivirus tools. Memory forensics allows investigators to capture and analyze the active processes, injected code, and network connections of such malware.

Rootkits and Kernel-Level Malware: Rootkits often operate at the kernel level and are designed to hide their presence from conventional security tools. They can manipulate memory structures to mask malicious processes or hooks. Memory forensics provides a method to detect these rootkits by analyzing the memory space used by the operating system and its kernel.

Malware Persistence: Malware may use memory to store persistent backdoors or covertly alter running processes to maintain control of a compromised system. By analyzing the memory image, investigators can uncover hidden processes, injected code, or unexpected changes to running applications that indicate malware activity.

Memory Volatility: Unlike hard drives, which retain data even when powered off, RAM is volatile. This means that once the system is powered down or rebooted, all data in memory is lost. Capturing memory while the system is still running is essential for preserving crucial evidence related to malware activity that may be wiped upon shutdown.

2. Techniques for Memory Forensics in Malware Detection

Memory forensics involves several key techniques and approaches to uncover malicious activities hidden within a system's memory. These include:

2.1. Capturing a Memory Dump

The first step in memory forensics is capturing a memory dump, which is a snapshot of the system's RAM at a specific point in time. This is typically done during an active investigation while the system is still running, as memory data is volatile and will be lost after the system is powered down.

Live Memory Capture: Tools like FTK Imager, WinPmem, and LiME (Linux Memory Extractor) can be used to capture a memory dump from a live system without interrupting its operation. This allows investigators to capture a snapshot of processes, network connections, and other critical artifacts before the system is shut down or rebooted.

Forensic Considerations: It is crucial to ensure that the memory capture is done without altering the system's state or corrupting evidence. Write-blocking tools and proper chain-of-custody procedures must be followed during the memory capture process to maintain the integrity of the evidence.

2.2. Analyzing Processes and Threads

After a memory dump is captured, investigators analyze it to identify running processes and threads. By examining the memory image, they can detect processes that are suspicious, unknown, or unlisted in the system's process table. Suspicious processes may include:

Injected Code: Malware often injects malicious code into legitimate processes to avoid detection. By analyzing the memory for anomalies in the process space, investigators can identify code that does not belong or has been inserted into running applications.

Hidden or Suspended Processes: Advanced malware may hide its processes from the operating system's task manager or the user's view. Memory analysis allows investigators to uncover such processes that are not visible in the normal process list.

Unusual Memory Usage: Malware may allocate unusual amounts of memory for certain processes or may exhibit behavior that differs significantly from typical processes. Detecting these anomalies can help identify malicious activity.

2.3. Identifying Malicious Code Injection

Memory forensics is particularly useful for detecting malicious code injection, a technique commonly used by malware to execute its payloads. Malware injects code into legitimate processes to avoid detection and increase persistence. Memory analysis allows investigators to:

Detect Injected DLLs or Code: Malware often injects malicious dynamic link libraries (DLLs) into legitimate processes. Investigators can scan the memory dump for unusual or suspicious DLL files loaded into memory, identifying the code's origin.

Analyze Code Injection Techniques: Understanding how malware injects code (e.g., through reflective injection or process hollowing) can help investigators detect and trace its operations in memory. Tools like Volatility and Rekall can be used to analyze code injection and uncover hidden malicious activities.

2.4. Network and Communication Analysis

Memory forensics can also uncover network connections and communication channels used by malware to communicate with remote attackers or servers. Many types of malware rely on external command-and-control (C&C) servers to receive instructions, exfiltrate data, or spread to other systems. By analyzing memory dumps, investigators can detect:

Active Network Connections: Active connections to suspicious or unknown IP addresses can be identified by analyzing the memory image's network stack.

C&C Communication: Investigators can identify patterns of communication between the infected system and C&C servers, including DNS queries, HTTP requests, and other types of traffic that could indicate malicious control.

Port Scanning and Exploit Attempts: Malware may attempt to scan for vulnerable systems or open ports. Memory analysis can reveal such network-related activities, including the detection of abnormal ports or services listening for connections.

2.5. Identifying Indicators of Compromise (IOCs)

Memory forensics is critical for identifying Indicators of Compromise (IOCs), which are pieces of evidence that point to the presence of malware or an attack. Common IOCs that can be identified through memory analysis include:

File Hashes: Memory forensics tools can help identify the hash values of files present in memory. These hashes can be compared with known malware signatures or checked against virus databases for matches.

Registry Keys and Artefacts: Malware often modifies system registries to maintain persistence or disable security mechanisms. Memory forensics can uncover altered registry keys, showing how malware has affected system configurations.

Network Artifacts: Memory dumps can reveal network-related artifacts such as IP addresses, domain names, and URLs used by malware to communicate with external servers.

By collecting and analyzing these IOCs, forensic investigators can build a more comprehensive understanding of the malware's tactics, techniques, and procedures (TTPs), which can be used to defend against similar attacks in the future.

3. Tools for Memory Forensics

Several specialized tools are used for memory forensics to assist in the capture, analysis, and interpretation of memory dumps:

Volatility Framework: One of the most widely used tools for memory forensics, Volatility provides a rich set of plugins for analyzing memory dumps and extracting valuable information such as processes, network connections, and injected code. It supports a wide range of operating systems, including Windows, Linux, and macOS.

Rekall: Rekall is an open-source memory forensics tool that is similar to Volatility but is designed to be faster and more efficient. It can analyze memory dumps, detect hidden processes, and uncover network connections.

FTK Imager: FTK Imager can capture memory dumps from live systems and create forensic images, which can then be analyzed using other memory forensics tools.

X-Ways Forensics: While primarily a disk forensics tool, X-Ways Forensics also has features for memory analysis, including the ability to examine system memory dumps.

Memory forensics is an essential technique for detecting and analyzing malware that hides in the volatile memory of a system. As modern malware becomes more sophisticated and uses techniques such as fileless execution, rootkits, and in-memory persistence, the importance of memory forensics in detecting these threats grows. By capturing and analyzing memory dumps, investigators can uncover malicious code, hidden processes, network communications, and other critical artifacts that are not visible through traditional file-based forensics. Memory forensics helps to complete the investigative puzzle, enabling digital forensics professionals to trace the full scope of a malware attack, identify Indicators of Compromise (IOCs), and provide actionable intelligence for mitigating future threats.

12.4 Responding to Cyberattacks: First Steps

Responding to a cyberattack promptly and effectively is critical to minimizing damage, preserving evidence, and preventing further intrusion. When a digital forensics team is called upon during a cyberattack, the first steps taken can significantly impact the overall outcome of the investigation and recovery process. In this section, we will explore the initial actions that must be taken when responding to a cyberattack, emphasizing the importance of a structured approach to the incident response process.

1. Immediate Detection and Identification of the Attack

The first step in responding to a cyberattack is recognizing that an attack is underway. Early detection is crucial, as it limits the window of opportunity for the attacker to cause damage, evade detection, or exfiltrate valuable data.

Monitoring Tools: Many organizations have security information and event management (SIEM) tools in place that monitor system logs, network traffic, and user behavior to identify suspicious activity. This could include unauthorized login attempts, unusual network traffic patterns, or the presence of known malware signatures. Alerts from these tools often trigger an incident response.

Anomaly Detection: In the absence of real-time monitoring, detecting unusual system or network behavior—such as unanticipated system crashes, unexplained file modifications, or unusual outbound network connections—can help identify potential attacks early.

Initial Assessment: The first responders must quickly assess the scope of the attack, determining whether the systems are still under active compromise and what assets are affected (e.g., servers, databases, workstations, etc.).

2. Containment and Isolation

Once an attack is identified, one of the key goals of the response team is to contain the attack and limit its impact. Allowing the attack to continue unchecked could result in the spread of malware, further unauthorized access, and even data exfiltration.

Segmentation of Network: If possible, isolate affected systems from the network by disconnecting them from the internet or local network. This step prevents the attacker from spreading malware or extracting data to external locations. Sometimes, completely shutting down or disabling specific services may be necessary to stop the attacker's actions.

Quarantine Malicious Processes: In cases of malware or active exploits, investigators should immediately isolate infected or compromised systems and examine them in a controlled environment to prevent further contamination of other systems. This may include stopping any suspicious processes or terminating unauthorized network connections.

Preventing Lateral Movement: In advanced cyberattacks, such as those carried out by APTs, attackers may attempt to move laterally across the network. The forensic team must prevent this by disabling access to network resources, blocking ports, and restricting account privileges where necessary.

3. Preservation of Evidence

One of the most critical aspects of responding to a cyberattack is the preservation of evidence. Any action that alters or deletes evidence can jeopardize the investigation and the potential for legal action. Preserving the integrity of the evidence ensures that it can be analyzed and used in court if necessary.

Creating Forensic Images: The first priority is to create a forensic image of the affected systems and devices. This includes capturing memory dumps, system images, and any relevant network logs or data on affected servers. Forensic imaging tools such as FTK Imager, dd, or EnCase should be used to ensure that the data is captured in a way that preserves its integrity and avoids tampering.

Documenting the Scene: A detailed log of actions taken during the incident response is essential. This includes noting the time of discovery, steps taken to isolate systems, and any changes made to the environment. This documentation serves as a chain of custody record and helps maintain the integrity of evidence throughout the investigation.

Write Protection: Use write-blockers to ensure that the original evidence is not altered in any way during the forensic imaging or analysis. This ensures that no evidence is inadvertently modified during the collection process.

4. Eradication of Malware and Remediation

Once the attack has been contained and the evidence has been preserved, the next step is to remove any malicious software or unauthorized access points. This is crucial to preventing further damage to systems or data.

Malware Removal: For known malware, utilize antivirus or endpoint detection tools to eliminate malicious files or processes. In some cases, manual removal or reinstallation of operating systems and applications may be required if the malware has deeply infected the system.

Account and Credential Cleanup: If the attacker has gained unauthorized access to user accounts or administrative privileges, it is essential to reset passwords, revoke access rights, and ensure that compromised accounts are properly secured. Affected accounts should be monitored for any unusual activity during this process.

Patching Vulnerabilities: After eradicating the immediate threat, the forensic team should work with IT and security teams to patch any vulnerabilities that were exploited during the attack. This may include installing updates, reconfiguring firewalls, or enhancing network security policies.

5. Investigation and Root Cause Analysis

After securing the environment, investigators should focus on conducting a thorough analysis of the attack to understand how the compromise occurred and the full extent of the damage. This step is critical for identifying the root cause of the attack and determining how the attacker gained access.

Timeline of Events: Investigators will work to reconstruct the timeline of the attack, identifying the point of entry, how the attacker escalated privileges, and the damage caused. Logs from security devices, systems, and network traffic are invaluable during this phase.

Forensic Analysis: Using the forensic images and data collected, investigators will perform a detailed examination to identify the methods used by the attacker, such as phishing, exploitation of vulnerabilities, or social engineering. This analysis also helps identify any data exfiltrated, systems compromised, or unauthorized changes made to files and configurations.

Collaboration with Threat Intelligence: By correlating attack patterns with known indicators of compromise (IOCs) and tactics used by other threat actors, investigators can gain insight into whether the attack is part of a larger campaign or linked to known cybercriminal groups.

6. Communication and Reporting

Effective communication throughout the incident response process is essential to ensure that stakeholders are kept informed and to comply with legal and regulatory requirements.

Internal Communication: Internal teams, including legal, management, and IT staff, must be kept up to date on the status of the incident and the actions being taken. This helps coordinate efforts and ensures that proper resources are allocated to the response.

External Reporting: Depending on the severity of the attack, the organization may need to report the incident to external bodies such as law enforcement, regulators, or industry-specific cybersecurity organizations. Reporting is essential for compliance with regulations like the GDPR, HIPAA, or PCI DSS, which may require breach notifications.

Incident Documentation: A comprehensive incident report should be created that outlines the nature of the attack, its impact, the steps taken to mitigate it, and any evidence collected. This report serves as a formal record of the attack and will be important for legal proceedings or insurance claims.

7. Lessons Learned and Preventative Measures

Once the immediate threat has been addressed and recovery is underway, it is important for the organization to conduct a post-incident review and develop strategies to prevent future attacks.

Root Cause Analysis: A detailed review of how the attack occurred is critical to improving security practices. By understanding how the attackers gained access, the organization can implement better defenses and detection measures to prevent similar incidents.

Enhanced Security Measures: Strengthening network security, implementing stronger user authentication, conducting regular vulnerability assessments, and providing staff training on cybersecurity best practices are essential steps in preventing future attacks.

Incident Response Plan Review: Following the attack, the organization should review and revise its incident response plan based on the lessons learned. This ensures a more efficient and effective response in the future.

The first steps in responding to a cyberattack—detection, containment, evidence preservation, eradication, and investigation—are critical to minimizing the damage and ensuring that a thorough investigation can take place. By acting swiftly and strategically, organizations can limit the scope of an attack, recover from the damage, and improve their defenses for the future. The role of digital forensics in this process is invaluable, as it ensures that evidence is preserved, and the root cause of the attack can be identified for corrective actions. Through a methodical and structured response, organizations can enhance their resilience against future cyber threats.

12.5 Tracing Malware Origins

Tracing the origins of malware is one of the most challenging and critical aspects of digital forensics, as it helps investigators understand how the malware entered the system, the methods used to propagate it, and the potential motives behind the attack. This process can provide crucial insights into the identity of the attackers, their infrastructure, and their broader objectives. In this section, we will explore the various techniques and approaches used in tracing malware origins and uncovering the history and motives behind a cyberattack.

1. Analyzing Malware Code

Malware analysis is often the first step in tracing its origins. By studying the behavior of malware, analysts can gather valuable information about its purpose, delivery mechanisms, and any identifying characteristics that could point to the creators or distribution methods. There are two main types of malware analysis: static analysis and dynamic analysis.

Static Analysis: This involves examining the malware's code without executing it. By deconstructing the binary or executable file, analysts look for patterns, embedded strings, or metadata that might reveal information about the malware's origin. Common indicators include hardcoded IP addresses, domain names, or even country-specific characteristics in the code. For example, malware might contain instructions to contact specific command-and-control (C&C) servers that could be traced back to known attackers or locations.

Dynamic Analysis: In dynamic analysis, malware is executed in a controlled environment (sandbox) to observe its behavior. By monitoring file modifications, registry changes, network communications, and system processes, investigators can uncover how the malware spreads, which systems it targets, and whether it communicates with external servers. Network traffic, particularly any connections to external servers, can provide clues to the malware's origin by exposing C&C servers or hosting infrastructure linked to the attackers.

2. Identifying Command-and-Control Servers

One of the most effective ways to trace malware origins is by investigating the communication between infected systems and their command-and-control (C&C) servers. These servers are used by attackers to control and issue commands to infected machines. By tracking the IP addresses, domain names, and URLs that the malware contacts, investigators can uncover the geographic location of the attackers and sometimes even their identities.

DNS Analysis: Malware often uses domain names to communicate with C&C servers, and these domains can be traced to specific organizations or regions. By performing reverse DNS lookups, analysts can uncover the IP addresses associated with the domains. The DNS records may also provide historical information about the domain's registration, including details about its owner and location.

Network Traffic Analysis: Network forensics tools such as Wireshark and TCPdump can be used to monitor outgoing traffic from infected machines. By analyzing packet data and looking for signs of communication with external servers, investigators can detect attempts to connect to known C&C servers. Additionally, analyzing the protocols used (e.g., HTTP, HTTPS, IRC, DNS tunneling) can provide further insight into the attacker's infrastructure and tactics.

IP Geolocation: Once an IP address is identified, investigators can use geolocation tools to determine its physical location. Tracking the location of the C&C server can help identify whether the attacker is operating from a particular country or region. In some cases, this information can help law enforcement agencies prioritize the investigation.

3. Investigating Malware Delivery Methods

Malware can enter a system through various methods, including phishing emails, malicious websites, drive-by downloads, or infected software. Understanding the delivery mechanism can provide clues about the attacker's identity, motivations, and previous operations. Tracing malware back to its delivery method involves examining the source of the infection and the methods used to bypass security measures.

Phishing and Social Engineering: Many cybercriminals deliver malware through phishing emails or malicious attachments. By analyzing email headers, file attachments, and URLs embedded in the messages, forensic investigators can trace the origins of these emails. For example, they may identify the sender's email address, the IP address used to send the email, or links that redirect to malicious websites.

Malicious Websites and Exploit Kits: In some cases, malware is delivered via compromised websites or exploit kits that take advantage of software vulnerabilities in browsers or plugins. By analyzing web server logs, investigating exploit kit signatures, and tracing IP addresses associated with the delivery mechanism, investigators can link the malware to specific threat actors or hacker groups known for using these techniques.

USB Drives and Physical Media: In targeted attacks, malware may be spread through infected USB drives or other physical media. Forensics teams may need to examine the infected devices themselves to gather evidence of how the malware was introduced. The investigation might involve recovering files from the USB drive, examining file timestamps, and identifying suspicious executable files that could have been dropped onto the system.

4. Examining Malware in the Context of Previous Attacks

Sometimes, malware strains are reused or repurposed by attackers, creating a trail that leads back to previous attacks or known adversaries. By comparing the malware in question to known malware families or examining similarities in tactics, techniques, and procedures (TTPs), investigators can build a profile of the attacker and their operations.

Signature Comparison: Cybersecurity companies and research institutions often maintain databases of known malware samples, including signatures, hashes, and behavioral patterns. By comparing a newly discovered malware sample with these databases, investigators can determine whether it has been used in previous attacks. If the malware matches a known signature, this can help trace the origin back to specific threat groups or campaigns.

TTP Analysis: Many advanced persistent threat (APT) groups and cybercriminal organizations have established patterns in their attack methodologies. By studying the malware's behavior and comparing it with documented TTPs, investigators can identify the attacker. For example, if the malware exhibits certain behaviors such as leveraging zero-day vulnerabilities or using specific encryption techniques, it might be linked to a particular hacking group or nation-state actor known for using these methods.

5. Tracking Cryptocurrency Transactions

In recent years, many cybercriminals and attackers have turned to cryptocurrencies to launder stolen funds or pay for malicious services. Some malware, such as ransomware, demands payment in Bitcoin or other cryptocurrencies. By tracing cryptocurrency transactions, investigators can often uncover the origins of the attack or the attackers themselves.

Blockchain Analysis: While blockchain transactions are pseudonymous, they are also transparent and publicly recorded. Investigators can track cryptocurrency transactions back to specific wallets and, through network analysis, potentially link the wallets to cybercriminal activities. In some cases, cryptocurrency exchanges may be able to provide information about the identity of the individuals behind the wallets, especially if they are using services that require Know Your Customer (KYC) verification.

Payment Trails: In ransomware attacks, attackers typically provide a wallet address to receive payments. By following the trail of cryptocurrency payments, forensic investigators can sometimes uncover patterns that link the attackers to other known incidents or even identify their geographical location.

6. Collaboration with International Agencies

Tracing the origins of malware often requires collaboration with law enforcement agencies, cybersecurity firms, and international organizations. Many cybercriminal groups operate across borders, making it difficult for a single jurisdiction to pursue them effectively. International cooperation allows investigators to share intelligence, pool resources, and bring cybercriminals to justice.

Collaboration with CERTs and CSIRTs: Computer Emergency Response Teams (CERTs) and Computer Security Incident Response Teams (CSIRTs) often share information about cyberattacks and vulnerabilities. Working with these organizations can provide access to global intelligence about attack methods and known threat actors.

Law Enforcement Agencies: Agencies like the FBI, INTERPOL, and Europol have dedicated units that investigate cybercrime and track malware origins. These agencies have the authority to request data from ISPs, coordinate with international police forces, and issue warrants for cybercriminal arrests.

Tracing the origins of malware is a complex, multi-faceted process that involves a combination of technical analysis, forensic investigation, and collaboration across various disciplines. By examining the malware's code, analyzing network communications, investigating delivery methods, and tracking historical attack patterns, investigators can uncover valuable insights into the attackers' identity and motives. Ultimately, the goal of tracing malware origins is to prevent future attacks, hold cybercriminals accountable, and strengthen the resilience of organizations and individuals against evolving threats in the digital age.

13. Reporting and Presenting Digital Evidence

Once digital evidence is collected and analyzed, the next crucial step is to present it clearly and effectively, whether in a legal context or to stakeholders. This chapter focuses on the art of forensic reporting and the best practices for presenting your findings. You'll learn how to structure forensic reports, ensuring that they are thorough, clear, and legally defensible. The chapter also covers how to translate complex technical findings into language that non-technical audiences can understand, including judges, juries, and other decision-makers. Additionally, you'll discover how to prepare for courtroom testimony as an expert witness, maintaining professionalism and credibility while presenting evidence in a compelling and persuasive manner.

13.1 Structuring a Forensic Report

A forensic report is a critical document in the digital forensics process, acting as the official record of an investigation. It serves as a comprehensive and detailed account of the steps taken, evidence collected, analysis conducted, and conclusions drawn. This report is essential not only for internal decision-making but also for legal proceedings, where it may be presented in court. The structure of a forensic report should follow a clear, logical format that allows readers, including legal professionals, to easily understand the findings and methodology.

Here, we will outline the key sections that should be included in a forensic report, along with considerations for presenting complex technical data in a clear and accessible manner.

1. Title Page

The title page is the first point of contact for the reader and should provide essential information about the case and the forensic investigation.

- **Case Identification**: Include the case number, investigation name, and any other identifiers relevant to the case.
- **Forensic Examiner's Information**: The name and professional title of the forensic examiner or investigation team, along with any relevant qualifications or certifications.
- **Date of the Report**: Clearly specify the date the report was generated.

- **Client/Agency Information**: Include the name of the client or agency requesting the investigation (e.g., law enforcement agency, organization, or company).

The title page should be formatted professionally and include a clear reference to the case for easy identification.

2. Executive Summary

The executive summary provides a brief, high-level overview of the entire investigation. It is typically written for a non-technical audience, such as legal professionals, management, or other stakeholders, and should focus on the key findings and conclusions.

- **Purpose of the Investigation**: A concise statement explaining the reason for the forensic investigation. This could include the type of cybercrime (e.g., hacking, data breach, fraud), or the specific issue being investigated.
- **Key Findings**: A summary of the most important results of the investigation, such as whether data was compromised, if a particular individual or entity is responsible, and if any evidence was successfully recovered.
- **Conclusions and Recommendations**: A brief outline of the conclusions reached and any recommended actions, whether for internal corrective measures or further legal action.

The executive summary should be clear, concise, and written in non-technical language, allowing stakeholders to quickly understand the significance of the report.

3. Case Background

This section provides context for the investigation and explains how the case was initiated.

- **Incident Overview**: A detailed description of the incident or event that triggered the investigation. This may include details like when the breach was first noticed, the type of system affected, and the method of discovery.
- **Initial Report**: The initial complaint or request that led to the forensic investigation, whether from an internal source or external entity.
- **Scope of the Investigation**: Define the scope and limitations of the investigation. This includes specifying which systems, devices, and data were analyzed, and clarifying any areas outside the scope of the investigation.

- **Key Objectives**: The goals of the forensic examination (e.g., to identify the source of a breach, recover lost data, confirm an individual's involvement in a cybercrime, etc.).

The case background section should give the reader a clear understanding of the investigation's origin and its focus.

4. Methodology

The methodology section is one of the most important parts of the report as it explains the forensic techniques and tools used during the investigation. This section should outline how evidence was collected, analyzed, and preserved, ensuring that the process can be verified and repeated if necessary.

- **Forensic Tools and Software**: List the specific forensic tools and software used, such as EnCase, FTK, or open-source tools like Autopsy. Include the versions of the tools and why they were selected for the investigation.
- **Evidence Collection Process**: Describe the procedures followed to collect digital evidence, such as the use of write blockers, chain of custody protocols, and imaging techniques. The description should emphasize the steps taken to ensure the integrity and admissibility of the evidence.
- **Data Analysis Techniques**: Explain the steps taken to analyze the collected data. This might include examining logs, recovering deleted files, conducting keyword searches, or performing network traffic analysis. Be sure to mention the forensic principles followed to ensure the analysis was thorough and unbiased.
- **Data Preservation**: Outline the steps taken to preserve evidence, including the storage methods and precautions to avoid evidence tampering. Discuss the chain of custody process in detail, as maintaining the integrity of the evidence is vital for legal proceedings.

The methodology section should provide enough detail for another professional in the field to understand the investigative process and replicate the findings.

5. Findings

The findings section is the core of the forensic report, detailing the results of the investigation. This section should be organized and presented in a clear, logical manner to allow the reader to follow the investigation's progression.

- **Evidence Collected**: Provide a comprehensive list of the evidence collected during the investigation. This could include digital files, system logs, email headers, network traces, and other forms of digital evidence. Each piece of evidence should be clearly labeled, referenced, and described.
- **Data Analysis Results**: Present the results of the forensic analysis in a clear, structured manner. This could include information on file timestamps, file system anomalies, deleted data recovery, network logs, or any other findings that were uncovered.
- **Linking Evidence to Individuals or Events**: Where applicable, discuss how the evidence ties back to specific individuals, devices, or actions. This could involve detailing how a specific user account was compromised, or how malware traces were found on particular machines.
- **Discrepancies or Limitations**: If there were any issues in collecting or analyzing evidence (e.g., corrupted files, encrypted data), be sure to note these in the findings section. This transparency adds credibility to the report and highlights any potential limitations in the investigation.

This section should be as detailed and precise as possible, presenting the evidence in an organized, logical fashion.

6. Analysis and Interpretation

In the analysis and interpretation section, the forensic examiner provides their expert analysis of the findings. This is where the investigator interprets the evidence in the context of the case and outlines what the findings mean.

- **Contextual Analysis**: Explain how the findings fit into the broader context of the case. This may involve linking data to specific actions, explaining the significance of certain findings, and identifying the sequence of events.
- **Conclusions Drawn from the Evidence**: Based on the analysis of the evidence, summarize the conclusions reached. This could include determining whether a breach occurred, identifying how the attack was carried out, or tracing the activities of a particular individual.
- **Corroboration with Other Sources**: If applicable, mention any external data or corroborative evidence (e.g., witness statements, physical evidence, or external intelligence) that supports the findings.

The goal of this section is to provide an expert interpretation of the evidence that links it back to the objectives of the investigation.

7. Conclusions

The conclusions section summarizes the main findings of the investigation and offers a final interpretation of the evidence. This section should be concise and clearly written, drawing from the findings and analysis.

- **Key Conclusions**: A brief summary of the primary conclusions drawn from the investigation. This could include identifying the responsible party, confirming the breach or cybercrime, and specifying the nature of the compromise.
- **Impact Assessment**: Discuss the impact of the incident based on the findings. This could involve analyzing the extent of the data loss, the level of disruption caused to the organization, or the broader consequences for the victims.
- **Recommendations**: Provide recommendations for remedial actions or future prevention. These could involve strengthening security measures, recommending system patches, or suggesting changes in policy or procedures to mitigate future risks.

The conclusions should be brief, summarizing the findings in a manner that aligns with the report's objectives.

8. Appendices

The appendices provide any supplementary information that supports the report. This could include detailed logs, screenshots, file hashes, data sets, or raw analysis results.

- **Raw Evidence Logs**: Any raw data collected during the investigation, such as file lists, system logs, or network traffic dumps.
- **Screenshots or Diagrams**: Visual aids that help illustrate key findings, such as a network topology diagram or screenshots of suspicious files.
- **Glossary of Terms**: If technical jargon or acronyms are used, a glossary can help ensure clarity for non-technical readers.

The appendices should be well-organized and clearly labeled, ensuring that all supporting materials are easily accessible.

A forensic report must be thorough, methodical, and clear to ensure its effectiveness in both internal reviews and legal proceedings. By following a structured format that includes all relevant sections—from case background to findings and conclusions—digital forensics professionals can produce reports that are not only comprehensive but also clear, organized, and actionable. The structure outlined above provides a solid foundation for creating forensic reports that meet the highest professional standards and stand up in a court of law.

13.2 Common Pitfalls in Documentation

In digital forensics, proper documentation is essential for ensuring that evidence is preserved, analysis is verifiable, and findings are presented clearly. Poor documentation practices can not only compromise the integrity of an investigation but also lead to legal challenges, including the inadmissibility of evidence in court. This section will highlight some common pitfalls in forensic documentation and provide guidance on how to avoid them.

1. Inadequate Chain of Custody Records

One of the most critical aspects of forensic documentation is maintaining an accurate and detailed chain of custody. The chain of custody refers to the record of who has handled the evidence, where it has been stored, and how it has been transported throughout the investigation. If the chain of custody is not properly documented, there can be doubts about the integrity and authenticity of the evidence, which can render it inadmissible in court.

Pitfall: Failing to maintain a complete and continuous record of all individuals who have handled evidence, the dates and times it was transferred, and the storage conditions. This can lead to gaps or inconsistencies in the documentation.

Solution: Ensure that every piece of evidence is documented with a unique identifier, and maintain detailed, chronological records of all movements and interactions with the evidence. This includes noting the individuals who collected, analyzed, and transported the evidence, as well as any temporary storage locations.

2. Lack of Proper Documentation of Evidence Collection

When collecting digital evidence, it's crucial to record the specifics of how and why particular data was chosen for examination. This includes documenting the collection methods, tools used, and any precautions taken to avoid altering the original evidence. Inadequate documentation of evidence collection can raise questions about the authenticity and integrity of the evidence.

Pitfall: Failing to document the tools and techniques used to collect evidence, leading to questions about whether the evidence was properly preserved and whether the proper forensic procedures were followed.

Solution: Always document the tools and methods used to acquire digital evidence. This includes the use of write blockers, imaging software, and any other technology involved. Detailed notes should also include the specific files, systems, or devices that were collected and the rationale for their inclusion.

3. Vague or Ambiguous Findings

In forensic reporting, vague or ambiguous language can lead to confusion and misinterpretation of the findings. Inaccurate or unclear documentation of forensic results can diminish the report's reliability, especially in legal proceedings where precision is crucial.

Pitfall: Using non-specific or overly general terms to describe evidence or analysis results. For example, saying "we found suspicious files" without providing detailed information about the files, their content, or why they are suspicious.

Solution: Be as specific and detailed as possible when describing findings. Instead of using terms like "suspicious," clearly outline why a file is suspicious, including its hash value, file name, metadata, and the context in which it was found. Provide precise details of the evidence, including file paths, dates, and any relevant attributes.

4. Failing to Update Documentation During the Investigation

Digital forensics investigations can be long and complex, and it's easy to overlook the need to consistently update documentation. Without regular updates, key details of the investigation—such as analysis techniques, evidence handling, or key findings—may be missed or forgotten, potentially affecting the credibility of the investigation.

Pitfall: Allowing documentation to fall behind as the investigation progresses. For example, delaying the recording of key observations, analysis steps, or evidence handling.

Solution: Keep real-time, ongoing documentation throughout the investigation. As new evidence is collected, analyzed, or tested, immediately record the relevant details. This will not only ensure that the documentation is accurate but also help to identify and correct any errors or inconsistencies early on.

5. Poor Use of Metadata in Documentation

Metadata plays an essential role in digital forensics, providing critical context about a file, such as its creation date, last modified date, author, and more. However, in many cases, forensic professionals may either overlook metadata or fail to document it properly. Incomplete or inaccurate metadata documentation can result in gaps in understanding the timeline or chain of events.

Pitfall: Failing to capture or document the metadata associated with digital evidence, which can be critical in establishing timelines or identifying sources of data.

Solution: Make metadata an integral part of forensic documentation. Record all relevant metadata associated with digital evidence, especially in cases involving file modifications, timestamps, or authorship. This helps to support findings and can be a key component in establishing evidence authenticity.

6. Inconsistent Formatting and Organization

Forensic documentation must be clear, consistent, and easy to navigate. Inconsistent formatting or a lack of organization can make it difficult for anyone reading the report—especially legal professionals or jurors—to understand the investigation process and results. A poorly structured report may also make it harder to cross-check data or locate relevant information.

Pitfall: Using inconsistent formatting, unclear headings, or disorganized sections in forensic reports. This can lead to confusion and errors, especially when the report is reviewed by multiple people or needs to be submitted to a court.

Solution: Follow a standardized structure for your documentation. Use clear headings, subheadings, and a logical flow of information. Make sure that evidence is referenced in a consistent and organized manner, and consider including a table of contents for longer reports.

7. Overlooking or Misinterpreting Legal Guidelines

While digital forensics often involves complex technical analysis, it is important to remember that the findings must align with legal guidelines. Failing to adhere to the legal framework or misinterpreting the rules of evidence can have serious consequences, particularly in court proceedings.

Pitfall: Documenting evidence in ways that fail to meet legal standards for admissibility. This includes missteps in handling evidence, improper documentation of chain of custody, or using methods that are not legally recognized.

Solution: Be well-versed in the relevant legal frameworks (e.g., Federal Rules of Evidence, GDPR, HIPAA) and ensure that all evidence handling and documentation meet these standards. Consult with legal experts to ensure that the evidence collection, documentation, and presentation comply with all applicable laws.

8. Not Documenting the Investigation's Limitations

Every investigation has limitations, whether due to technological constraints, incomplete data, or external factors. Failing to document these limitations can create the impression that the investigation was more comprehensive or conclusive than it actually was.

Pitfall: Omitting or underreporting limitations in the investigation process, which can lead to unrealistic expectations about the results or the reliability of the evidence.

Solution: Clearly document any limitations encountered during the investigation. This could include missing data, inaccessible devices, or unverified sources. By acknowledging these limitations, you ensure the report's transparency and help set realistic expectations for what the findings can confirm.

9. Lack of Evidence Correlation or Cross-Referencing

In complex investigations, multiple pieces of evidence may need to be cross-referenced or correlated to build a coherent case. Failure to properly correlate different data points or evidence sources can result in missed connections and incomplete conclusions.

Pitfall: Presenting evidence in isolation, without connecting it to other data points or events within the investigation.

Solution: Always cross-reference evidence and establish clear links between different data sources. For example, if a suspicious email leads to the discovery of malware on a device, explain how the two are connected and provide the relevant timestamps, email headers, or logs to corroborate the findings.

10. Rushing to Finalize Reports

Forensic investigations are often time-sensitive, but rushing through documentation can lead to errors or omissions. A rushed report may miss important details, introduce inconsistencies, or fail to fully explain the analysis process.

Pitfall: Writing or finalizing reports too quickly, sacrificing thoroughness and clarity for speed.

Solution: Set aside adequate time for writing and reviewing the report. Take time to proofread for clarity, check for accuracy, and ensure all relevant evidence is included. Where necessary, seek peer review or consult with colleagues to ensure the report is comprehensive and accurate.

Effective documentation is a cornerstone of digital forensics and must be handled with care. By avoiding these common pitfalls, forensic investigators can produce thorough, credible, and legally sound documentation that ensures the integrity of the investigation and the admissibility of evidence in court. Attention to detail, clarity, and adherence to best practices will help avoid critical errors that could compromise an investigation.

13.3 Presenting Evidence in Layman's Terms

In digital forensics, one of the most important challenges forensic investigators face is presenting technical evidence in a way that is accessible and understandable to non-experts. Whether the audience consists of jurors, lawyers, or the general public, the ability to communicate complex technical findings in simple, clear terms is essential. The ultimate goal is for the evidence to be easily understood, compelling, and persuasive, regardless of the technical background of the audience. This section explores the methods and strategies for effectively translating technical jargon into layman's terms, ensuring that the evidence is not only presented clearly but also resonates with a broad audience.

1. Avoiding Jargon and Technical Terminology

Digital forensics relies heavily on specialized language and technical terminology that may be completely unfamiliar to those outside the field. Terms like "hash values," "write blockers," "file system metadata," or "sector-level analysis" can confuse and alienate a lay audience. To ensure that the evidence is understandable, it is crucial to avoid or simplify technical jargon.

Pitfall: Using complex technical terms without providing an explanation, leading to confusion and misunderstanding.

Solution: Simplify the language by explaining technical terms in plain language or substituting jargon with familiar terms. For instance, instead of saying "hash value," explain it as a "unique digital fingerprint of a file." When using unavoidable technical terms, ensure to briefly define them so the audience can follow along without feeling overwhelmed.

2. Using Analogies to Explain Technical Concepts

Analogies are a powerful tool for making complex concepts more relatable. By drawing comparisons between unfamiliar digital forensic processes and everyday situations, you can help the audience grasp abstract ideas with ease. Analogies create a mental bridge between the technical and the familiar, making the evidence more accessible.

Pitfall: Failing to use analogies or explanations that resonate with the audience, which could leave the audience lost in the technical details.

Solution: Choose analogies that align with the audience's everyday experiences. For example, to explain how data is stored and retrieved from a computer, compare it to how books are organized in a library. Each file is like a book, and the file system is the library's catalog, which helps you locate the book (data) you need. This approach helps the audience understand technical processes without getting bogged down in the details.

3. Visual Aids and Diagrams

Visual aids are an invaluable tool in simplifying the presentation of digital evidence. Graphs, charts, screenshots, flow diagrams, and other visual elements can help break down complex data and processes into digestible, easily understandable formats. In some cases, showing rather than telling can make the difference between confusion and clarity.

Pitfall: Overloading the audience with text-heavy slides or reports, which can overwhelm them and obscure the main points.

Solution: Use visuals strategically to complement your verbal explanations. Diagrams that illustrate file structures, network traffic, or timelines can help convey key points more effectively than words alone. When presenting evidence from digital devices, showing screenshots of the evidence (such as a file listing or email log) alongside simple explanations can clarify the context. Ensure that visuals are clean, labeled clearly, and free of unnecessary technical details.

4. Telling a Story with the Evidence

One of the most effective ways to present forensic evidence in a way that's both engaging and easy to follow is by framing it as a story. A compelling narrative helps the audience understand the context of the evidence and the sequence of events that led to the findings. It provides a clear beginning, middle, and end, showing how the investigation unfolded and how the digital evidence ties into the larger story.

Pitfall: Presenting evidence in a disjointed, technical manner without a clear narrative, which can confuse the audience and make the case harder to follow.

Solution: Construct a narrative that places the evidence within the context of the investigation. Start with the issue or incident that prompted the investigation, describe the steps taken to collect and analyze the evidence, and conclude with the findings that led to the final conclusion. For example, if the investigation uncovered a deleted file, explain how the file was traced back to the suspect, reconstructed, and how this piece of evidence fits into the broader context of the case.

5. Relating Evidence to Real-World Impact

It is often helpful to connect the technical evidence to its real-world implications. By demonstrating how the evidence fits into the broader context of the investigation—such as the impact of a cybercrime on victims or businesses—investigators can help the audience understand why the evidence is important.

Pitfall: Presenting evidence without linking it to its broader significance, which can make the findings feel abstract or disconnected from the real-world consequences.

Solution: Frame the evidence in a way that highlights its relevance to the case's outcome or the harm caused by the criminal activity. For example, if a hacker's IP address is traced through forensic analysis, explain how this leads to identifying the suspect and how the victim's system was compromised. By providing context, the evidence becomes more meaningful and relatable to the audience.

6. Simplifying Technical Findings without Oversimplifying

While simplifying the language and concepts for a lay audience is essential, it's important to strike a balance between accessibility and accuracy. Oversimplifying technical findings can undermine the credibility of the investigation or mislead the audience about the significance of the evidence.

Pitfall: Over-simplifying evidence to the point where critical technical details are lost or misrepresented.

Solution: Maintain accuracy while simplifying. For example, when describing how data was recovered from a damaged hard drive, you can explain the process without going into excessive technical detail. A clear explanation might be: "We used specialized software to recover the data that was lost when the drive was damaged," rather than delving into the specifics of file carving or sector-level analysis. The key is to provide enough information to convey the method used and its reliability without overwhelming or confusing the audience.

7. Keeping It Concise and Focused

In many cases, especially when presenting in a courtroom or to stakeholders who may have limited time or attention, it's important to be concise and focus only on the most relevant aspects of the evidence. Avoid overloading your audience with too many details or irrelevant information, as this can detract from the core message.

Pitfall: Providing excessive detail that distracts from the main findings, leading to a loss of focus.

Solution: Prioritize the most important aspects of the evidence that directly support the case or investigation. Be mindful of the time constraints and the audience's attention span. Present evidence in bite-sized chunks that build logically toward your conclusion, while omitting unnecessary technical details that don't contribute to the overall message.

8. Practice and Feedback

Finally, one of the best ways to ensure that evidence is presented in layman's terms is through practice. Rehearse your presentation, and if possible, seek feedback from non-experts to gauge how well your explanation is understood. Practice will help you refine your delivery, identify potential areas of confusion, and ensure that the evidence is both compelling and comprehensible.

Pitfall: Presenting without practice or seeking feedback, which can result in unclear explanations or a lack of confidence during the presentation.

Solution: Run mock presentations for colleagues or non-technical individuals to test your communication. Ask for constructive criticism to identify where explanations might need improvement. This feedback will help refine the presentation and ensure it resonates with the intended audience.

Presenting complex forensic evidence to a non-expert audience is a crucial skill for digital forensic professionals. By avoiding jargon, using analogies, visual aids, and storytelling, forensic experts can make technical evidence accessible and compelling. It's essential to focus on clarity, conciseness, and context while maintaining the integrity and accuracy of the evidence. By mastering the art of presenting evidence in layman's terms, forensic professionals ensure that their findings are not only understood but also impactful in legal proceedings and beyond.

13.4 Expert Witness Testimony: Dos and Don'ts

In the realm of digital forensics, one of the most critical aspects of presenting evidence is expert witness testimony. Whether in a courtroom, deposition, or other legal settings, an expert witness's role is to provide professional, unbiased opinions based on their knowledge and expertise. Their testimony can significantly influence the outcome of a case, making it essential to understand the dos and don'ts of giving expert testimony. This section highlights key best practices and pitfalls to avoid to ensure that your testimony is effective, credible, and persuasive.

1. Do: Be Well-Prepared

Preparation is the foundation of effective expert testimony. Being well-versed in the details of the case, as well as your findings, ensures that you can present your opinions clearly and confidently. This includes thoroughly reviewing all the evidence, understanding the case details, and knowing the key questions you may be asked. Additionally, anticipating cross-examination and preparing for potential challenges to your credibility is essential.

Pitfall: Failing to thoroughly prepare or review evidence, which can lead to confusion, inconsistent testimony, or missed details that could undermine your credibility.

Solution: Prepare meticulously by reviewing all case files, data, and prior testimony. Make sure you understand every detail of your findings and their implications. If you are asked to speak about a specific tool, methodology, or concept, be prepared to explain it in simple terms, providing context that supports your findings.

2. Don't: Overstate Your Qualifications

As an expert witness, it is important to maintain professionalism and credibility. One of the most common mistakes is overstating qualifications or exaggerating expertise. While it is crucial to assert your qualifications to establish credibility, claiming more knowledge or experience than you possess can damage your reputation and undermine your testimony.

Pitfall: Over-inflating your qualifications or knowledge, which can lead to challenges on your credibility and can backfire under cross-examination.

Solution: Be honest and accurate about your qualifications and expertise. If you don't know the answer to a question, it is better to admit uncertainty rather than providing incorrect or speculative answers. Demonstrating honesty about your capabilities fosters trust with the court.

3. Do: Keep Your Testimony Objective and Unbiased

As an expert witness, your role is to provide impartial, factual information. Your testimony should be grounded in objective facts and findings, and you should avoid any appearance of bias or advocacy for either party. Even if you are hired by one side, your duty is to serve the truth, not to "help" the hiring party win the case.

Pitfall: Allowing personal biases or assumptions to color your testimony, which can damage your credibility and the weight of your findings.

Solution: Approach your testimony as an impartial expert. Stick to the facts and let the data speak for itself. If you are asked to provide an opinion, base it strictly on the evidence and your professional knowledge. Ensure that your testimony is consistent and not influenced by external factors.

4. Don't: Use Technical Jargon Without Clarification

While digital forensics relies on complex terminology and technical jargon, it is important to remember that a courtroom is not filled with experts. The judge, jury, and even opposing counsel may not have a technical background, and using overly complex language can confuse the audience and undermine the effectiveness of your testimony.

Pitfall: Using technical jargon without providing explanations or definitions, which can alienate and confuse non-technical listeners.

Solution: When testifying, use clear, concise language that can be easily understood by a non-expert audience. If you must use technical terms, always define them in simple terms. For instance, instead of saying "the hash value matched," explain it as "the unique identifier for the file was the same, which confirms its integrity." This ensures that everyone in the courtroom can follow your testimony and grasp the importance of your findings.

5. Do: Stick to Your Area of Expertise

As an expert witness, it is crucial to only testify on topics that fall within your area of expertise. Venturing into areas outside your specific knowledge can lead to confusion and could jeopardize the effectiveness of your testimony. If asked questions beyond your expertise, it is best to refer to other experts who are qualified in those areas.

Pitfall: Offering opinions outside your area of expertise, which can undermine your credibility and lead to questions about your qualifications.

Solution: Know the boundaries of your expertise and stay within them. If asked a question that is beyond your scope, politely acknowledge that it falls outside your area of expertise and suggest that the court consult a different expert if necessary. Being transparent about your limits demonstrates professionalism and integrity.

6. Don't: Get Defensive or Emotional

In the adversarial setting of a courtroom, expert witnesses may face aggressive questioning or attempts to discredit their testimony. While it's natural to feel defensive when your findings or credibility are challenged, it's important to remain calm, composed, and professional throughout the process. Becoming emotional or defensive can weaken your credibility and give the impression that you are not objective.

Pitfall: Responding emotionally or defensively to challenges, which can harm your credibility and make you appear unprofessional.

Solution: Maintain composure at all times, even if you feel your testimony is being unfairly questioned. Focus on answering questions calmly and professionally. If you are challenged, respond with factual, evidence-based answers and avoid getting personal. A composed demeanor reflects confidence in your findings and reinforces your credibility as an expert.

7. Do: Be Clear About the Limitations of Your Findings

Every forensic investigation comes with certain limitations, whether in the tools used, the data available, or the assumptions made. It's important to be upfront and transparent about these limitations during your testimony. Acknowledging the scope of your work helps manage expectations and shows that your findings are grounded in reality, not speculation.

Pitfall: Overstating the scope or accuracy of your findings, which could lead to challenges during cross-examination and damage your credibility.

Solution: Clearly communicate any limitations or uncertainties in your findings. For instance, if data was lost or if certain files couldn't be recovered, explain this limitation to the court. Acknowledging these aspects provides a more accurate picture and reinforces your professionalism.

8. Don't: Be Unprepared for Cross-Examination

Cross-examination is a pivotal moment in legal proceedings, where the opposing counsel seeks to challenge your testimony. Being unprepared for this phase can lead to uncomfortable situations and result in damaging inconsistencies or errors.

Pitfall: Being caught off guard during cross-examination, which can undermine your credibility.

Solution: Anticipate potential challenges to your testimony and be prepared with clear, concise answers. If you don't know the answer to a question, it's acceptable to say so, but ensure your response is calm and confident. Being well-prepared for cross-examination helps demonstrate your expertise and professionalism.

9. Do: Make Your Testimony Accessible and Understandable

The ultimate goal of expert testimony is to provide the court with clear, understandable, and actionable information. While you must maintain accuracy, you should always aim to present your findings in a way that is not overly technical or abstract. Your testimony should help the court understand the significance of the evidence and how it impacts the case.

Pitfall: Making your testimony too technical, which may lead to confusion and reduce its impact.

Solution: Present your findings in a way that resonates with both legal professionals and non-experts. Break down complex processes, use analogies or examples, and keep your explanations focused on the key issues relevant to the case.

Expert witness testimony is a critical aspect of digital forensic investigations. By adhering to best practices, such as staying objective, being prepared, and presenting complex information in an understandable way, forensic experts can significantly influence the outcome of a case. Equally important is avoiding the pitfalls of overstating qualifications, using excessive jargon, or becoming defensive. By following these dos and don'ts, digital forensic experts can ensure that their testimony is not only credible but also compelling and persuasive.

13.5 Visualizing Evidence with Charts and Graphs

In the world of digital forensics, the ability to communicate complex findings clearly and effectively is essential, especially when presenting evidence in a legal setting. One of the most powerful tools for enhancing the clarity of your testimony is the use of visual aids such as charts and graphs. These visual tools can transform raw data into easily understandable formats, helping the court to quickly grasp the significance of the evidence. This section delves into the importance of visualizing digital forensic evidence, best practices for creating effective visual aids, and common pitfalls to avoid when using charts and graphs in your forensic reports and testimony.

1. The Power of Visual Evidence

Charts, graphs, and other visual aids are invaluable tools for simplifying complex data. In a digital forensic investigation, evidence can often be vast and intricate, such as network traffic logs, file system structures, or time-based data sequences. When left as raw data, this information may overwhelm a judge or jury. By converting it into visual formats, you make the information more accessible, making it easier for non-experts to understand the significance of your findings.

Visuals are particularly effective at highlighting trends, relationships, and anomalies within the data. For example, a graph showing spikes in network traffic at a particular time can help establish a timeline of events during an incident. Similarly, pie charts or bar graphs can be used to depict the distribution of data across devices, applications, or time periods, helping to clarify the investigation's key points.

Pitfall: Overloading your audience with too many visuals, or making visuals that are overly complex, which can confuse rather than clarify.

Solution: Use visuals strategically, focusing on key data points that support your central findings. Aim for simplicity and clarity, ensuring that each visual has a clear purpose and adds value to your argument.

2. Types of Visual Aids in Digital Forensics

Several types of charts and graphs can be used to represent digital evidence effectively. Below are some of the most commonly used visuals in digital forensic presentations:

Timeline Charts: These are particularly useful in digital forensics as they can display events in chronological order. For example, a timeline can illustrate the sequence of actions taken on a device, including file modifications, logins, and network access points. This is crucial for demonstrating a chain of events or tracking activity related to cybercrimes.

Pie Charts: Pie charts are often used to represent the distribution of data across different categories. In forensics, they can show, for example, the proportion of data stored on various devices, or the breakdown of types of files (documents, images, videos, etc.) found during an investigation.

Bar Graphs: Bar graphs can help illustrate comparisons between different data points or groups. A bar graph might be used to show the number of data access attempts across different users or to compare the amount of data retrieved from multiple devices.

Network Diagrams: For network forensics, network diagrams are extremely effective in visualizing the flow of data between devices. These diagrams can demonstrate how a breach occurred or how data was exfiltrated from a compromised system.

Heat Maps: Heat maps are often used to represent the intensity of data points over a geographic area or within a specific timeframe. For instance, in mobile forensics, heat maps can visually represent location data, showing the frequency of visits to certain places over time.

Pitfall: Using visuals that are too abstract or that lack context, making it hard for the audience to understand the connection between the data and the conclusions.

Solution: Ensure that each visual aid is well-labeled, with clear captions, titles, and legends. Provide enough context for the audience to understand what the visual represents and how it supports your findings.

3. Best Practices for Effective Visualization

To ensure that your visuals are impactful and serve their intended purpose, it's essential to follow best practices when creating and presenting them:

Simplify Complex Data: Rather than presenting all the raw data, focus on key highlights that align with your investigative findings. A clear, simple graph that illustrates a key point is much more effective than a complicated table full of unnecessary details.

Consistency in Design: Use consistent color schemes, fonts, and formatting across all visuals. This enhances readability and ensures that your audience can easily follow the presentation without being distracted by inconsistent designs.

Provide Context: Don't just present visuals without explanation. Ensure that each chart or graph is accompanied by a narrative that explains what the visual represents, how it was created, and why it's relevant to the case.

Highlight Key Findings: Use annotations, arrows, or text to draw attention to the most important aspects of the visual. For example, if a network diagram is used, highlight the compromised node or unauthorized data transmission with a different color or size to make it stand out.

Ensure Accuracy: Ensure that all the data presented in charts and graphs is accurate and correctly represents the findings. Any inconsistencies between your testimony and the visuals can undermine your credibility.

Pitfall: Overcomplicating visuals with too many data points or excessive annotations, which can detract from the central message.

Solution: Prioritize clarity and focus on presenting only the most relevant data. Avoid excessive detail that doesn't contribute to your key argument. Keep annotations to a minimum to ensure the visual remains digestible.

4. When to Use Visual Aids

Knowing when to use visuals is just as important as creating them. The goal is to use visuals when they will help clarify complex evidence, highlight trends, or make your testimony more persuasive. However, overuse of charts and graphs can lead to confusion or make your presentation seem cluttered.

Use visuals in the following scenarios:

To Present Complex Data: When you're dealing with large volumes of data (e.g., network logs, file system structures), visuals can be incredibly helpful in summarizing the information in a digestible form.

To Show Trends or Patterns: Visuals such as timelines or line graphs are particularly effective when demonstrating a sequence of events or identifying patterns in the data that would otherwise be difficult to explain with words alone.

To Emphasize Key Points: Visual aids should support the central points of your testimony, such as demonstrating a link between the suspect and the crime scene through digital evidence.

Pitfall: Using visuals for every data point, which can overwhelm the audience and distract from the critical evidence.

Solution: Use visuals sparingly and only when they can add value. Focus on the critical pieces of evidence that will make a significant impact on the case.

5. Avoiding Pitfalls in Visualizations

There are several common pitfalls to avoid when using charts and graphs in your forensic presentations:

Cluttered Visuals: Avoid overcrowding visuals with too much information. If a graph or chart has too many data points or annotations, it can become hard to interpret and may even confuse the audience.

Misleading Graphs: Ensure that your graphs accurately represent the data. Avoid manipulating the scale or design to exaggerate or understate certain findings, as this can damage your credibility.

Lack of Labeling: Charts and graphs should always be clearly labeled with titles, axes, and legends. A visual without clear labels can confuse the audience and make it difficult to understand the significance of the data.

Solution: Keep your visuals clear, simple, and properly labeled. Make sure that they highlight the most important aspects of the case and that they are easy to interpret.

Visualizing evidence with charts and graphs is an essential skill for any digital forensic investigator. By converting complex data into easy-to-understand formats, you can enhance the effectiveness of your testimony and ensure that your findings resonate with the court. However, to be truly effective, it is essential to follow best practices for creating clear, relevant, and accurate visuals. By using visuals strategically, you can elevate your case and help the court understand the critical evidence that supports your findings.

14. Future Trends in Digital Forensics

The field of digital forensics is constantly evolving as new technologies emerge and cyber threats become more sophisticated. In this chapter, you'll explore the future of digital forensics, including the impact of artificial intelligence and machine learning on evidence analysis, automation in investigative processes, and the growing significance of IoT devices and smart technologies. You'll also learn about the rise of blockchain for securing evidence integrity and how it may revolutionize digital investigations. The chapter concludes with a look at the ethical and legal challenges that lie ahead, preparing you for the rapidly changing landscape of digital forensics and the critical role it will continue to play in the fight for justice.

14.1 AI and Machine Learning in Forensic Analysis

The application of Artificial Intelligence (AI) and Machine Learning (ML) in digital forensics represents a transformative shift in the way investigators analyze and interpret vast amounts of data. These technologies, which have gained significant traction in recent years, offer forensic professionals powerful tools to process, identify patterns, and predict behaviors in ways that were previously unimaginable. AI and ML are beginning to redefine traditional methods of digital forensics, enhancing efficiency, accuracy, and the scope of analysis.

1. The Role of AI in Digital Forensics

Artificial Intelligence, which involves programming systems to think and make decisions like a human, plays a significant role in forensic investigations by automating tasks that would typically take investigators hours or even days. AI can analyze large volumes of data quickly, identifying patterns, anomalies, and correlations that may be difficult for human investigators to detect. By incorporating AI, forensic experts can examine data at a deeper level, uncovering hidden evidence, making quicker conclusions, and improving investigative accuracy.

AI systems are particularly adept at tasks like natural language processing (NLP), image recognition, and anomaly detection. For example, AI can be used to sift through large datasets, including emails, text messages, and social media posts, to detect specific keywords or patterns related to an investigation. In image forensics, AI can automatically identify and analyze suspicious or illicit images, such as identifying fake documents, detecting altered images, or flagging potentially harmful content.

Pitfall: Over-reliance on AI without proper oversight can lead to misinterpretation of results or failure to detect nuanced evidence. AI systems require thorough validation and expert input.

Solution: Use AI as a supplementary tool, not as a replacement for human judgment. Ensure that all AI-generated findings are verified and corroborated by traditional investigative methods.

2. Machine Learning in Forensic Investigations

Machine Learning, a subset of AI, involves systems that learn from data and improve their predictions or analysis over time without being explicitly programmed. In digital forensics, ML algorithms are used to detect patterns, recognize anomalies, and make predictions based on historical data, which is essential for identifying potential threats or uncovering evidence that might otherwise go unnoticed.

Machine learning excels in tasks like classifying and categorizing large datasets, detecting unusual patterns of behavior, and identifying suspicious or malicious activity. For instance, ML can be used to detect malware, track unusual network traffic, or uncover hidden connections between seemingly unrelated data points. The more data ML systems are exposed to, the better they become at identifying patterns, which makes them ideal for investigating ongoing cybercrimes or handling large-scale data analysis.

- **Malware Detection**: ML models can analyze files, emails, and network traffic to detect new or unknown types of malware, even without relying on traditional signature-based methods.
- **Anomaly Detection**: ML systems are great for flagging unusual behavior within a network or on devices. For instance, if a user's account suddenly starts downloading unusually large files or accessing data they typically don't, an ML system can highlight this for further investigation.
- **Predictive Analysis**: ML algorithms can be used to predict criminal behavior or assess risks, such as identifying patterns of hacking activity or predicting the potential spread of a cyberattack based on historical data.

Pitfall: Training machine learning models requires high-quality, annotated data. Poor or biased training data can result in inaccurate or incomplete predictions.

Solution: Use diverse and clean datasets to train models and ensure ongoing evaluation and refinement of the ML algorithms. Cross-validate predictions with expert human analysis to avoid biases.

3. Benefits of AI and ML in Digital Forensics

The integration of AI and machine learning in digital forensics offers several significant advantages:

Increased Efficiency: AI and ML can dramatically speed up the analysis of large volumes of digital evidence. For instance, AI-powered tools can quickly scan terabytes of data for specific information, helping investigators focus on relevant evidence faster than traditional manual methods.

Advanced Data Processing: AI and ML excel at analyzing complex, unstructured data, such as multimedia files, emails, and social media content. They can uncover patterns, relationships, or hidden evidence that would be difficult for a human investigator to spot within a short timeframe.

Enhanced Accuracy: By leveraging machine learning algorithms, investigators can reduce human error and increase the reliability of forensic findings. AI tools can continuously learn from new data, improving their ability to identify digital evidence over time.

Scalability: AI systems can scale to handle large datasets, making them ideal for handling cases involving massive amounts of data, such as large-scale cyberattacks, financial fraud investigations, or cloud-based forensics. This scalability enables investigators to keep up with increasingly sophisticated cybercrimes.

Pitfall: An over-dependence on AI and ML models can lead to the neglect of critical human oversight, especially in complex cases where context and subjective judgment are necessary.

Solution: Combine AI and ML tools with human expertise. Forensic experts should interpret the results generated by AI and machine learning systems to ensure proper conclusions are drawn from the analysis.

4. Challenges of Implementing AI and ML in Digital Forensics

While the benefits of AI and machine learning in digital forensics are clear, there are several challenges that need to be addressed:

Data Privacy Concerns: The application of AI and ML in digital forensics often requires access to large amounts of data, including private or sensitive information. Ensuring that these systems comply with data protection regulations, such as GDPR and HIPAA, is critical to maintaining privacy and legal compliance.

Bias and Ethics: Machine learning algorithms can inherit biases from the data they are trained on, leading to skewed results or misidentification. For instance, a biased AI system might incorrectly flag certain behaviors or users as suspicious based on historical patterns that are not universally applicable.

Lack of Transparency: AI and ML systems are often seen as "black boxes" due to their complex algorithms and decision-making processes. This lack of transparency can pose challenges in forensic investigations, where it's crucial to understand how evidence was processed and why certain conclusions were drawn.

Pitfall: Not fully understanding the underlying AI or ML model could lead to improper use or misinterpretation of results in legal proceedings.

Solution: Invest in explainable AI (XAI) technologies, which aim to make AI models more transparent and understandable. Forensics experts should be trained to explain how AI and ML models work, ensuring that their findings are credible and interpretable in court.

5. The Future of AI and ML in Forensic Analysis

The role of AI and machine learning in digital forensics is still evolving, and we can expect to see even more advanced applications in the future. As AI systems become more sophisticated, they will be capable of automating even more aspects of forensic analysis, allowing investigators to focus on higher-level decision-making and strategy. Some potential future trends include:

Real-Time Forensics: AI systems could evolve to perform real-time forensics, analyzing data streams and network traffic as they occur, allowing investigators to respond to cybercrimes immediately.

Integration of AI and Blockchain: AI may be used to analyze blockchain data and transactions, providing deeper insights into the flow of illicit cryptocurrency or identifying patterns within decentralized networks.

Self-Learning AI: Future AI systems will likely become more autonomous, self-learning from each investigation to continually improve their detection capabilities. This will lead to more accurate and reliable findings over time.

In conclusion, AI and machine learning are poised to revolutionize the field of digital forensics by enhancing the speed, efficiency, and accuracy of investigations. By automating routine tasks, detecting complex patterns, and predicting future behaviors, these technologies can help forensic professionals stay ahead of increasingly sophisticated cyber threats. However, as with any technological advancement, it is crucial to ensure that AI and machine learning tools are used responsibly, with proper oversight, to ensure that they remain accurate, ethical, and reliable.

14.2 The Role of Blockchain in Evidence Integrity

Blockchain technology, often associated with cryptocurrencies like Bitcoin, is increasingly being explored for its potential to enhance the integrity of digital evidence. Blockchain provides a decentralized and immutable ledger system, making it an attractive solution for digital forensics, where maintaining the chain of custody and ensuring the authenticity of evidence is critical. In digital forensics, evidence integrity refers to ensuring that the evidence has not been altered, tampered with, or corrupted during its collection, preservation, and analysis. Blockchain offers a unique way to address these challenges by leveraging its core features: decentralization, immutability, and transparency.

1. Understanding Blockchain and Its Core Features

Blockchain is essentially a distributed digital ledger where data is recorded in "blocks" and linked together in a chronological order to form a chain. Each block contains a cryptographic hash of the previous block, timestamped data, and a list of transactions or records. These blocks are stored across a decentralized network of computers, ensuring that no single entity has control over the data.

The key features that make blockchain relevant for evidence integrity are:

Decentralization: Unlike traditional centralized systems, blockchain operates on a network of distributed nodes. This means there is no central point of failure, and no single party can manipulate the system, making the data more secure and resistant to tampering.

Immutability: Once data is added to a blockchain, it cannot be altered or deleted without the consensus of the network participants. This creates an unchangeable record of events that can serve as a trustworthy source for proving the integrity of digital evidence.

Transparency: Blockchain provides transparency by making the data visible to all participants in the network. This can be particularly useful in maintaining the chain of custody for digital evidence, as all transactions (or data modifications) are recorded in a way that can be verified by authorized parties.

2. Blockchain for Chain of Custody in Digital Forensics

The chain of custody is one of the most critical aspects of handling digital evidence. It refers to the documentation and handling of evidence from the moment it is collected until it is presented in court. The goal is to demonstrate that the evidence has not been altered or tampered with during its handling, ensuring its admissibility in legal proceedings.

Blockchain can be leveraged to improve the chain of custody by:

Recording Evidence Collection: Every time evidence is collected, its information (e.g., the time, location, and person who collected it) can be recorded on a blockchain. This provides a timestamped, verifiable record that proves the evidence's authenticity from the moment it was first encountered.

Tracking Movement of Evidence: As evidence moves through various stages of investigation and analysis, each transfer or change in its possession can be logged on the blockchain. For example, when evidence is handed from one investigator to another, the event can be recorded in the blockchain with the identity of the person receiving the evidence and the time of the transfer.

Preventing Tampering: Blockchain's immutability feature ensures that once an evidence record is added, it cannot be altered or deleted without leaving a trace. If anyone attempts to tamper with evidence or modify the chain of custody, it would be immediately detectable.

This immutable and transparent record-keeping system helps create a clear, auditable history of the evidence, reducing the risks associated with human error or malicious tampering.

Example: A digital forensic investigator collecting a hard drive could record key information such as the device's serial number, the date and time of collection, and the investigator's name on the blockchain. Any subsequent transfer of that device to another investigator or lab would also be recorded in real-time. The blockchain would then provide an immutable, tamper-evident history of the evidence's handling.

3. Blockchain for Ensuring the Authenticity of Digital Evidence

In digital forensics, one of the key concerns is ensuring that the evidence presented in court is authentic and has not been tampered with. Blockchain can provide a solution to this problem by offering a secure and verifiable record of the evidence's existence and contents.

Hashing Evidence: Blockchain can be used to record the cryptographic hash of digital evidence, such as files, emails, or other digital artifacts. A hash is a unique identifier for a file that changes if the file is modified. By storing the hash of a file on the blockchain, investigators can later verify that the file has not been altered by comparing the hash value stored in the blockchain with the hash value of the file at the time of presentation.

Time-Stamping Evidence: Blockchain's timestamping feature allows digital evidence to be securely time-stamped when it is first collected, ensuring that its existence is recorded at a specific point in time. This helps prevent any disputes regarding when the evidence was obtained or whether it was fabricated or altered after the fact.

Ensuring Data Integrity: By storing evidence or its cryptographic hash in a decentralized blockchain, digital forensics teams can protect the evidence from unauthorized access, tampering, or alteration. Any changes made to the evidence will be detected because of the nature of blockchain, where any modification to data in a block will change its cryptographic hash, which would not match the original stored hash.

Example: If investigators collect a video file from a suspect's device, they can create a hash of the video file and store this hash on a blockchain along with a timestamp. Later, when the file is presented in court, the same hash can be generated from the file, and the integrity can be verified by comparing the hashes. If the hashes match, the file can be confidently considered authentic.

4. Blockchain and Transparency in Forensic Investigations

Blockchain's transparency provides a crucial advantage in forensic investigations, particularly when it comes to auditing evidence and ensuring accountability.

Auditability: All actions and transfers involving digital evidence can be publicly or privately audited, depending on the blockchain configuration. This makes it easier to track the handling and manipulation of evidence over time, ensuring that all parties involved are accountable for their actions.

Access Control and Permissions: Blockchain can also be used to manage permissions and access control for sensitive evidence. For example, only authorized individuals or organizations can access certain data on the blockchain, and any access or modification attempts are logged and visible to all network participants.

Decentralized Verification: Since blockchain is decentralized, no single entity or person controls the evidence, and multiple parties can verify the authenticity of the evidence. This provides a higher level of trust and reduces the risk of malicious activities from any single party involved in the investigation.

5. Potential Use Cases for Blockchain in Digital Forensics

Blockchain's potential for improving evidence integrity extends beyond just tracking chain of custody and hashing evidence. Some other innovative use cases include:

Smart Contracts for Evidence Handling: Smart contracts are self-executing contracts where the terms are written directly into lines of code. These could be used to automate the transfer of digital evidence, ensuring that certain conditions (such as approval by authorized individuals) must be met before evidence is handed over or accessed.

Decentralized Evidence Repositories: Blockchain could facilitate the creation of decentralized evidence repositories, where evidence can be securely stored and accessed across jurisdictions, enabling collaboration among different agencies while maintaining data integrity.

Forensic Provenance Tracking: Blockchain can enable the tracking of the provenance (or origin) of digital evidence, ensuring that investigators have a full record of how evidence was obtained and its integrity verified at every stage.

Blockchain technology holds significant promise for ensuring the integrity of digital evidence, improving the chain of custody, and guaranteeing the authenticity of data throughout the investigative process. Its core features—decentralization, immutability, and transparency—offer robust solutions to challenges traditionally faced in digital forensics, such as tampering, unauthorized access, and data manipulation. While blockchain adoption in forensic practices is still emerging, its potential to revolutionize digital evidence handling is clear. By incorporating blockchain into forensic investigations, professionals can create a more secure, transparent, and trustworthy framework for dealing with digital evidence in both legal and investigative contexts.

14.3 Forensics for IoT and Smart Devices

The rapid growth of the Internet of Things (IoT) and the proliferation of smart devices have introduced new complexities to digital forensics. From smart homes and wearables to connected vehicles and medical devices, these technologies are creating a massive volume of data that can be crucial for investigative purposes. As these devices collect, store, and transmit sensitive information, they also present unique challenges for forensic investigators seeking to extract, preserve, and analyze digital evidence.

In this chapter, we explore the evolving field of IoT forensics, the types of evidence that can be obtained from these devices, the tools and techniques required for their analysis, and the associated challenges.

1. Understanding IoT and Smart Devices in Forensics

IoT devices are objects that are embedded with sensors, software, and other technologies that enable them to collect, exchange, and process data. These devices can range from simple objects like smart thermostats and fitness trackers to more complex systems like smart cars, home security systems, and industrial machines. Smart devices, on the other hand, typically refer to interconnected objects such as smartphones, smartwatches, and home assistants that often serve as interfaces for interacting with the broader IoT ecosystem.

The data generated by IoT and smart devices often includes timestamps, location data, sensor readings, user interactions, and even audio and video recordings. These can serve as valuable evidence in a range of investigations, including criminal cases, civil disputes, fraud, and even national security matters. However, the diversity of devices and data types poses a number of challenges for investigators in terms of collecting, analyzing, and ensuring the integrity of the evidence.

2. Types of Evidence in IoT and Smart Devices

The digital evidence collected from IoT and smart devices can be broadly categorized into the following types:

Sensor Data: Many IoT devices contain sensors that collect data about the physical world, such as temperature, humidity, motion, or pressure. For example, a smart thermostat can provide data about when someone was home or when the temperature was adjusted. Similarly, motion sensors in a security camera could be used to confirm the presence of an individual at a particular time and place.

Location Data: Many IoT and smart devices, especially wearables and smartphones, generate GPS data. This data can be used to trace an individual's movements and establish their whereabouts during a particular event or time frame. For instance, a GPS-enabled fitness tracker may show the exact route taken by a suspect during a crime.

Communications Logs: Smart devices often log user interactions, such as text messages, phone calls, and even voice commands. In the case of voice assistants (like Amazon's Alexa or Google Home), these logs can include records of conversations, commands issued by the user, and interactions with other smart devices.

Multimedia Evidence: Many IoT devices, such as smart cameras or doorbells (e.g., Ring), capture video and audio recordings. This data can be crucial in criminal investigations, providing a visual record of events, potential suspects, and even conversations.

Application and Usage Data: Data from apps and services running on smart devices can provide a deeper understanding of a user's behaviors, preferences, and interactions. This could include activity logs, app history, transaction data, and other forms of metadata.

Device Configuration and Firmware Data: Investigators can also extract data related to the configuration of the device itself, such as firmware versions, user settings, and device-specific settings that can provide additional context or clues about the device's usage and the timeline of events.

3. Challenges in IoT and Smart Device Forensics

While IoT and smart devices offer rich sources of evidence, they also introduce several challenges that forensic investigators must overcome:

Data Volume: The sheer volume of data generated by IoT devices can be overwhelming. With millions of devices constantly collecting and transmitting data, identifying and isolating the relevant evidence becomes a daunting task. Investigators must be able to filter through this massive amount of data and focus on the critical pieces that will aid their investigation.

Data Fragmentation: IoT devices often store data in a decentralized or fragmented manner, sometimes across multiple platforms or devices. For example, data from a smart home may be distributed across several devices (e.g., security cameras, thermostats, lighting systems) and cloud-based storage services. This fragmentation can make it challenging to piece together a complete picture of events.

Proprietary Formats and Encryption: Many IoT devices use proprietary data formats or encrypt their data, making it difficult for investigators to access and interpret the information. Without the proper decryption keys or tools, extracting useful evidence from these devices can be nearly impossible. Forensic professionals must stay updated on the latest methods and tools for breaking through encryption or proprietary formats.

Lack of Standardization: Unlike traditional computing systems, IoT devices often lack uniformity in terms of operating systems, software, and communication protocols. This lack of standardization means that forensic investigators may have to deal with a variety of device-specific issues, making each investigation unique and requiring specialized knowledge and tools.

Legal and Privacy Issues: As IoT devices are deeply integrated into people's personal lives, there are significant privacy concerns. Accessing private data from these devices, especially without proper authorization or legal warrants, can lead to legal challenges. Investigators must navigate complex privacy laws and ensure that their activities comply with relevant regulations, such as the General Data Protection Regulation (GDPR) or the Health Insurance Portability and Accountability Act (HIPAA).

4. Tools and Techniques for IoT Forensics

Several tools and techniques have emerged to address the challenges posed by IoT and smart devices. These tools help investigators extract, analyze, and preserve data from a wide variety of devices:

Forensic Imaging Tools: Tools like FTK Imager, X1 Social Discovery, and OSForensics can be used to create forensic images of IoT devices and extract data in a forensically sound manner. These tools allow investigators to create exact copies of the data, ensuring that no changes are made to the original evidence.

Data Recovery Software: In cases where IoT devices are damaged, investigators can use specialized data recovery tools to recover lost or deleted files. For example, tools like Recuva or DiskDigger can be used to recover deleted data from flash memory or hard drives used in IoT devices.

Mobile Forensic Tools: Many IoT devices, such as smartphones, wearables, and tablets, are analyzed using mobile forensic tools like Cellebrite, Magnet AXIOM, and Oxygen Forensics. These tools allow investigators to extract data from mobile devices, including call logs, messages, application data, and geolocation information.

Cloud Forensics Tools: Since many IoT devices rely on cloud storage, forensic investigators often need to extract data from cloud services. Tools like CloudForensics or X1 Cloud can assist in identifying, collecting, and preserving evidence from cloud-based platforms that store IoT data.

Network Analysis Tools: IoT devices typically communicate over local networks or the internet. Tools like Wireshark, TCPDump, and NetFlow can capture and analyze network traffic, helping investigators detect unusual activity, unauthorized access, or potential evidence of data exfiltration.

Dedicated IoT Forensics Tools: Some companies have developed specialized tools for IoT forensics, such as the IoT Inspector or FTK Imager, which are designed to handle specific IoT data formats and protocols.

5. Future of IoT and Smart Device Forensics

As IoT and smart devices continue to evolve, so too will the field of forensics. Future advancements may include:

Advanced Artificial Intelligence (AI) and Machine Learning: AI and machine learning algorithms can help forensic investigators automate the analysis of large data sets generated by IoT devices, identifying patterns and anomalies that would otherwise be difficult to detect manually.

Standardization of IoT Data Formats: As IoT forensics becomes more established, there may be a push toward standardizing data formats and protocols across devices. This would make it easier for forensic investigators to work with different types of devices and collect evidence more efficiently.

Blockchain for IoT Evidence Integrity: Blockchain technology could be used to ensure the integrity of data collected from IoT devices, providing a secure, immutable record of evidence from its collection through to its presentation in court.

The field of IoT and smart device forensics is growing rapidly in response to the increasing complexity and interconnectivity of the digital world. As more devices become connected, they offer a wealth of potential evidence for investigators, but also introduce significant challenges related to data volume, fragmentation, and security. By utilizing the right tools and techniques, digital forensics professionals can overcome these challenges and ensure the integrity of IoT data, providing crucial evidence in both criminal and civil investigations. As technology advances, so too must forensic practices, ensuring that investigators remain equipped to handle the evolving digital landscape of IoT devices.

14.4 Automation in Digital Investigations

As the field of digital forensics evolves and the volume of data to be analyzed continues to grow, the need for faster, more efficient methods of conducting investigations becomes increasingly important. Automation in digital investigations is a transformative approach that leverages cutting-edge technologies to streamline processes, enhance efficiency, and improve the accuracy of evidence collection and analysis. By automating repetitive tasks and utilizing machine learning, artificial intelligence (AI), and other advanced tools, forensic investigators can save time, reduce human error, and focus on the more complex aspects of their cases.

In this chapter, we explore the role of automation in digital forensics, the tools and technologies driving this change, its advantages and limitations, and the future of automation in forensic investigations.

1. The Role of Automation in Digital Forensics

Automation plays a crucial role in digital forensics by addressing several key challenges faced by investigators:

Handling Large Volumes of Data: Modern digital investigations often involve vast amounts of data, including gigabytes or even terabytes of files, communications, and system logs. Manually sifting through this data can be time-consuming and prone to human error. Automation allows for the processing of large data sets at scale, helping investigators quickly identify and isolate relevant evidence.

Repetitive Tasks: Many forensic tasks are routine and repetitive, such as file hashing, data duplication, or examining multiple files for specific keywords. These tasks can be automated using scripts, algorithms, or specialized software, freeing up investigators to focus on more strategic and complex aspects of the investigation.

Consistency and Accuracy: Automation reduces the possibility of human error, which can be critical in ensuring the integrity and accuracy of forensic findings. Automated systems can consistently apply established protocols, perform redundant checks, and verify the chain of custody to ensure that evidence is handled correctly and remains admissible in court.

2. Tools and Technologies Enabling Automation

Several tools and technologies are at the forefront of driving automation in digital forensics. These tools integrate automation into key stages of the forensic process, from data acquisition to analysis and reporting:

Automated Forensic Tools: Forensic software tools like FTK Imager, Autopsy, and EnCase offer features that automate various steps in the investigation. These tools can automatically create disk images, recover deleted files, and even detect specific types of evidence, such as child exploitation material or malware. They streamline the analysis process by automating searches for specific keywords, file types, or metadata.

Machine Learning and AI: Machine learning (ML) and AI are increasingly being used in digital forensics to improve data analysis and evidence identification. For example, AI-powered tools can be trained to identify patterns and anomalies in data, such as unusual network traffic or fraudulent activity in financial records. These systems can also assist in classifying and tagging data, speeding up the process of reviewing large data sets and helping investigators prioritize critical evidence.

Automated Log Analysis: Log files are a crucial source of evidence in many digital investigations, yet manually analyzing thousands or millions of logs can be overwhelming. Automation tools, such as Splunk or ELK Stack (Elasticsearch, Logstash, Kibana), use predefined rules and AI-driven algorithms to analyze logs for suspicious activities, enabling investigators to detect anomalies or security breaches in real-time.

Data Correlation and Visualization: Automation tools can also be used to correlate and visualize data from different sources. For instance, a forensic investigator may need to link data from various devices, network traffic, and cloud-based logs. Automation tools, such as CaseNotes or Magnet AXIOM, use sophisticated algorithms to correlate data and present it in easily interpretable visual formats like timelines, graphs, or charts. This can help investigators quickly identify patterns and connections between different pieces of evidence.

Automated Reporting: The process of generating forensic reports can be a time-consuming task, often requiring investigators to manually document every step of the process, the methods used, and the evidence discovered. Automated reporting tools can generate comprehensive forensic reports based on predefined templates, pulling data directly from forensic investigations. These reports are structured, clear, and consistent, making it easier for legal teams to interpret and present evidence in court.

3. Advantages of Automation in Digital Investigations

The implementation of automation in digital forensics provides several key benefits:

Efficiency and Speed: Automation significantly reduces the time required for investigators to process and analyze digital evidence. This enables quicker response times in both criminal and corporate investigations, which can be crucial in preventing further damage, identifying suspects, or recovering stolen data.

Cost Reduction: By automating routine tasks, forensic teams can reduce the need for manual labor and optimize their resource allocation. This can lead to significant cost savings, especially in large-scale investigations that involve a high volume of data.

Improved Data Accuracy: Automated tools minimize human error, which can be especially critical when handling complex or large amounts of data. Automated systems can ensure consistent adherence to forensic protocols, maintaining the integrity of the evidence and reducing the risk of errors that could affect the outcome of an investigation.

Increased Coverage and Scope: Automation allows investigators to cover more ground in less time. By automating data analysis, investigators can focus on reviewing and interpreting critical evidence rather than getting bogged down with repetitive tasks. This leads to more thorough investigations, increasing the chances of finding important evidence that might otherwise be overlooked.

Standardization and Consistency: Automated systems follow predefined rules and protocols, ensuring that evidence collection and analysis are standardized across investigations. This increases the credibility and reproducibility of forensic processes, making it easier for investigators to present findings in court.

4. Limitations and Challenges of Automation

While automation provides several benefits, it also presents challenges and limitations that must be addressed:

Complexity in Handling Novel Cases: Automated systems may struggle with unique or novel cases that require human expertise and intuition. For example, AI systems may have difficulty analyzing encrypted data, dealing with non-standard file formats, or interpreting complex evidence in highly sophisticated attacks. In these cases, human intervention and expert analysis remain indispensable.

False Positives and Negatives: Automated systems are not perfect and may produce false positives or negatives. For example, an automated system may flag a legitimate file as suspicious, wasting time for investigators, or fail to identify a significant piece of evidence due to a lack of understanding of the specific context. It is crucial to ensure that automated tools are constantly updated and fine-tuned to minimize these errors.

Over-reliance on Technology: Over-reliance on automated tools can lead to a lack of critical thinking or expertise in the investigative process. While automation can streamline tasks, investigators must maintain their understanding of forensic principles and practices to avoid missing important insights that automated tools might overlook.

Security and Privacy Concerns: Automation systems, particularly those that leverage cloud services or AI, could be vulnerable to cyberattacks, data breaches, or unauthorized access. It's essential for investigators to ensure that automation tools are secured and comply with data privacy regulations.

5. The Future of Automation in Digital Investigations

As technology continues to evolve, so too will the role of automation in digital forensics. Some potential developments include:

Advancements in AI and Machine Learning: Future developments in AI and machine learning will likely result in more sophisticated forensic tools that can better analyze large datasets, detect anomalies in real-time, and predict patterns of criminal behavior. These tools will also become more adaptive, learning from previous cases to improve their accuracy and effectiveness.

Integration of Automation with Blockchain: Blockchain technology can be used to automate evidence tracking and chain of custody, providing tamper-proof records of evidence from its collection to its presentation in court. The combination of automation and blockchain could revolutionize how digital evidence is handled and authenticated.

Automated Incident Response: With cyberattacks becoming increasingly sophisticated, the future of automation in digital forensics may include fully automated incident response systems. These systems could identify, contain, and remediate cybersecurity incidents in real-time, providing immediate response capabilities to prevent further damage.

Expanded Use of Robotics: In the future, robotic systems could be used to physically interact with devices, collect data, and analyze evidence in environments where human access is difficult or dangerous, such as in cases involving hazardous materials or crime scenes with complex setups.

Automation is fundamentally transforming digital forensics, offering speed, efficiency, and consistency in an increasingly data-driven world. While automation cannot replace the need for human expertise, it can significantly enhance the investigative process, enabling forensic professionals to manage the growing complexity and volume of digital evidence. As technology continues to advance, automation will play an even more critical role in the success of digital forensic investigations, ensuring that justice is served faster and more effectively.

14.5 The Future of Privacy and Forensic Ethics

As the digital landscape continues to evolve, privacy and ethics are becoming increasingly critical in the field of digital forensics. Investigators face the challenge of balancing the need to uncover crucial evidence with the responsibility to protect individuals' privacy rights and maintain ethical standards. The growing complexity of digital data, coupled with advancements in technology such as cloud computing, the Internet of Things (IoT), and artificial intelligence, presents new opportunities and challenges for the digital forensics community. As we look toward the future, it is vital to consider the implications of these changes for privacy, ethics, and the role of digital forensics in ensuring justice.

1. The Changing Nature of Privacy in the Digital Age

Privacy, once considered a relatively straightforward concept, is increasingly becoming a complex issue in the digital age. The rise of pervasive technologies such as smartphones, wearable devices, smart home systems, and the IoT has dramatically expanded the scope of personal data that can be captured, shared, and analyzed. The data collected by these devices often includes not just simple records, but sensitive and intimate details about an individual's life, health, behavior, and interactions.

For digital forensic investigators, these developments pose significant challenges in ensuring that privacy rights are respected. On the one hand, investigators are tasked with collecting evidence from a wide range of devices and systems, while on the other, they must navigate the growing body of privacy laws and regulations that govern how personal information is accessed and used.

As technologies advance, the future of privacy in digital forensics will likely see increasing tension between the need for law enforcement to access digital evidence and the protection of individual privacy rights. Investigators will need to develop new strategies to ensure compliance with legal standards while also safeguarding sensitive personal information.

2. Emerging Legal and Regulatory Frameworks

As digital forensics continues to expand, so too does the body of law that governs it. Key privacy regulations such as the General Data Protection Regulation (GDPR), California Consumer Privacy Act (CCPA), and Health Insurance Portability and Accountability Act (HIPAA) impose strict rules on the collection, storage, and use of personal data. These laws are designed to give individuals more control over their personal information and protect them from misuse.

The future of forensic investigations will require investigators to have a strong understanding of these legal frameworks to navigate the complex privacy landscape. Additionally, as more regions and countries adopt their own privacy laws, cross-border investigations will become increasingly complicated. Investigators will need to stay informed about these changing regulations and consider how international privacy standards might impact their ability to access and use digital evidence.

One emerging trend in the regulation of privacy and digital forensics is the concept of data sovereignty, which refers to the idea that data should be subject to the laws of the country where it is stored. As cloud computing and global data storage become more widespread, ensuring that investigators comply with the laws of different jurisdictions will be crucial in maintaining ethical standards.

3. The Ethical Dilemmas of Digital Evidence Collection

Ethical issues in digital forensics often arise from the very nature of evidence collection. For example, investigators may need to access sensitive information that is critical to an investigation, such as personal messages, emails, or location data, which may contain deeply private or potentially harmful content. The ethical dilemma lies in balancing the need for this evidence with respect for the individual's right to privacy.

Moreover, forensic investigators must adhere to ethical principles such as non-discrimination, confidentiality, and objectivity. However, as digital forensics increasingly involves sophisticated technologies like AI and machine learning, these technologies may inadvertently introduce biases or errors into the analysis, further complicating the ethical landscape.

In the future, the development of ethical guidelines and best practices will be crucial to ensure that digital forensics professionals act with integrity and fairness. Investigators will need to be mindful of not only the potential consequences of their actions but also the broader implications for privacy rights and social justice.

4. Forensic Investigations in an Era of Encryption

As encryption technologies continue to evolve and become more widely adopted, digital forensics professionals will face new challenges in accessing encrypted data. Many devices, particularly smartphones and cloud-based services, now use end-to-end encryption to secure user data. This encryption can prevent investigators from accessing critical evidence, particularly in cases involving criminal activity, terrorism, or national security.

The ongoing debate surrounding encryption presents both ethical and legal considerations. On one hand, encryption is essential for protecting user privacy and data security, while on the other, it can hinder law enforcement's ability to access evidence necessary for investigations. Governments around the world are debating whether or not to mandate "backdoors" or alternative means of accessing encrypted data. However, the implementation of such measures poses significant ethical concerns, as they could compromise the security of digital systems for all users.

In the future, digital forensic professionals will need to navigate these challenges with care, ensuring that their methods of data collection and analysis respect both legal rights and ethical principles. Investigators must balance the need to unlock encrypted data for justice with the responsibility to prevent broader security risks or the violation of individuals' privacy rights.

5. Ensuring Accountability and Transparency in Digital Forensics

As automation and AI play an increasing role in digital forensics, it will become increasingly important to ensure accountability and transparency in forensic processes. Automated tools can provide efficiencies and assist investigators in analyzing vast amounts of data, but these tools must be transparent and auditable. Investigators must be able to explain how a particular piece of evidence was identified, how a tool arrived at a particular conclusion, and how conclusions were drawn based on that evidence.

This push for accountability will likely involve the development of more robust documentation and reporting standards. Investigators must be able to demonstrate that their methods were sound, that privacy and ethical considerations were taken into account, and that all necessary steps were followed to preserve the integrity of the evidence.

In the future, forensic investigators may also be required to explain how automated systems arrived at their conclusions, especially if the evidence is being used in a legal proceeding. This will require a higher level of transparency in how forensic tools operate, the algorithms they use, and the data they rely on.

6. The Role of Digital Forensics in Protecting Human Rights

Digital forensics plays an essential role in the protection of human rights, particularly in the context of cybercrime, human trafficking, and the investigation of state-sponsored espionage or abuses. However, ethical concerns arise when forensic methods are used in ways that could infringe upon individuals' rights. For example, surveillance systems and mass data collection could be used in ways that violate civil liberties, disproportionately target marginalized groups, or lead to false accusations.

The future of digital forensics will require professionals to be ever more vigilant in ensuring that their work is aligned with human rights principles. This will mean advocating for the responsible use of technology and ensuring that investigative practices are not only legally compliant but also ethical and fair.

7. Conclusion: A Delicate Balance Between Privacy, Ethics, and Justice

The future of digital forensics lies in finding the delicate balance between protecting individuals' privacy and advancing justice. As technologies continue to evolve, the forensic community will face new challenges in maintaining ethical standards while embracing innovations in automation, AI, and encryption.

To ensure the responsible application of digital forensics, investigators will need to be well-versed in both the technical and ethical aspects of their work. They must prioritize transparency, accountability, and respect for privacy while remaining committed to uncovering the truth and ensuring justice is served.

Ultimately, the future of digital forensics is not just about technological advancements but also about maintaining the integrity and ethical foundations upon which the profession is built. The role of digital forensic investigators will continue to evolve, but their responsibility to uphold privacy, protect human rights, and act ethically in the face of advancing technology will remain paramount.

In the modern age, every interaction leaves a digital trail, and understanding how to uncover, analyze, and interpret these trails is critical in the pursuit of truth. ***E-Evidence: Mastering the Science of Digital Forensics*** is your definitive guide to navigating the complex and ever-evolving world of digital evidence.

Written by **Esterino Falcone**, a seasoned digital forensics expert with decades of experience, this book bridges the gap between theory and practice. From the fundamentals of preserving evidence integrity to tackling cutting-edge challenges like cloud forensics and cryptography, E-Evidence equips you with the knowledge and tools needed to excel in investigations.

Inside, you'll discover:

- The foundational principles of digital forensics and its role in modern investigations.
- Step-by-step guidance on collecting, preserving, and analyzing electronic evidence.
- Insights into specialized areas like network forensics, mobile device investigations, and malware analysis.
- Strategies for presenting findings effectively in legal and professional contexts.
- A forward-looking perspective on the future of digital forensics, from AI to IoT.

Whether you're a budding investigator, a cybersecurity professional, or simply intrigued by the science of solving digital mysteries, this book provides a comprehensive roadmap to mastering the art of digital forensics.

E-Evidence: Mastering the Science of Digital Forensics is more than a technical guide— it's a call to uncover the truth, safeguard justice, and adapt to the fast-paced digital world.

Turn the page, and begin your journey into the fascinating realm of e-evidence today.

To my dear readers,

Thank you for choosing to embark on this journey with me through the intricate and fascinating world of digital forensics. Writing **E-Evidence: Mastering the Science of Digital Forensics** has been both a labor of love and a mission to share the knowledge I've gained over the years with those eager to learn, grow, and make a difference in this ever-evolving field.

Your time and curiosity are precious, and it means the world to me that you've chosen to invest them in this book. Whether you're a seasoned professional, a student of technology, or simply intrigued by the mysteries of digital evidence, I hope this book provides you with valuable insights, practical tools, and a deeper appreciation for the science and art of uncovering the truth.

I am truly inspired by the global community of investigators, technologists, and justice-seekers who strive to make the digital world safer and more transparent. You are the reason I wrote this book, and your passion for learning fuels my own drive to contribute to this field.

As you turn the final page, I hope you carry forward not only the knowledge you've gained but also a sense of purpose and curiosity to continue exploring the boundless possibilities of digital forensics.

From the bottom of my heart, thank you for being part of this journey.

With gratitude,

Esterino Falcone

www.ingramcontent.com/pod-product-compliance
Lightning Source LLC
LaVergne TN
LVHW081751050326

832903LV00027B/1903